Research for Indigenous Survival

Indigenous Research Methodologies in the Behavioral Sciences

Best wishes,

Lori Lambert

Books by Lori Lambert

Lambert, L., & Toby, R. (2009). *Gungalu Warrior Dreaming. Rockhampton, Queensland, Australia* (Unpublished manuscript at the request of the family).

Lambert, L (2008). *In Our Own Voice.* (12 Narratives focusing on culture and health for Grades 8-12). Seattle, WA: University of Washington.

Lambert, L., & Wenzel, E. (2007). Issues in Indigenous Health. In R. Labonte & J. Greene (Eds.), *Critical Issues in Public Health.* New York: Routledge.

Lambert, L. (2005). *Cheyenne Daughter.* Bloomington, IN: Authorhouse.

Lambert, L., & Walsh, C. (2002). *Heart of the Salmon, Spirit of the People: Ethnicity, Pollution, and Culture Loss.* Bloomington, IN: 1st Books Library.

Lambert-Colomeda, L. A. (2000). *Keepers of the Central Fire: Issues in Ecology for Indigenous peoples.* Boston: Jones and Bartlett.

Lambert-Colomeda, L. A. (1996). *Through the Northern Looking Glass: Breast Cancer Stories told by Northern Native Women.* New York: National League of Nursing Press.

Research for Indigenous Survival

Indigenous Research Methodologies in the Behavioral Sciences

by Lori Lambert, Ph.D.

published by
Salish Kootenai College Press
Pablo, Montana

distributed by
University of Nebraska Press
Lincoln, Nebraska

Cover illustration credits: Front cover: wolf beaded by Lori Lambert; upper left, Mark Warcon, photo by Dr. Carol Baldwin; lower left, Evelyn Mat,,,t Hernandez, photo by Frank Tyro; upper right, Rachel Bjorklund; lower right, Frank Finley, photo by Lori Lambert. Back cover: Australian aboriginal painting by Wingla Brian Fisher.

Thanks to Martha Kohl of the Montana Historical Society and Geff Wyatt, Wyatt Design, Helena, Montana, for help with the text design. Thanks to Corky Clairmont, Pablo. Montana, for help with the cover design.

Library of Congress CIP data:
Lambert, Lorelei A.
    Research for indigenous survival: indigenous research methodologies in the behavioral sciences / by Lori Lambert, Ph.D.
    pages cm
    Includes bibliographical references and index.
    ISBN 978-1-934594-12-4
    1. Indigenous peoples–Research–Methodology. 2. Indigenous peoples–Research–Moral and ethical aspects. 3. Indigenous peoples–Research–Australia–Methodology. 4. Indigenous peoples–Canada, Northern–Methodology. 5. Indians of North America–Montana–Methodology. 6. Social sciences–Methodology. 7. Psychology–Methodology. 8. Storytelling. I. Title.
    GN380.L36 2014   305.80072'1–dc23

                                                        2014026119

Distributed by University of Nebraska Press, 1111 Lincoln Mall, Lincoln, NE 68588-0630, order 1-800-755-1105, www.nebraskapress.unl.edu.

Table of Contents

Dedication

For Memere, a much-loved storyteller; for my family: Frank Tyro, Emily Colomeda, Regina Colomeda, Ted Colomeda, Sydney Colomeda-Watt, Eric Burrell, and Gabriella Anderson… you bring the joy into my life.

To Indigenous communities all over the world, we are still here!! (Lori)

Acknowledgements

The heart of this work comes from the Indigenous participants in Queensland, Australia; Tadoule Lake and Churchill, Manitoba, Canada; and on the Flathead Indian Reservation in Montana. They have given me advice, stories, and ideas about Indigenous cultural research. Without their help, this work would not have been possible.

I am grateful to Dennis Carder, J.D. (Cherokee), former Project Director for the Andrew W. Mellon Fellowship for tribal college faculty with the American Indian College Fund; Cole St. Albans (Jicarilla Apache & Ojibwa), of the American Indian College Fund and the Andrew W. Mellon Foundation; Dr. Ed Galindo (Shoshone), consultant with American Indian College Fund; and Dr. Shawn Wilson (Cree) for their interest in this research and providing the support that made this work and research possible. The American Indian College Fund has enabled Native researchers, students, and faculty in tribal colleges to pursue issues of importance to all Native scholars.

Countless Indigenous researchers have smoothed my way, and their theories and ideas have given me confidence, that this is the Red Road to follow when doing Indigenous Cultural Research.[1]

I am inspired by the research and ideas of Dr. Beatrice Medicine (Lakota), Dr. Charles Menzies (Tsimshian & Tlingit), Dr. Shawn Wilson (Cree), Dr. Margaret Kovach (Cree), Linda Tuhiwai Smith (Maori), Dr. Oscar Kawagley (Alaskan Inupiaq), Dr. Greg Cajete (Tewa), Frank Finley (Salish), Dr. Thundering Hill (Choctaw), and Dr. Baglee Chilisa. I am also grateful to my dear friends and colleagues from Salish Kootenai College for their unending support: especially Dr. Carol Baldwin, Department Head Psychology, who accompanied me to Australia and the Hudson's Bay, Canada. This work would not have been possible without her inspiration. Mary Bigbow (Chippewa Cree), and Co Carew (Apache), SKC faculty in the Social Work Department continue to give me encouragement. Mark Warcon and Deanne Warcon Toby (Northern

Cheyenne, South Sea, Murri), opened the doors to their South Sea
Island Community in Joskeleigh, Queensland. They have shared
their culture and have been dear friends since 1999. Robert Toby of
Rockhampton, Queensland, a cultural leader of the Gungalu Aboriginal people, helped me to access his people as participants for
this work. Dr. Luana Ross (Salish), past President of Salish Kootenai
College and Carmen Taylor (Salish), past Academic Vice President
of Salish Kootenai College, gave me encouragement, advice, and
friendship over many years. Thank you also to the Confederated
Salish and Kootenai Tribal Council for their permission to interview tribal members on the Flathead Indian Reservation. Thank
you to Dr. Jera Stewart, psychologist from Confederated Salish and
Kootenai Tribal Health Department for her support. Finally to my
husband, Dr. Frank Tyro, Media Director at Salish Kootenai College, for his unending love, encouragement, and technical advice
over these many, many years.

I am also indebted to the eagle eyes of two dear friends and
colleagues who helped edit this work: Dr. Marlene R. Warner,
who was my Ph.D. dissertation adviser from 1992-1994, and Dr.
Thundering Hill (Choctaw) who I met at a science and religion
conference in 1995. At last a special thank you to Bob Bigart, edi-
tor for Salish Kootenai College Press. Like Beaver who finds the
fire in sticks, Bob has found my many errors and my gems, and for
that I am grateful.

I also want to thank my children, Regina Marie, Emily Ann,
and Robert Edward (Ted), for their love and support through my
many academic endeavors. I hope that I was their role model. As
my son, Ted, says, "My mom has many talents, but cooking is not
one of them. I always thought that macaroni and cheese was supposed to have little powder puffs of uncooked cheese."

I need to acknowledge my many huskies, who, with loyal
hearts, loving eyes, and warm bodies, have kept me warm and
taught me how to be patient: Katiya Wolf, Attu, Jake Boy, Molly,
Honey Bunch, Yogo Sapphire, Sitka Alaska, and Denali.

I am always learning from my students and I appreciate their
amazing and scholarly work, especially those at Salish Kootenai
College who major in psychology and social work. They continue
to inspire me, and, because of them, I continue to do this work. I especially want to mention Corinna Littlewolf (Northern Cheyenne),
who was my student research assistant for this project, Shawnee

Skunkcap (Blackfeet), Roberta Arcenio (Salish), and Charmaine Curtis-Bingham (Salish). They were the first graduates from Salish Kootenai College bachelor's program in psychology in 2011 and were the first students to "endure" the Indigenous Research Methodologies Class. They have overcome enormous challenges and I am proud to call them colleagues and scholars:

> Lori, I love to do research now. I didn't think I would love it so much, but you showed us how to do it from our own hearts, minds, and communities (anonymous student, personal conversation, 2011).

Preface
by Dr. Eduardo Duran

After many years of working in clinical/healing settings all over Indian country (by the way it's all Indian country), I am in the process of becoming more immersed in research projects. Even as clinicians, most of us are required to take many courses in research methods along with statistics as part of the training towards higher degrees. These courses have a tendency to socialize students into thinking in logical positivistic fashion. The new way of thinking at times replaces the students' way of being in the life-world and tends to invalidate Indigenous epistemologies. I am honored at the opportunity to write this preface to Lori Lambert's book in which she courageously examines research in Indigenous communities.

Lori hits the ground running as the saying goes. In chapter one she makes the case of researchers being the new neocolonial authorities even when the "so called objects" of the study disagree with the research findings. The fact that western empiricism is the gold standard for doing research in Indigenous communities is an obvious colonial practice that for some reason has been out of radar contact for most researchers. Many Native researchers are aware of this neocolonial practice but their voices are squelched by academic settings with the threat of not graduating and later by the grueling tenure requirements. By the end of many years of adhering to these requirements many researchers are then compelled to continue with the practice of colonizing Indigenous peoples by the requirements of funding institutions.

In her later chapters, Lori addresses Indigenous epistemology as this applies to research in our communities. She deals with how animals are part of the life-world and how they teach how to live as well as how research can be formulated to include their wisdom in the search for new knowledge. Oral tradition and learning from the land itself are deep sources of knowledge that must be included in research methods as well as in the analysis of data that may not adhere to logical positivistic requirements. Indigenous psychology has existed and continues to exist in Indigenous communities, and the knowledge that has been passed on from oral tradition must not be considered anecdotal, and invalidated by David Hume and his empiricism.

In my experience, I have found that many Western institutions involved in research pay lip service to Indigenous methodologies and approaches. Once Indigenous people try to implement Indigenous ideas, the powers that be insist that all Indigenous ideas be filtered through Western empirical lenses if the project is to proceed. Unfortunately, most research projects proceed in a colonial fashion even when under the guise of community participatory research, which in my view is never truly participatory as long as the funding agents are operating from a Western epistemological framework. Colonial oversight of most research prevails and much effort is spent in trying to disguise the power intrusion from colonial funding sources.

The last chapters deal with decolonizing eyes and centering tribal knowledge as part of the research. I agree completely that tribal and other agencies that are part of the Native community must control research activities. That said, there are some agencies and agents who operate from a colonial mindset and their philosophy is deeply imbedded with colonial ideology. The past 500 years of colonization have left a deep imprint of internalized oppression and identification with the oppressor. Tribal agents operating from this ideology may be in a position to approve research, but they will serve to ensure that the research serves the interests of the research methods and the funding agency. Researchers and funders must wash their hands from the obvious colonial practice that uses scientific objectivity as a smoke screen to cover the neocolonial research practices being imposed on Native people use this activity.

Decolonizing research methods must begin with traditional Indigenous epistemologies that are the root metaphors that have been the driving force behind Indigenous research for millennia. These root metaphors and Indigenous methods must stand on their own or side by side with Western approaches and not beneath the boot of David Hume and his lack of insight into worldviews that differ from the Western philosophical tradition. In order to move research into this Indigenous paradigm it will require that principle investigators emerge from the Traditional knowledge keepers and not only from the academy. It will be a truly amazing time when funding sources will actually fund research that is not tied to an academic setting or requiring someone with a degree from one of these institutions.

Meanwhile, as we await for true research competency and real participatory research (that is community controlled by community members who are striving to decolonize themselves) we will continue to search for knowledge in the only way that we know how. A saving grace in this process is the awareness that we may be engaging in neocolonialism. This awareness can serve as the delimitation section of the results paper in which the awareness can act as the bracketing strategy as is prescribed by phenomenological practices. Lori's book is a step towards realizing a true Indigenous approach to research. I am grateful to her for having the courage to press the paradigm and every amount of pressure on the existing paradigm will be helpful in shifting research methods to a more humane and useful way of seeking knowledge.

Eduardo Duran, Ph.D.
Bozeman, Montana
September 9, 2012

Introduction

Indigenous peoples have the responsibility and right to restore, revitalize, use, develop, and transmit to future generations their languages, oral traditions, songs, philosophy, knowledge, writing system, and literature, and their heritage and visions (Battiste, 2000, p. 286).

Indigenous people are the tribal people in independent countries whose distinctive identity, values, and history distinguishes them from other sections of the national community. We are the descendents of the pre-colonial inhabitants of a geographical area and retain some or all of our cultural values, history, and lifeways, and, despite our legal status, retain some or all of our social, economic, cultural, and political institutions. These are the elements, which distinguish Indigenous people from other sections of the national community.

Indigenous research methodologies in the behavioral and social sciences include ethno-psychology,[2] and focuses on Indigenous people and their behavior. As a medical ecologist/anthropologist, I use the word Indigenous to refer to that, which is native and place-based, not transported from other regions. Indigenous psychology generally advocates examining knowledge, skills, and beliefs Indigenous people have about themselves and understanding them and their natural environments. In this way, Indigenous research methodologies in ethno-psychology are aligned with anthropology and the social sciences. They emphasize examining psychological phenomena in an ecological, historical, and cultural context. Indigenous psychology research methods and treatments ought to be developed for each cultural, Indigenous, and ethnic group.

Indigenous methodologies are an alternative way of thinking about the research process, and they differ from the Western approach since they flow from tribal knowledge (Smith, 1999; Wilson, 2008; Kovach, 2009). "Although these methodologies vary according to the ways in which different Indigenous communities express their own unique knowledge systems, they [Indigenous methodologies] do have common traits" (Louis, 2007, p. 130). They involve a tribal epistemology, meaning that information is gained through a relationship with Indigenous people in a specific community. While these research methods and methodologies are aligned with several Western qualitative approaches, there are distinctions. Some of those distinctions include a relationship with the source of the research data, or the person who knows and tells the story. Another distinction is the relationship that the researcher has with the story, how it is told, and how the knower and the researcher interpret the story. I believe that researchers who conduct research with Indigenous communities have accountability to that community's ethics, epistemology, ontology, and methodology. Our sense of community and place, the beat of our drums, and our hearts and minds connect us to one another. Having said that, Indigenous research methodologies in psychology cannot take place without a discussion of culture, identity loss, colonization, land loss, and dislocation.

Because the passion for doing research with an Indigenous methodology comes from the heart of the researcher, this focuses my work from the cultural knowledge, beliefs, behaviors, experiences, and realities of the Canadian Northeast Woodlands First Nations. They are my ancestors, the Mi'kmaq, Abenaki, and Huron-Wendot peoples. The Mi'kmaq and Abenaki are two of the five tribes[3] that belong to the Wobanaki Confederation and are known as the "People of the Dawnland." The Dawnlands, or in our language of Mi'kmaq, Mikmaki, "red earth country" are found on the northeastern shore of North America from Maine to Nova Scotia and New Brunswick. I am more aligned to the Mi'kmaq than the other first nations of my heritage. Our Creation Story follows:

How Niscaminou Made the Mi'kmaq

Niscaminou, the Sun, the Very Great, made the
sky and the stars, and flung the Great White Spirit
Road like silver lace across the heavens. Sometime
after he made the sky and the stars he made the

earth, the tall trees and the flowers. He made the mountains to rise above the land and poured the sea into the hollow places. He made the rocks and the sandy shores. He made the rain and the fog; the snow and the dew, and the wind that moves over the earth. Then, after he had made the sky and the earth, the flowers and the tall trees, he made the Indians.

...They were red-brown like the red-brown earth; tall and strong; and were warm with the Sun's rays.

They were the first people on earth and they were Mi'kmaq (Robertson, 1969, p. 21).

In 1621 Chrestien Le Clercq, a Recollet priest and one of the first European explorers to meet the Mi'kmaq people on the east coast of Cape Breton, described how the Mi'kmaq already knew how to read and write (Le Clercq, 1910, pp. 85-86). Le Clercq, was one of the first missionaries to learn the Mi'kmaq language and was able to speak with the people about their history and knowledge of writing and reading letters. He wrote about their history in *Nouvelle Relations De La Gaspesie* (1691), which was published in Paris, France. In the Mi'kmaq's own history there are clear references to visitors who had come in ships long before Cabot and Cartier (Whitehead, 1991, pp. 8-9; Chiasson, 2006, p. 165). The Mi'kmaq told LeClerq that our Mi'kmaq nation had been settled by visitors from overseas, long before the coming of the Europeans. They told him that people came and were shipwrecked in a storm and they lost everything of value and lost hope of returning to their own country. The stranded visitors used furs of animals to clothe themselves and built an elaborate town within an enclosure on Cape Dauphine. Although, it is well known through Mi'kmaq oral histories and artifacts left at L'Anse aux Meadows in Labrador, that the Vikings ventured to the northeastern shores of Canada in the tenth century, 1000 A.D., it was a short-lived adventure that left no known effect on Native life (Mann, 2011).

Paul Chiasson, a Yale-educated architect and Cape Breton native where eight generations of his Acadian family had lived, stumbled on an old road that led up a mountain he had never explored and may have confirmed this oral history in 2002. Cape Breton is one of the oldest points of exploration and settlement in the Americas with a written history that dates back to the first days of European discovery. Chiasson discovered the ruins of an entire town site that thrived on Canadian shores of Cape Breton well before the European Age of Discovery. Two years of investigative work followed and uncovered evidence of written language, clothing, technology, and religion with deep cultural ties to China. He unveiled the first substantial evidence that the Chinese may have been in the New World before Columbus (Chiasson, 2006). However, there are those such as Hanam (2006) who doubt Chiasson's claim that the ruins exist, or that they are Chinese in origin, although only the aerial photographs were examined and not the oral history of the Mi'kmaq people themselves.

The greatest character in Mi'kmaq mythology is Gluscap. In oral histories, Chiasson (2006) learned that the cultural hero, Gluscap came to the Mi'kmaq by ship. He is remembered as a transformer, not a god, but someone whose leadership gave rise to the legend. He taught the Mi'kmaq how to live and told them that European settlers would take the lands from them (Hager, 1895; McDonald, 1999; Chiasson, 2006).

Compelling evidence that Gluscap was Prince Henry Sinclair, not a Chinese explorer, comes from the legends of the Knights Templar: In 1398, a Scottish Prince, a Templar Knight, named Henry Sinclair, Earl of Orkney, sailed from Europe to Nova Scotia in what is now Canada. Legends the Mi'kmaq tell say that his arrival coincided with the appearance of Gluscap, "He remained all winter near Cape d'Or, and that place still bears the name of his wigwam" (Pohl, 1974, p. 143).

Gluscap was the manifestation of what the People desired to be. He was the embodiment of the People's achievements. He did great deeds and taught the Mi'kmaq all they knew. For example, he showed them how to make bows and arrows, canoes, and wigwams, how to hunt and fish, how to read and write. Gluscap did not die, but he went away and will come back when the People need him (Robertson, 1969).

In a more recent history of the Mi'kmaq, Alex Christmas tells this story:

> They [Mi'kmaq] were among the first peoples to discover Europeans on their shores, and for centuries the Mi'kmaq have been forced to adapt to changes brought by the newcomers. Like other Aboriginal peoples, their land was taken, first for

lumbering, then for settlement. Disease drastically reduced their population. The expansion of European settlements reduced their territory…

Between 1942 and 1949, 2,100 Mi'kmaq living in some 20 locations—reserves scattered in rural areas and urban peripheries—were pressured to relocate to Eskasoni or to Shubenacadie. The size of each reserve doubled.

Relocation affected the life of the Mi'kmaq in Nova Scotia more than any other [Canadian] post-Confederation event, and its social, economic and political [and emotional] effects are still felt today (Alex Christmas, quoted in Canada, Royal Commission on Aboriginal Peoples, 1996, pp. 400-401).

In a Mi'kmaq[4] paradigm of epistemology, axiology, and ontology, I liken the Indigenous research methodologies process to the ceremony of crafting a Micmac potato basket used in Aroostook, Maine, for hundreds, maybe thousands of years. In fact, archeological evidence has discovered a 3,000 year-old design of the Micmac potato baskets in Cape Breton. Just as the researcher must prepare for the research, the preparation of crafting the basket begins with the knowledge or epistemology of the whole community and how to locate the appropriate Black Ash tree. When the tree is found, prayers are offered and songs are sung as the tree is cut.

The preparation respects the ethics or the axiology of not taking the basket designs of another basket maker or tribe. It is the conceptual design, the reality or the ontology of the basket in the mind and hands of the basket weaver and how that vision appears in the reality of the completed basket. A Micmac potato basket holds many things beside potatoes. As it is being crafted, stories are told, including stories of traditional environmental knowledge, tribal and family memories, culture, histories, songs, and ceremonies. In the end, the basket itself encompasses the history of the tribe, the basket maker's family, and demonstrates the utmost reverence for the basket maker and the results of the research project.

Although I have never made an ash splint, men in the Saulnier and Therriot family, who are my Mi'kmaq and Acadian relatives on my grandfather's side, were well known in Nova Scotia for making brown ash splint baskets. Today, Richard Silliboy carries on the craft and tradition of premier Micmac basket making from Aroostook County, Maine. Richard's grandfather taught him the skills and ceremonial preparation needed to make a beautifully crafted basket: how to go into the woods and chose the suitable brown ash tree. Author Kathleen Mundell found that "Many basket makers have a trained eye for picking out a good tree." Richard observed, "I guess finding a good tree is like a mechanic picking out a good car. It's experience and doing it over and over and knowing what the wood is going to be like" (Mundell, 2008, p. 34). These days, Richard sees this local, functional knowledge as a declining art. He explains, "....we need to learn how to go out into the woods and select trees that are suitable for basket making. This is an art all by itself, an art that is known by very few people" (Mundell, 2008, p. 37):

> Black Ash...likes to have its feet wet. In floodplain forests and edges of swamps, black ash mingles with red maples, elms, and willows. It is never the most common tree—you only find it in scattered patches—so it can take a long day of tromping over boot-sucking ground to find the right tree...
>
> And yet it's not enough to simply find black ash; it has to be the right one—a tree ready to be a basket (Kimmerer, 2013, p. 143).

Like the crafting of a Micmac potato basket, Indigenous methods of research emphasize preparation, and focus on the ways in which all the interrelated parts fit together to facilitate the goals of the research; the relationships among the research participants, and the end results, which make the research (and the potato basket) valuable to the community. This is the formal procedure and preparation for my own research, and it is the preparation I teach to my own young researchers. To me, Indigenous research is a celebration of culture and knowledge: "The practice of culture, a uniquely human construction, endows the world of cultural participants with symbolic meaning" (Loppie, 2007, p. 278).

Indigenous research refers to research that directly impacts the culture, life, and well being of Indigenous people and their communities. It may assemble data that attempts to describe Indigenous people, their heritage, and their culture: "....it may affect the human and natural environment in which Aboriginal Peoples live" (Castellano, 2004, p. 99).

I believe that the role of Indigenous cultural research in ethno-psychology is an attempt to comprehend behavioral phenomena and issues that occur in a particular place with a particular group of people who are unique to that place: "It is ludicrous to imagine that the emotional functioning of people in different cultures is basically the same. It is just as ludicrous to imagine that each culture's emotional life is unique" (Shweder, 1991, p. 252).

What follows is a personal journey that includes the theories and ideas of Indigenous cultural research methodologies that impact psychological behaviors. They are grounded in the writings of many, many other Indigenous researchers who have contributed to the emerging literature: Menzies, 2001; Wilson, 2008; Smith, 1999; Kovach, 2009; Trimble & Medicine, 1993; Martin, 2003; Castellano, 2004; Loppie, 2007; Cajete, 2000; Kawagley, 1995; Deloria, 2006; Duran, 2006; Duran & Duran, 1995; Gonzalez y Gonzalez & Lincoln, 2007; Cole, 2002; Dana-Sacco, 2010.

In the early 1990s when I researched my doctoral dissertation, *Through the Northern Looking Glass: Breast Cancer Stories Told by Northern Native Women* (Lambert-Colomeda, 1996), the literature on Indigenous methodologies was in embryonic stages. No formal theory or methodology existed that was considered Indigenous. The closest methodologies akin to what I sought to accomplish were Feminist Research Methodologies, which gave a voice to marginalized Native women of the north. It is non-hierarchical, non-manipulative, and is based on the commonalities and relationships with women participants (hooks, 1984; Harding, 1991). I appreciated the concept that research could be done from a woman's perspective, on women's issues, and give a voice to marginalized women. But the methodology didn't expand the holistic view that spoke to my spirituality, to the heart of my community, my culture, and of Native women and Native researchers in particular. Today, promising literature on Indigenous research methodologies has emerged from Indigenous scholars working in mainstream universities in Australia, Canada, New Zealand, and the United States (Kovach, 2009; Wilson 2008; Chilisa, 2012; Loppie, 2007; Battiste, 2000). Additionally Aboriginal women from Canada have written on the subject of Indigenous feminism. They indicated that Indigenous feminist analysis and activism must seek to attain social justice along gender lines, class, race, and sexuality (Suzack, Huhndorf, Perrault & Barman, 2010).

One important point is the integrity of the story: "Stories are not separate from theory; they make up theory and are, therefore, real and legitimate sources of data and ways of being" (Brayboy, 2005, p. 430).

And so we see that Indigenous people are driving their own agendas rather than the academies and Western research:

> The old order of research—positivist, empirical, and driven by the agenda of the academy, has not served Indigenous populations whose interests are currently geared towards surviving and thriving through self-determination and control over resources including cultural and knowledge resources (Ermine, Sinclair, & Jeffery, 2004, p. 9).

I envision that this work may create a smoother research path for Indigenous scholars, and will contribute to their becoming expert researchers by applying Indigenous methodologies to their work; I hope they learn to love research that gives voice and self-determination to their own communities, and that they develop their own Indigenous conceptual frameworks as the path that they follow to conduct research. They will have the capacity to build the framework for a proposal from their own passion, values, "Place," and Indigenous or tribally centered epistemology. The past colonizing policies of the West and of European invaders toward Indigenous people are rooted in imperialism, white supremacy, and a desire for material gain. Indigenous scholars are working towards social change for their communities. In our global world, university graduates need an understanding of both Western and Indigenous research methodologies. The Mi'kmaq call this dual perspective "Two-eyed Seeing." We live in a multicultural world and balance on the cusp of many cultures. Two-eyed seeing reflects how two cultures view the world and understand the benefits of both lifeways. Indigenous components view the world in a holistic way, encompassing culture, spirituality, Native knowledge, ceremonies, language, and how cultures are passed down and strengthened through oral traditions. It relates to the stories, geography, culture, language, and history of a place. Western research methodologies do not convey the same rich meanings.

One eye is strictly human, relating to our own abilities as Indigenous humans to see and think about things rationally. The other eye is concerned with hearing, seeing, and learning from Other, whatever that might be, as in two different sources of "authority" and two different sources of data. Indigenous people have always done the kind of physical world seeing (research) that Western science does. But we have always done this other type of seeing, too, and valued what we learned through the spiritual realm. The spiritual world seeing may include dreams and visions and intuition and listening to what the Land says to us, to what bird behavior or song tells you, or paying attention to what a bear shows you, or other events in the natural world. Dr. Thundering Hill believes that many Western scientists either pluck that other eye out as if shot with an arrow, or turn a blind eye. The value for Indigenous researchers is seeing how Western science has "evolved" into a culture all its own with its own rites, rituals, and ways.

Wilson (2008, p. 51) observes "There is a definite perception among Indigenous peoples worldwide that they were among the most researched group of people on Earth during this time [1970s]" (Huggins, 1998; van den Berg, 1998). And yet, non-Indigenous people continue to speak for us even in matters that do not concern them:

> While non-Indian historians and some Indians have made careers speaking for tribes and interpreting cultures besides the one to which they belong, many Indians will not write about tribes other than their own, even if they have insights into those cultures. When it comes to speculating on Others' motivations and world-views, many Indians are simply uncomfortable and won't do it (Mihesuah, 1998, p. 12).

Nevertheless, emerging research literature from Indigenous scholars like Linda Smith and Shawn Wilson, seeking to decolonize Indigenous people through their own research with tribes other than their own, is beginning to come of age in the forefront of mainstream universities:

> An important aspect of this emerging style of research is that Indigenous peoples themselves decide exactly what areas are to be studied. It is time for research that is conducted by or for Indigenous people to take another step forward (Wilson, 2008, p. 15).

To guide my own research methodology I applied an Indigenous epistemology of group discussions, called Sharing or Talking Circles. I use these terms interchangeably as a means of sharing ideas and experiences (Loppie, 2007; Kovach, 2009; Smith, 1999; Chilisa, 2012; Martin, 2003).

Circles suggest inclusiveness and the lack of a hierarchy namely, interconnectedness, continuity, and equality:

> Everything we do, we do in a circle. The symbol of the circle holds a place of special importance in Native lifeways. According to our elders' teachings, the seasonal pattern of life and renewal and the movement of animals and people were continuous, like a circle, which has no beginning and no end. Our tipi and wigwams are formed in a circle (personal conversation, anonymous Mohawk elder, 2000).

So it is with the sharing circle. Sharing circles use a healing method in which all participants (including the facilitator) are viewed as equal and information, spirituality, and emotionality are shared (Lavallée & Poole, 2010). It is a method that is familiar and comforting for many Aboriginal participants in Canada who have knowledge of this practice (Restoule, 2004). Healing circles are often used as part of ceremony and as a way of healing (Stevenson, 1999), and in these contemporary times, are increasingly used by Indigenous researchers (Baskin, 2005; Restoule, 2004; Martin, 2003).

In a research setting, although both the focus group and the sharing circle are designed to gain knowledge through discussion, the principles behind a sharing circle are quite different. Circles are acts of sharing all aspects of the individual—heart, mind, body, and spirit—and permission is given to the facilitator to report on the discussions (Nabigon, Hagey, Webster & MacKay, 1999). All comments directly address the question or the issue, not the comments another person has made. In the circle, an object that symbolizes connectedness to the land, for example, a stick, a stone, or a feather, can be used to facilitate the circle. Only the person holding the "talking stick" has the right to speak. Participants can indicate their desire to speak by raising their hands. Going around the circle systematically gives everyone the opportunity to participate. Silence is also acceptable and any participant can choose not to speak (Running Wolf & Rickard, 2003).

On the other hand, "Healing circles differ from talking circles in the protocol and expectations. Participants [in healing circles] are encouraged to tell specific types of stories centred [sic] on themes of suffering, trauma, loss, grief, and healing, and there is increased tolerance for and expectation of intense affect as these stories are recounted" (Kirmayer & Valaskakis, 2009, p. 452).

My concerns are similar to those shared by Cardinal (2010), which are the ethical obligations, relationship, and responsibility to the community and the work. These are central in my inquiry, and speak to the complexities of struggling with the questions of researcher's right to tell.

The findings of my inquiry may add to the innovative literature of Indigenous Cultural Research and narrative inquiry, and their connections. Additionally, as I write, I am cognizant of the mental health disparities affecting us all. For the Nova Scotia Mi'kmaq, as for many other Indigenous groups, removal from their lands was emotionally traumatic:

> Centralization was doomed to failure and it took a heavy toll before finally being abandoned.... Over 1,000 Mi'kmaq were forcibly removed from their communities, losing farms, homes, schools and churches in the process. During the post-war period we also saw the introduction of residential school systems, which was intended to take away our youth and make them non-Mi'kmaq. As in other areas of Canada, this approach did not succeed, but it did serve to disorient and demoralize three generations of our people (Alex Christmas, quoted in Canada, Royal Commission on Aboriginal Peoples, 1996, p. 405).

Chapter 1
Thoughts on Indigenous Research

Responsible research means staying for tea (University of Alaska Fairbanks, Center for Alaska Native Health Research, n.d.).

Traditional Western research methodologies have established the researcher as the "authority," an expert who can describe and predict changes in a society even if the "objects" of the study disagree with the findings. Indigenous scholars who were educated in mainstream universities, and who also understand Indigenous ways of seeking knowledge, are challenging these western assumptions and methodologies of research (Castellano, 2004).

In Indigenous languages there is no word that has a similar concept to the English word "research." It is a process of telling stories and remembering our history and understanding how the world works. Perhaps we should rename research in our own languages: "The word 'research' has too much racist and colonial baggage attached to it to be used in an Indigenous context....we must find new words to liberate and decolonize our processes for....gathering and sharing knowledge" (Absolon & Willett, 2005, p. 114). Albert Marshall, a Mi'kmaq elder from Cape Breton, calls it *Toqwa'tu'kl Kjijitaqnn* in the Mi'kmaq language. It refers to bringing knowledges together. I will write more about this concept later. The time is long overdue to bring Indigenous knowledge, perspectives, and voices to all levels of research. It is critical that Indigenous people are full participants in research projects that concern them and share in an understanding of the aims and methods of the research, and distribute the results of research in their communities: "It is essential that Aboriginal Peoples and their organizations put forward, not only concerns, but also solutions to the ethical problems that too often have made research affecting them inaccurate and irrelevant" (Castellano, 2004, p. 100).

Indigenous voices are emerging with literature from Indigenous scholars working in mainstream universities and focusing on Indigenous research methodologies. There are still many non-Indigenous researchers who conduct their research **on** Aboriginal people rather than **with** Aboriginal people. Some researchers have even mastered the form of respectful consultation, but lack the in-depth real respect that should be shown to Aboriginal people. The researchers depart the community; write their dissertations or books, and Native people never benefit from their contributed stories and participation (Menzies, 2001; Smith, 1999; Wilson, 2008; Kovach, 2009; Loppie, 2007; Chilisa, 2012; Porsanger, 2004).

For the past several years, Indigenous and Aboriginal researchers have been applying age-old and honored methodologies to give a strong voice to research methodologies in our communities. It is my belief that Indigenous research must produce new knowledge and information that can benefit our communities, move our communities forward, and create stronger communities of decolonized residents filled with self-determination and self-worth.

Because of soul wounds (Duran, 2006), feelings of depression, and low self-esteem, some my own students have committed suicide. Their deaths are a tragic loss to their community, to their tribe, family, and the next seven generations that will never be. I feel helpless and at a loss of what to say. In many communities there exist similar feelings of helplessness, low self-esteem, incidents of spousal abuse or child abuse, and worsening drug abuse (Mark Warcon; Ila Bussidor; Caroline Bjorklund, personal conversations, 2012).

While respecting members of the community, I am motivated to understand mental health issues in Indigenous communities through the eyes and cultural paradigm of the people themselves. Today more than ever, there is a much greater need for Indigenous ways of being and knowing about science, mental health, and psychology. The methods of researching these issues are through the eyes of Indigenous scholars. It is essential that we, as Indigenous researchers, recognize, and appreciate the resilience of others who have not succumbed to these social, and emotional problems. As Wilson (2008) reminds us, when we research the positive aspects of a community, positive behaviors will follow.

"The term 'research' is inextricably linked to European imperialism and colonialism. The word itself, 'research,' is probably one of the dirtiest words in the indigenous world's vocabulary" (Smith,

1999, p. 1). As Western research methods have come under scrutiny by Indigenous scholars, there has been a reframing of research paradigms and programs by Indigenous academics, researchers, and thinkers (Martin, 2003). The negative implications that past researchers have earned emanated from their unethical practices in Indigenous communities:

> ...we are over-researched and this has generated mistrust, animosity and resistance from many Aboriginal people.....until recent times, research conducted in Aboriginal lands was done without the permission, consultation, or involvement of Aboriginal people. The same is especially true for research conducted on or about Aboriginal people generating what I call 'terra nullius research'. In this research, we are present only as objects of curiosity and subjects of research, to be seen but not asked, heard or respected (Martin, 2003, p. 203).

Smith (1999) wrote that Indigenous people are the most researched people in the world:

> Researchers enter [our] communities armed with goodwill in their front pockets and patents in their back pockets, they bring medicine into villages and extract blood for genetic analysis. No matter how appalling their behaviours, how insensitive and offensive their personal actions may be, their acts and intentions are always justified as being for the 'good of mankind' (Smith, 1999, p. 24).

There exists a paucity of Indigenous researchers in the social sciences such as mental health providers, licensed social workers, and substance abuse counselors in Native American communities in the United States and Australia. In Canada in 2013 only 3% of the 15, 218 university freshmen were Aboriginal (Prairie Research Associates, 2013; Australian Institute of Health and Welfare, 2012). Not only is mental health care deficient in these communities, but they also need culturally appropriate expertise in understanding how to collect and interpret information on mental health care and mental health in particular. For example, in Canada in 2001, Aboriginal students represented only 0.7% of all first-year medical students in Canada, but First Nations, Inuit, and Metis comprise 4.5% of the Canadian population. The number of aboriginal students in medical school and other health professions including nurses, dentists, physiotherapists, occupational therapists, nutritionists, and pharmacists is only one-sixth of the total needed to reflect the overall population (Canadian Council on Learning, 2008).

With the suicide epidemic increasing on Indian reservations and Canadian reserves (United States Department of Health and Human Services, Indian Health Service 2013; Canada, Public Health Agency of Canada, 2006) and among urban Indian people, it is imperative that we, as Indigenous educators and researchers, train and educate our graduates in issues of the social sciences and Indigenous research.

Among Canadian First Nations population the suicide rates are twice the national average and show no signs of decreasing. However, these rates differ from community to community. Some communities have had "epidemics" of suicide, while others have had few or no suicides for several years.

In 1997 a survey conducted by the government of Canada found that 16% of First Nations adults living on reserves experienced major depression, compared to 8% of the general Canadian population, and suicides are twice as high for Aboriginal people in Canada (Canada, Public Health Agency of Canada, 2006, pp. 164-168).

Additionally, statistics from Kowanko, de Crespigny, Murray, Groenkjaer, & Emden (2004), and Elliott-Farrelly (2004) indicated that the general health status and life expectancy of Australian Aboriginal people are markedly lower than the non-Aboriginal population. Mental health disorders are pervasive, especially related to alcohol and other drugs, and the suicide rates are two to three times higher in Aboriginal people in Australia.

My former collaborative work with Aboriginal health care providers and community workers in Queensland (1999-present), and with First Nations in Arctic Canada, where I carried out my doctoral research (1993), brought to light many of the same mental health problems that we face on Indian reservations and with urban Indian people in the United States: predominately, issues of self-destruction such as suicide, alcohol and drug abuse, depression, anger, lack of empowerment, Post Traumatic Stress Disorder, and low self-esteem:

> The high rates of alcohol and substance abuse, mental health disorders, suicide, violence, and behavior-related chronic diseases in American Indian and Alaska Native (AI/AN) communities is well documented….[American Indians and Alaska Natives] are significantly more likely to report past-year alcohol and substance use disorders than any other race, and suicide rates for AI/AN people are 1.7 times higher than the U.S. all-races rate. Domestic violence rates are also alarming, with 39% of AI/AN women experiencing intimate partner violence—the highest rate in the U. S. (United States Department of Heath and Human Services, Indian Health Service, 2013, p. 1).

Those issues have illuminated even more zealously the call for Indigenous research methods. I hope that this work will change the negative impression of our communities held in the writings of Western researchers. I pray it meets the needs of Native and non-Native academics by providing guidelines for Indigenous research in cooperation with Indigenous communities. I expect it will provide the structure to empower a variety of Indigenous communities where many members feel that the colonial academic model of data gathering and processing, marginalizes community members, and misses essential cultural understanding. This process skews data collection and interpretation and prevents the holistic story from being told, which in turn impairs the healing process (Blood & Heavy Head, 2007). To reinforce this concept, many studies in psychology, human services, and other social sciences conducted on Indigenous people, as opposed to conducted with or by Indigenous people, focus on negative aspects of life, as identified by outside researchers: "The research agenda is set from outside the community" (Wilson, 2008, p. 16).

We recognize the negative behaviors that people in these small villages and communities exhibit, but there are positive things happening as well. For example, there are celebrations of sobriety on the Flathead Indian Reservation (F. Auld, E. Matt, personal conversations, 2012), workshops that focus on suicide prevention and parenting, and many tribal members graduating with degrees in psychology, social work, and drug counseling. Data from the American Indian Higher Education Consortium in 2003-04, indicate a total of 17,190 students were enrolled in tribal colleges and universities (TCUs). Overall TCU enrollment waned slightly with the economic challenges facing the nation, but by 2009-10, enrollment had reached a record 19,070 students—an 11 percent increase. Although only eight TCUs offer degrees in social science and psychology, these programs have experienced the greatest growth (American Indian Higher Education Consortium, 2012, p. 13).

On Indian reservations and among urban Indian people, the increasing rates of suicide, bullying, and substance and spousal abuse, make it imperative that we, as Indigenous educators and researchers, train and educate our graduates in issues of Indigenous psychology and research methodologies that focus our research on the positive aspects of culture and issues in our communities. Many families and individuals are resilient. They will not just survive. They will thrive with culturally appropriate support.

The heart of any Indigenous research begins with "Place" and within that "Place" is "Oneself" and the heart of research. Indigenous research methodologies differ from the Western approach because they flow from a place, an Indigenous place, a tribe, a community. They flow from place-based tribal knowledge. They are central and specific for each place. While they may be aligned with several Western qualitative approaches, there are distinctions. Some of those distinctions include a relationship between the gatherer of data and the source telling the research story or data. Another distinction is the relationship that the researcher has with the story being told, how it is told, and how the informants or participants and the researcher have formed a relationship with the story, or how each individual interprets the story (Wilson, 2008). As this emerging work progresses in the mainstream, we are learning of the complex nature of Indigenous research methodologies:

> Indigenous research has four dimensions: (1) It targets a local phenomenon instead of using extant theory from the West to identify and define a research issue; (2) it is context-sensitive and creates locally relevant constructs, methods, and theories derived from local experiences and indigenous knowledge; (3) it can be integrative, that is, combining Western and indigenous theories; and (4)...its assumptions about what counts as reality, knowledge, and values in research are informed by

an indigenous research paradigm (Chilisa, 2012, p. 13).

In Western models, traditionally, the research project and the data are separate from the researcher. The researcher is a unemotional onlooker. There is no relationship to the data, to the culture of the informants, or to the informants per se. Quite the opposite in Indigenous models, the researcher is included in the research process. The researcher's voice, culture, and story are heard: The "Oneself," if you will, the heart of the research, and the passion of why the researcher wants to do that research.

Another aspect of how Indigenous methodologies differ from Western methods is how the methodology is focused on relationships; the relationship to the community, to the person giving the data, and to the data itself. Indigenous methodology is being accountable to that community. As S. Wilson wrote (2001), we need to ask ourselves:

> ....how am I fulfilling my role in this relationship? What are my obligations in this relationship? ....Does this method [of research] allow me to fulfill my obligations in my role? Further, does this method help to build a relationship between myself as a researcher and my research topic? Does it build respectful relationships with the other participants in the research? (pp. 177-178).

Generally, in Western research paradigms, the researcher is an observer of the phenomenon, and their voice is not heard. In fact, the Western objective approach takes the researcher away from the relationships. According to S. Wilson (2001), "An Indigenous paradigm comes from the fundamental belief that knowledge is relational. Knowledge is shared with all of creation… It is with the cosmos, it is with the animals, with the plants, with the earth that we share this knowledge. It goes beyond this idea of individual knowledge to the concept of relational knowledge" (pp. 176-177). Kovach (2009) described the preparation and the experiential aspect of the research as a process, grounded in inward knowledge. It is going inward into oneself and finding out who we are and what are our experiences. It is a dance between our hearts and mind.

Historically, Indigenous people have always been "researchers." In the simplest terms, research is observing a phenomenon (problem statement), making a hunch (hypothesis), forming a question (research question), and systematically searching for the answer (methodology). It involves seeking knowledge, learning to hear, to see, to be aware, to use and trust our perceptions, and observing if the observable facts can be repeated. This kind of circular thinking links with the Western scientific method as well (Cajete, 2000).

Information from *The Encyclopedia of American Indian Contributions to the World* by Keoke & Porterfield (2002) addresses many of the inventions and scientific contributions made by Native people of the Americas including how Native people contributed much to the science of animal husbandry, agriculture, astronomy, architecture, and mechanics of tools and inventions. I would argue that our ancestors engaged in research to discover how the world works. How did Native women determine that smoked buckskin is waterproof? How did they ascertain that beans, squash, and corn grow better when planted together? How did they learn that they could change the patterns of the horse coat by breeding a white horse with a black horse?:

> Native people have been good observers. They understood that things were always in process, that things were always being created and then destroyed and then created again in new forms (Cajete, 2000, p. 36).

From observations on earth to the celestial signs above, Indigenous cultures have made predictions concerning astronomical events, for example, the coming of an eclipse, or the arrival of comets. Inuit hunters of the North applied star navigation during the long winters, when no earthly signs were visible to show them the way to hunt polar bears, seals, and birds on the ice. In the South Pacific the Indigenous peoples from Australia, New Zealand, and the islands, monitored the sky to show them the way across vast expanses of ocean.

In other sciences like agronomy or agriculture, Indigenous people developed the potato, squash, corn, and beans, and improved their taste and texture. Maize or corn cannot reproduce itself because the kernels are wrapped in the husk. It is thought by scientists that Indians developed it from its closest genetic relative, the mountain grass called teosinte. Teosinte is not an edible plant and its ears are smaller than the ears of baby corn found in many

Chinese dishes. For decades, archeologists and anthropologists have argued how this amazing feat was achieved (Mann, 2011).

In the field of engineering, Native peoples of the Americas built amazing stone cities like Machu Pichu, or the pyramids of the Maya. They invented the tipi, the igloo, longhouse, and wigwam, which are so strong that, even in a windstorm, they never fail (Keoke & Porterfield, 2002).

The Salish people living in the Rocky Mountain areas invented their style of tipi, built with lodgepole pines and buffalo hides or deer hides. After contact, tipis were constructed of canvas (R. Bigcrane, personal conversation, 2011). The Blackfeet tribes of northern Montana and Canada developed very wide based tipis because of the constant wind. Both canvas and hide styles can withstand the winds of winter storms. One of my engineering friends, who wishes to remain anonymous, pointed out that the way air moves around the cone shaped tipi gives it its strength. When the wind blows sideways to the tipi, as it often does on the Great Plains of the United States, the wind blows faster around the bottom, where it is wider. The wind blows slower around the top where it is narrower. The air pressure is greatest at the top of the tipi, pushing down, and very lowest at the bottom of the tipi where there is a relative vacuum compared to the top. The result is that the harder the wind blows, the harder the tipi is going to be pushed down against the ground.

The Sayisi Dene houses were not permanent. The people moved with the circle of the seasons following the movement of animals. It was their circle of life. Dene needed homes they could put together and take down easily. Dene made tipis. In the winter they used more poles to make their tipis. Between the poles they pushed in moss to keep out the winter wind. During the summer the Dene often lived in lean-tos (C. Bjorklund, personal conversation, 2011).

Robert Toby, Jr. is the cultural preservation officer for the Gungalu people of Queensland. I asked him if he would write a few words for this chapter on how his people survived in Australia: "Over tens of thousands of years, Indigenous Australians have observed, analyzed, synthesized and applied learned sets of knowledge and skills to similar and new situations, thus passing on from generation to generation, base knowledge and its application that has evolved over time. When white settlers snatched the land and its resources, Indigenous Australians began to integrate western technologies into traditional practices. For example, Robert Toby senior [his father], a Gungalu elder from the Dawson and Callide Valleys in Queensland, talked about his mother changing the possum trap, using the tails of the horse [to hold the trap door] rather than native animal sinew." During a walkabout interview with him a few years ago, I learned of how his family lived in the 1920s. We were in a field walking in the bush trying to find the stumps, which were next to his birthplace. He told the story of how his family camped next to a small billabong. "They had canvas tents, an old wood stove, [which was still standing there]. They had to know how to get water from the billabong, and how to hunt for food" (R. Toby, Sr., personal communication, 2006):

> Over hundreds of generations they adapted to these different, changing environments, and in turn they learned how to manipulate them to augment the food supply. As hunter-gatherers, they lived off the land with a precise and intimate knowledge of its resources and seasonal patterns (Macintyre, 1999, p. 11).

Our ancestors needed a researched knowledge of math, engineering, and their environment or Place to create these structures. These activities required careful observations regarding the ecology, making hunches, experimenting by trial and error, and they gained knowledge from these activities. They may not have had the word "research" in their language, but they understood if they carefully observed and made hunches or theories, they would be taught with Indigenous eyes how the world worked. However, over time, and through the influence of Western lifeways, this Indigenous research process was abandoned and forgotten by many tribal people as the concept of research became highly Westernized. The purpose of research became a scholarly, theoretical model of pure knowledge acquisition designed for the "Self" rather than shared with members of the community. The research agenda of Western researchers, especially with regard to Native people, was often to organize, define, and preserve Indigenous people in the context of Western thought (Smith, 1999).

Local knowledge systems are based on the shared experiences, customs, values, traditions, lifestyles, social interactions, ideological orientations, and spiritual beliefs specific to Native communities.

These are forever evolving as new knowledge is obtained or generated (University of Alaska Fairbanks, n.d.).

For some Western scholars, still following the traditional Western research paradigm and ways of thinking, it may come as a surprise to learn that Indigenous methodologies have been designed by Indigenous scholars within Western academic institutions, and not in the jungle or rainforest, or snow-covered tundra: "…indigenous approaches to research on indigenous issues are not meant to compete with, or replace, the Western research paradigm; rather, to challenge it and contribute to the body of knowledge of indigenous people about themselves and for themselves, and for their own needs" (Porsanger, 2004, p. 105). Today, Indigenous people are beginning to reclaim their research heritage by placing more emphasis on the role of research in ensuring our existence as unique tribal nations because of research efforts embedded in our historical past:

> …American Indians have been exploited by non-Indians [researchers], who have established successful careers, won writing awards, have been called the nation's leading experts on Indians, and who have fed their families by writing "about" American Indians. A fair question is, "what have they given Indian people in return?" (Fixico, 2003, pp. 125-126).

Today, Native people are beginning to reclaim their research heritage by placing more emphasis on the role of research in ensuring our existence as unique tribal nations. The National Congress of American Indians outlined the foundation that drives this work. These are the values embedded in Indigenous research:

1. Indigenous knowledge is valid and should be valued.
2. Research is not culturally neutral.
3. Responsible stewardship includes the task of learning how to interpret and understand data and research.
4. Tribes must exercise sovereignty when conducting research and managing data.
5. The research must benefit Native people (National Congress of American Indians, 2009, p. 12).

Henderson (2009) wrote that Indigenous research methods generally emphasize the ways in which interrelated parts fit together to facilitate the goals of the research, the relationships among the research participants, and the end results. There is a difference between methods and methodology, albeit some researchers use the terminology interchangeably. However, the methodology is the study of how methods are used. The methods are the tools researchers use to gather data. For example in the Indigenous model, the method may include individual face-to-face interviews, talking circles, healing circles, and methods of how the data is disseminated to the community.

These make the research valuable to the community. A new class of Indigenous researchers has emerged and we are doing research that is passionate, tribal, cultural, and beneficial to our communities:

> [As indigenous researchers we must]…intentionally build community capacity while learning to incorporate Indigenous ways of knowing into the work. In addition to respecting important values such as trust, reciprocity, self-determination, and long-term commitment, research relationships with Native communities…require participation in research review processes that are tribally [or community] controlled (Dana-Sacco, 2010, p. 63).

Chapter 2
We Have Always Learned from Animals: What Can Coyote and Platypus Teach Us?

If you talk to the animals they will talk with you and you will know each other. If you do not talk to them you will not know them, and what you do not know you will fear. What one fears, one destroys (George, 2012, p. 2).

In the past and even today, Native people continue to learn many behaviors from their relationship to the environment, and from observing the animals. When the Navajo tell stories that bears taught them how to do something or Grandmother Spider taught the Navajo women to weave, these stories are being validated by Western science (Deloria, 1995).

People of the Great Plains tell Coyote stories when there is snow on the ground; people in the Northwest along the coastal regions tell Raven stories; and Micmac/Mi'kmaq people tell Gluscabie stories, all of which have a moral or message.

In 1992, at the American Advancement of Science Conference in Chicago a new field was introduced call zoopharmacogynosy. Zoopharmacognosy refers to the process by which animals self-medicate, by selecting and using plants, soils, and insects to treat and prevent disease. Coined by Dr. Eloy Rodriguez, a biochemist and professor at Cornell University, the word is derived from roots zoo, pharma, and gnosy. Biser (1998) wrote that some species ingest non-foods, such as toxic plants, clay, or charcoal, to ward off parasitic infestation or poisoning. M. A. Huffman reported chimpanzees eat certain bushes as an emetic, and, in order to remove parasitic worms from their intestines, substantial evidence indicates that they swallow the whole leaves of certain rough-leaved plants (Reynolds, 2005, pp. 41-43).

Starks & Slabach (2012) indicated that humans have been eating clay since the time of the ancient Egyptians. There is no documentation, however, on which species initially learned the practice.

The Inuit of Arctic Canada learned to hunt seals by observing the behaviors of polar bears hunting at seal breathing holes. The bear knew that the seal was ready to breathe through the hole when the hair on the bear's muzzle moved. This hunting style was adapted by polar Inuit who fashioned a stick with a wishbone and a feather. As soon as the feather moved, they knew the seal was coming to take a breath on the surface of the ice, and they were ready with their harpoons (C. Jonkel, C. Bjorklund, personal conversation, 2011).

The Murri people, Indigenous people of Australia, have similar stories of how they learned from animals. For example Myee the Bogong Moth woman, who didn't heed advice, lost her beautiful colors when she traveled up the mountains to the snow demonstrating that when children misbehave, there are consequences (McKay, 2001, pp. 78-79).

The first Platypus was born of a mother duck and a father water rat. As an interracial baby, it was rejected until the mother found a place of safety and acceptance in the Blue Mountain Ranges (McKay, 2001, pp. 57-60).

Another example of watching and researching the world we live in occurred a few years ago on the Navajo Indian Reservation in Arizona. Some older people were asking questions: Why is there an increased population of deer mice? A few years ago the United States had a major outbreak of hantavirus. The Navajo people watched nature that year and saw that there was a lot of rain; unusual for the desert. It caused the pinion pines to produce an abundance of pine nuts, the food source for deer mice, which in turn caused a population explosion of mice, which carried the virus. The virus was deposited in the dust with urine and saliva. Children who played in the dust were the first ones to acquire the virus. Many young Navajo, who were infected by the virus, died. The Navajo elders had a theory that the rain had somehow caused the epidemic and they were right on target. In Navajo stories, mice are considered to be the bearers of an ancient illness that even predates the bubonic plague in the Navajo region. Healers say that when mice enter the home, they put people at risk of infection, as people come into contact with mouse droppings and urine. The illness enters through the mouth, the nose, or the eyes, and it usually attacks the strongest and healthiest of the Navajo people. Therefore, traditional medicine prescribes avoiding mice, keeping them out of the hogans, and isolating food supplies. Some Navajo medicine people, called haatalli in their language, predicted the 1993 hantavirus outbreak. Their oral tradition says that in 1918 and 1933-34, there were similar outbreaks. After an increase in rainfall there was an increase in the pinion crop and that provided food for the overpopulation of mice (Moon-Stumpff, 2010). In the recent past, mainstream science and the National Science Foundation have generally discounted traditional environmental knowledge, but these stories and experiences emanate from generations of Indigenous people watching and living in a Place.

There are innumerable instances of items of so-called "folk wisdom" which were dismissed by "scientific information" turning out to be truer than the science which at first discounted them. That folk wisdom was simply the distillation of many generations of experience (Bruchac, 2005, p. 87).

Indigenous wisdom and research continues to inform Western science. As mentioned previously, it has been shown from studies on climate change, that Western scientists, especially in the Arctic of Alaska, have begun to depend on native knowledge and research (Wohlforth, 2004). Another example of Indigenous knowledge informing Western science involves an Ojibwa elder, Ogimakwe, who was interviewed by Mary Magoulick, a folklorist at Georgia College in Milledgeville, Georgia. The elder described a lesson she learned from a group of trees: how the older trees give protection to the younger trees:

> I was looking one day [looks and gestures outside] and I was noticing all these trees they reach out and they touch each other, that's how they grow. They don't grow straight up, you know. They grow tall into the sky towards the Creator, but they also reach up to touch each other. And they, all the little ones, they'll grow right next to the big ones... And they [the bigger trees] hug 'em, they protect 'em, you know (Ogimakwe, quoted in Magoulick, n.d.).

Recently, Western scientist Dr. Susan Simard at the University of British Columbia discovered through testing of carbon transfer, that the older trees provide carbon to saplings by common underground mycorrhizal networks (Simard, 1997). Thus being Mother trees to the smaller saplings.

By watching polar bears or moths and other animals, we continue to learn about the world around us: "Salish people say that the thunder wakes the bears from hibernation. Our elders[5] taught us that the Blue Jay has an important message if we listen. We can see the changes in the earth and the animals and plants because the earth speaks to us through the animals and plants" (R. Bigcrane, personal conversation, 2011).

Chapter 3
Oral Histories, Stories, and Art as Data

I will tell you something about stories,
[he said]
They aren't just entertainment.
Don't be fooled,
They are all we have, you see,
all we have to fight off
illness and death (Silko, 1977, p. 2).

Stories as Data

Stories or narratives are the origin of American Indian oral tradition and are the means for sharing knowledge and passing it from one generation to another. Stories build bridges between two interpretations of an event. Scores of tribal histories are older than we are, and many are told by watching and listening to the Land, as my friends Thundering Hill and Roy Bigcrane have pointed out. Countless stories are thousands of years old, and carry the wisdom of all those years. Stories were extensively used as a teaching method for children as well as adults and they function to connect issues that are central to the individual, community, and social process (Cruikshank, 1990). Through tribal stories, the elders have passed down examples of appropriate behavior, knowledge, and philosophies central to their tribe (Battiste & Henderson, 2000; Brant-Castellano, 2000). Although stories are traditionally used to highlight lessons in morality or of confirming identity, in this work stories are used to tell of peoples' experiences. Since time immemorial, Indigenous cultures and tribal stories have been passed down from generation to generation (Trimble, Sommer & Quinlan, 2008).

Creation stories tell us how the world came to be—they remind us of who we are and of our belonging, for example, animal stories: "There are stories that hold mythical elements, such as creation and teaching stories, [for example, how the animals made the world safe for humans,] and there are personal narratives of place, happenings, and experiences as the...(Aunties and uncles) experienced them and passed them along to the next generation through oral tradition" (Kovach, 2009, p. 95). There are stories that have been told to others for safekeeping, like the stories told of the Plains Wars, the Sand Creek Massacre, the Washita Creek Massacre, and Custer's battle. These stories live in the hearts of the Cheyenne people so they can be told to future generations. Stories are told of personal experiences. Blackfeet writer Little Bear (2000) wrote "Storytelling is a very important aspect of Native America. It is not just the words and the listening but the actual living of the story" (p. xii). These are the stories we collect in our research data.

Kovach (2009) wrote that narratives are the primary means for passing down knowledge within tribal and Indigenous communities. Stories are our primary means of relating to one another. We would not survive without stories. Stories can tell us how to relate in a community and to be part of a community. In his writings, Mehl-Madrona (2011) indicated that Australian Aboriginal elders inform us that there are many layers of story and how to discern when to use each layer of the story and for what healing:

> Each research project needs to undertake a number of processes in order to set the project within the context of the story (P. Croft-Warcon, personal communication, 2011).

Those of us who are not from the specific tribe telling the story can never understand the context of that story. It is through the culture and the history of the tribe that the story is understood. For example in 2004 Albert Marshall, Mi'kmaq elder, told me that we will never understand a Navajo Coyote story unless we are Navajo. Whenever human beings gather, we tell stories, stories of weddings, funerals, stories of events and of people we know. Stories shape our brains. Stories allow us to bridge from Indigenous knowledge to scientific knowledge (Mehl-Madrona, 2010). For example, oral histories tell of when there were giants on the earth, stories of giant deer, elk, and beaver (Trimble, et al., 2008). Today, Western science is discovering the fossil remains of these animals.

In the late Pleistocene era, North America's forests and plains were filled with lumbering mastodons, armored rhinos, great dire wolves, saber tooth cats, ten-foot long armadillo like creatures, beavers the size of armchairs, turtles that weighed almost as much as cars, and sloths that were able to reach tree branches twenty feet tall (Mann, 2011).

Legends and myths are alternative forms of history. They are stories whose origins are lost in time about actions that may be foreign to the non-Indigenous experience of how the world works (Trimble, et al., 2008). Other concerns in telling stories are stories sacred to the community. Not everyone is permitted to tell them nor is everyone allowed to listen.

Oral history is an additional category of story. It is a term with many meanings. In its generic form, the term oral history has come to mean any talk, any telling of events that have happened in the past. Other meanings focus on traditional Indigenous knowledge, oral narrative, oral stories of events, and oral tradition. All of these meanings refer to events that have been passed down from generation to generation (Trimble, et al., 2008). Oral histories tell us about life in the past and can be traditional stories that are quite specific about the cultural past and hold cultural specific significance for the community: "They represent a continuing commitment to oral transfer of knowledge in indigenous cultures" (Trimble, et al., 2008, p. 103). How stories are told may be prescribed by protocols; for example, the Salish and Pend d'Oreilles cannot tell Coyote stories unless there is snow on the ground. As researchers, we may question who is allowed to tell stories and to whom. How is the information allowed to be told and when?

Some communities (Murri, South Sea Island, Australian Aboriginal) tell us that oral histories are memories of the past that are told in the present by certain Story Keepers in their community. Sometimes the stories are of a personal nature or family traditions such as the oral histories passed down from the experiences of ancestors and may include tribal culture or how to do certain bead or basket work; they can tell of ceremonies, prayers, medicine plants, sacred places, and of wars. Some stories may date back hundreds and thousands of years, back to time immemorial. Oral histories are specific to the culture of each Indigenous community, and often each individual family. In many tribes the leaders select who will be the next "Keeper" of certain oral histories after the present Keeper passes over:

Indigenous oral history can contain information
that, whether in the form of traditions or included
as part of first-person memories, is sacred to the
tribe. Questions about who is allowed to tell the
information, who is allowed to hear the information, how and when the information is allowed to
be told, and who is allowed to have access to the
information for the long term are among the most
important for practitioners of indigenous oral history (Trimble, et al., 2008, p. 17).

Indigenous scholars and researchers also identify themselves
through their stories within their research projects (Lavallée, 2009).
Fixico (2003) wrote that stories among American Indians consist of
at least five parts: time, place, character, event, and purpose. Each
part connects the other parts for the storyteller to weave the story.
Many Indigenous scholars use narrative and storytelling as the primary method of supporting research objectives and community
goals at the same time. Stories can assist researchers as openings for
a variety of methods of data gathering and knowledge seeking such
as openings for conversations or sharing circles (Trimble, et al.,
2008; Wilson, 2008; Weber-Pillwax, 2004). Stories as data are important and one key to collecting these data is hearing the stories.
One can hear a story and go through the motions of being attentive
and acting engaged to allow participants to talk and tell their story.
"Hearing" the story means having a relationship with the story and
the teller, and knowing that there is value to the story. The stories
are the guardians of accumulated knowledge within communities:
"…for many Indigenous people, stories serve as the basis for how
our communities work….and reminders of our individual responsibilities to the survival of our communities" (Brayboy, 2005, p.
427). So in the true methods of Indigenous people, I begin this
work by gathering stories of time, place, characters, experiences,
and journeys. I gather these stories through sharing circles.

Recall that there is a difference between sharing circles and a research focus group. Sharing circles are places where the participants
tell their stories. For example, among the Cree, ancestors who have
died are present in the circle. Food is served. The circle may take
many hours and everyone can contribute to the story. It is not just
the researcher's agenda. It is the agenda of the community. An elder may lead the circle. Everyone participates and the circle directs

how the story is told. The researcher lets the story flow without interrupting. The power is with the people telling the story and not the researcher, although the researcher may ask questions to enhance understanding of the story (Weber-Pillwax, 2004; Dana-Saco, 2010).

Wilson (2008) and Kovach (2009) tell us that as Indigenous researchers we should collaborate with community leaders by asking key questions. For example, how they want the researcher to tell their story; how they want to collaborate with the researcher to ensure that the community's needs are met with the research and that the community moves forward past historical trauma; and how the community wants the data to be disseminated:

> Storytelling also taught us about resistance to colonialism—our people have resisted even when legislation attempted to assimilate our children. All stories have something to teach us. What is most important is to learn to listen, not simply hear, the words that storytellers have to share (Thomas, 2005, p. 241)

It is morally and ethically right for the community to own the stories that are collected as data, not the researcher, not the university, or the government. Community members have trusted the researcher, and have shared their stories with the researcher.

All stories have something to teach us. What is important is to listen to the stories, to really listen and not just hear the words. In Western research methodologies, researchers have often entered communities to ask themselves, "What can the stories from this community do for me, for my dissertation, for the book I want to write?" Rather they should be asking, "How can I convey the community's stories to empower this community?" Countless numbers of Indian people regard the telling of stories as a sacred ceremony (Wilson, 2008; Silko, 1977; Tafoya, 1997). For example:

> Every time we tell a story it's a ceremony. In English, we translate it that when you tell a story you "wet it with your breath." You give it life, just as when you give water to a seed it blossoms (Tafoya, 1997 p. 135).

Art as Data

Stories and art, according to artist and Australian Aboriginal woman Pam Croft-Warcon, can help with mental healing. She told me that telling stories and creating art helped with her own self-identity and mental healing. She is the only Australian Aboriginal person who holds a Ph.D. in Visual Arts. I have known her for over twenty years and consider her my friend. She once told me that one can uncover stories of trauma and happiness within a community from art stories. Her Mud Map series of Rockhampton and the Sand Hills, of Queensland, Australia, where she makes her home, is a personal story of belonging. It is about reconciliation, and is a visual narrative of what she has learned about her life journey. Her work is also a personal healing tool, which aids the understanding and acceptance of the events of her life while at the same time teaching her to love her physical, emotional, and spiritual self. Pamela discusses her mud map series as stories:

> Each mud map is likened to cultural text, as a fluid interactive process which records past and present journeys imprinted within the Australian landscape. The maps trace the tracks of animals and peoples, connections and relationships to spaces and places, symbols, patterns and colours...The crabs imprinted their presence as they foraged for food, so too did the Ibis and seagulls. This evidence of water and animals became stories, recorded in the mud like texts that have been imprinted within the artwork (Fredericks, 2006, p. 15).

These are visual stories that live on in memory and reality long after the artist passes on:

> Australian Aboriginal art is one of the oldest continuing art traditions in the world. Much of the most important knowledge of aboriginal society was conveyed through different kinds of storytelling—including narratives that were spoken, performed as dances or songs, and those that were painted (EDSITEment!, National Endowment for the Humanities, n.d.).

These concepts were also reiterated by groups of unnamed Aboriginal artists across Canada:

> Art can be medicine, a survival tool, an antidote. Art is our identity, our place, a sign of our presence on this planet. It is medicine as it helps healing because we've been through so many things. Art is for the people. It can help build communities.

Making art is participating in creation. It is making oneself available to the spirit, the vision, the invisible, the imagined.

Art is about historical recovery—who we are in a place we've never left. Art is a tool for reclaiming, renaming and reframing history.

Art can turn your life around. It saves lives. Art can be a therapy for communities and survivors. We've gone through a lot…

Aboriginal arts are the economics of the soul —self-worth, respect and honour (Trepanier, 2008, p. 15).

Chapter 4
Preparing Ourselves, Our Relationships, and Learning from Place

We are part of the world as much as it is part of us, existing within a network of relations among Entities... This determines and defines for us rights to be earned and bestowed as we carry out rites to country, self and others... [Oodgergoo, Australian poet and activist, explains:] "All living things, be they mammals, birds, reptiles, insects or trees are our sisters and brothers and therefore we must protect them. We are their custodians. We not only share with them, we also guard them" (Martin, 2003, pp. 209-210).

In the previous chapters, I wrote how we, as Indigenous people, learn from Place. This chapter will further elaborate on that concept. My friend and colleague Roy Bigcrane tells me that Places on the Flathead Indian Reservation, where we live and work, are imbued with spirits. The mountains, the forests, the lake, the animals, and the rivers give us knowledge if we are willing to observe, hear, and learn. We often talk of the water and forest spirits. We learn from our homelands and our Place. Understanding our Indigenous places makes us who we are as Indigenous people. Within these places are our relationships, the bones and spirits of our ancestors, and our connections to our past.

My Grampa knew that wilderness Places had things to teach us. He took my brother and me for long walks in the woods along the Charles River or around Lake Attitash[6] to watch, and listen for animals. He asked us questions like, "Who lives in the 'creaking tree'?" or "What do you think made the holes under the trees?" and "What species of fish swim in the rivers?" He taught us to fish for catfish, and thread the worms on the hook with skill, not like a "sissy." As I write I can imagine us walking with him and the voice of his teachings. He made us maps of the forest and made us use them to discover hidden treasures. Because of his teachings, I am never frightened traveling in the forests.

Locating oneself in Place as a researcher is a key component within the Indigenous research framework (Absolon & Willett, 2005; Baskin, 2005; Restoule, 2004). Many of us introduce ourselves by who we are, where we are from, who our ancestors are. This identification allows people to know us, which helps to establish trust, to locate our genealogy, and to define our position as a researcher (Martin, 2003; Absolon & Willett, 2005). Dr. Thundering Hill indicated that we should also introduce ourselves to the Land and the Places where our participants live in order to form relationships with their environments (personal communication, Dr. Thundering Hill, 2012). To that impression, I would add that we should introduce ourselves to the lands where our ancestors died, or were massacred.

Wilson (2008) and others (Letendre & Caine, 2004) indicate that an Indigenous methodology means answering to all of your relations, and fulfilling those relationships around you. Only after the researcher develops the beliefs that serve as a foundation to an Indigenous research paradigm can one begin to define the specific methods that fit with the methodology.

The research path begins with the central home of the research, the community, the Place. This includes building relationships with members of the community as well as having respect for that community, and learning about the people in the community and what their culture is like. It begins with an ethnographic point of view of living and working in the community.

I have lived in many places in my life, for instance, the Philippines, Canada, the Arctic, and the four communities I researched for this work. Each community is unique. Each has its own culture, ceremonies, geography, language, ways of dressing, ways of living in the world, and laws. Although there are differences, there are also similarities, as evidenced from the interview responses. Like the ceremony of making the Mi'kmaq potato basket:

> The research that we do as Indigenous people is a ceremony that allows us a raised level of consciousness and insight into our world.

> ....The source of a research project is the heart/
> mind of the researcher... A 'good heart' guarantees
> a good motive, and good motives benefit everyone
> involved (Wilson, 2008, pp. 137 & 60).

The ceremony itself includes the tools the researcher uses to do the work. It is the ritual of everyone thinking the same thing, as in the talking circles [or yarning] called thinking alike. It is what the researcher does, and what is learned, and how it changes the researcher: "If research doesn't change you as a person, then you haven't done it right" (Wilson, 2008, p. 135).

Lori's Voice

> *I sit in my camp by the shore of the lake and watch the*
> *sun rise in the quiet of the dawn (Close, 2009, p. 7).*

Kwai, Kwai Metalawin. Weli esti puk? And so I begin with the story of my own journey, not to be boastful or self-important, but to introduce myself in a traditional way through my life story, and brief history. It is our way of having others learn about us, and our family. We are all related.

My Indian name is Otter. In Mi'kmaq it is called *Kiw'nik*. Many tribes believe Otters express joy for all. Part of the Otter's vibrant energy is associated with its deep connection to water, where they spend most of their time and where they are very fast and agile swimmers. Often they are seen floating on their backs with their paws sticking out of the water or playfully sliding on their bellies or doing acrobatics. The name suits me as I am a swimmer, love being in the water, and have a playful nature. Once, in the middle of an interview I was having with a Shaman in Finland's arctic north, the Shaman told me I had "Otter Power" and that I was a "Power Woman" and to use my power wisely. What is remarkable to me is that Chief Henri Membertou also had Otter as his helper animal. Membertou was the first Mi'kmaq to be baptized as Catholic (Lescarbot, 1907). Chief Henri Membertou is one of my ancestors.

In our Mi'kmaq language our land is called *Ndakinna*. We are the Dawnland People from where the sun rises over the east coast of Canada. The Abenaki call it Alnombak or Aln8bak (8 is an old Jesuit symbol for a nasalized, unrounded o). My family is a blend of French immigrants who journeyed to New France, today called Canada, in the 1600s. They called themselves Acadian and settled in the bountiful lands of Nova Scotia, New Brunswick, and Quebec. They intermarried with the Native populations of Mi'kmaq, Huron, and Abenaki First Nations and called themselves by the names of the places where they settled...Bras D'Or Lakes, Nova Scotia; Cocagne, New Brunswick; Madawaska, Quebec; Eskasoni, Nova Scotia. My paternal grandmother's family comes from the Huron-Wyandot Cord Clan located on the Isle d'Orleans, a community organized by the Jesuits for the converted Hurons in Quebec. No one ever spoke of her family's ties to First Nations as they may have been in denial. Or in those days, it was not good to be Indian. My mother's family is Abenaki from the Deer Clan and descendents of Mi'kmaq and Acadians. We were connected to them ever since I can remember. Although, I did not grow up on a reservation or a reserve, in summer my family traveled from Massachusetts to Canada, Vermont, and New Hampshire. My brother and I roamed the lakes, forests and woods of the Dawnlands, the Aboriginal territory of the Abenaki and Mi'kmaq. Our grandfather taught us how to live in the woods, to catch catfish with a worm. When the catfish stung us with its dangerous spines, he taught us to rub the stung area on the catfish belly to get relief. He taught us to read "treasure maps" and find hidden riches that he had placed under the "creaking tree." He never smoked or drank whiskey in the woods. He took us to Lake Attitash, named by the Abenaki for the blueberries that grow there. As we picked, we ate more than we gathered; our tongues and teeth told the tale when our grandmothers asked us, "Where are the blueberries?" We could only smile with purple teeth and tongues.

We listened to the Mi'kmaq stories of the Great Celestial Bear and how her blood changed the fall foliage from green to red. We swam in cobalt blue mountain lakes; ate the amazing woodland plants and animals. We went "mucking" in the low tide mud flats and gathered clams on Plum Island. Before they were cooked, we raced our lobsters across the floor of the camp and, if we were brave, we removed the bands of elastic holding their pincer claws. When they turned bright red, they were ready to eat, and we dipped their succulent bodies into bowls of hot butter, and devoured them as juices and butter ran down our chins and arms onto a newspaper-covered table. Our great grandmother, Memere, helped us find the little shell in the stomach that she said was the image of Mali or the Mi'kmaq Virgin Mary. She told us stories in French, which was her first language. She was a Mi'kmaq-Abenaki woman whose culture had been ripped from her family by the Jesuits. She remembered a handful of medicine plants, not her culture, language, or ceremonies. Memere was a strict Catholic and she celebrated St. Anne's Day, the patron saint of the Mi'kmaq people. When I was born, she gave me my middle name for St. Anne. If I close my eyes, I can still see her wearing her wine-colored dress reserved for Sunday Mass. I have heard her tribal language spoken by other tribal members, but I can only speak a few words. She gave me the gift of knowing some medicine plants and the gift of wonder, and curiosity, but she was unable to share her ceremonies or many of the old stories. However, her stories of Gluscabe, the Corn Mother, the Girl who Married a Bear, and the Great Celestial Bear are ones I know and cherish, and I dance at powwows in the regalia of the Northeast Woodlands women. We didn't realize how lucky we were. We were not rich, but we had enough and we were wealthy in culture and family.

Every summer, Memere's promises to her patron saint were kept as we drove the long pilgrimage from Massachusetts to Ste Anne de Beaupre, Quebec. She was happy to pray in her French language, to stand in awe at the immense basilica, to visit with her relatives in the territory of the Mi'kmaq. My brother and I also stared in wonder at the bones said to be the arm of St. Anne located behind the golden statue of Jesus' grandmother. The majestic basilica that stands today reminds me of the Notre Dame Cathedral in Paris. It is an elaborate structure built in the Norman Gothic style of architecture, unlike the little wooden chapel built by the early settlers:

> The first chapel was built on this site by early settlers in 1658 to house a miraculous statue of St. Anne. By 1688 it had become a site of local pilgrimage, and by 1707, Native Americans (who in Canada are called the First Nations) were coming to venerate the saint they called "Grandmother in the Faith."
>
> The first miracle attributed to the intercession of St. Anne at Beaupré was the cure of a crippled workman in 1658. This was soon followed by the deliverance of a group of sailors from a storm (Canadascope, 2111, p. 2).

Memere insisted that I attend Catholic school, which I did for 12 years and although I was popular and a good student, I was told that I was "not college material because of my [Otter Spirit] play-fulness." Today, it is an honor and privilege to teach and live on the Flathead Indian Reservation where my students, friends, and colleagues have introduced me to their lands, culture, stories, lan-guage, and ceremonies. I am grateful for their warm friendships. Although I was raised away from many of my Canadian relatives and ancestors, I was determined to give voice to my First Nations families who had no voice for 500 years after contact. The Catho-lic Church, Jesuits, and Canadian government told them how to live, what to believe, how to be spiritual, how to kill the Indian inside—and took their lands. Today, although many of their off-spring are suffering from what Duran (2006) calls "soul wounds," many others have adapted to mainstream life:

> By the early part of this century, the Mi'kmaq of Nova Scotia lived on 40 small reserves scattered around the province. Much of the income earned by Mi'kmaq families came from work in indus-try or agriculture. Some Mi'kmaq operated their own farms and sold their surplus, while others hired themselves out as labourers on non-Aborigi-nal farms. Many others went annually to harvest blueberries in Maine, a migration pattern that still exists to a limited extent. As the wage economy be-came more important, the amount of time spent hunting, trapping, fishing and making handicrafts declined (Alex Christmas, quoted in Canada, Roy-al Commission on Aboriginal Peoples, 1996, pp. 400-401).

Through my work, I have released the historical anger and trauma of our past, and have progressed into the 21st century. Today, all over the world, Indigenous people are reclaiming their voices. Indigenous knowledge has value and importance to western lifeways. My obligation to my ancestors, friends, and the partici-pants in this project weighs heavy. Because of this, I have danced with my heart and mind to understand our common journey: "It is the knowing and respectful reinforcement that all things are related and connected. It is the voice from our ancestors that tell us when it is right and when it is not. Indigenous research is a life changing ceremony" (Wilson 2008, p. 61).

Chapter 5
Indigenous Psychology as a Behavioral Science

*The medicine is already within the pain and suffer-
ing. You just have to look deeply and quietly. Then you
realize it has been there the whole time.*
— *saying from Native American Oral Tradition
(Duran, 2006, p. 49).*

Indigenous psychology, also called ethno-psychology is a branch of the behavioral/social sciences. Basically, Indigenous psychology is described by Kim and Berry (1993, p. 2) as "the scientific study of human behavior (or the mind) that is native, that is not transported from other regions, and that is designed for its people." An increasing number of social scientists have come to realize the pervasive influence of culture on human behavior. It has become imperative for culture to be included as an important variable in all psychological research, theory, and practice (Kim, Yang & Hwang, 2006; Nebelkopf & Phillips, 2004; Organista, Marin & Chun, 2010; Matsumoto & van de Vijver, 2011). However, in numerous mainstream university courses, Indigenous students are forced to study existing psychological theories that represent the psychology and cultural traditions of Europe and North America. These courses are not appropriate with Indigenous ways of being and thinking.

Grayshield & Mihecoby (2010) postulated that before anyone can begin to apply conventional psychological principles and theories to an ethnocultural group, they must first understand its unique lifeways and thought ways. Pan-Indian generalizations about Native Americans abound in the literature. Trimble, et al. (2008) wrote that in order to accurately learn of tribal cultures, researchers must live in and be exposed to the culture, customs, traditions, and ethnicity of the community where they hope to gain knowledge.

Indigenous psychology advocates examining knowledge, skills, and beliefs as well as the cultural concepts that groups have about themselves, in their natural environment. Theories, concepts and methods are developed to correspond with Indigenous psychological phenomena (Kim & Berry, 1993; Duran, 2006; Ranzijn, McConnochie & Nolan, 2008). Indigenous psychology includes beliefs that Indigenous groups may have concerning mental health behaviors. For example, some Indigenous groups in Haiti believe that bad spirits cause mental illness (Videbeck, 2014, p. 127), and in the Philippines witches put spells on people and cause them to behave in a certain way (Dr. Santos Colomeda, personal conversation, 1966).

Others have described mental illnesses as "soul loss," "spirit possession," or use descriptive categories such as the "physiological imbalance," "insufficient vitality," "breach of taboo," or "cultural confusion" (Tseng, 2001, p. 157). In one certain place in Australia mental illness is not discussed as such. It is called Womba, and "No one likes to be branded with the word Womba" (Jeffries, personal conversation, 2011). Womba may also refer to a range of issues including social and emotional wellbeing. Some Indigenous people may also have their own tribal language words that they use within their tribally based context of place (B. Fredericks, personal conversation, 2012).

In *Healing the Soul Wound,* one of Eduardo Duran's patients indicated that violence is a spirit that can move from place to place and across generations unless someone with "medicine" does something about it (Duran, 2006).

Indigenous psychology seeks to use appropriate methods from a particular place to research issues in mental health and behavioral issues, and to create new knowledge regarding these issues. Although Kim, Yang, & Hwang (2006) identified 10 characteristics of Indigenous psychology, the three most relevant to this work are: (1) Examining psychological phenomena in ecological, historical, and cultural context. (2) The starting points of research in Indigenous psychology can be identified as indigenization from without and indigenization from within, which to me indicates that research methodologies must be accomplished from an Indigenous paradigm and within Indigenous communities. (3) Indigenous psychology needs to be developed for each individual, cultural,

Native, and ethnic group. Other characteristics from Kim, Yang, & Hwang are listed in the footnotes.[7]

To understand and better respond to the mental health of Indigenous people one needs to reflect upon what mental health means to Indigenous people. Reyhner (1992) points to the need for community involvement in healing and wellbeing. There is a correlation in Indigenous families and their perception of disease:

> Native cultures teach that the individual does not have the power to get well or sick all on her own, because illness occurs through participation in a life of many constraints. We are born into families with particular beliefs, cultures, values, and habits....We tend to think, relate, live, and feel the way our families do (Mehl-Madrona, 2003, p. 32).

But many families have been wounded in countless ways because of colonization, culture, and language loss. Called historical trauma, intergenerational trauma, or soul wounding, it is held responsible for substance and spousal abuse, suicides, and numerous maladaptive behaviors. Yet, people are working together in American Indian and First Nations communities across North America to heal these traumas. For example, culturally focused intervention programs like the Historical Trauma and Unresolved Grief intervention developed by the Takini Network of the Navajo works to restore an attachment to traditional values in an effort to address the transfer of trauma across generations (Yellow Horse Brave Heart, 2003).

However, to be truly successful, all agencies and programs working with Indigenous people globally have to work with cultural identity. Treating the symptoms of ill health, including addiction and mental health issues, does not heal the root causes of historical trauma and colonization or treat the soul wound (Duran, 2006; Lavallée & Poole, 2010). Healing in each community is unique, just as each community, and tribe is unique. To understand the needs of each community, researchers and agencies ought to seek out information from the community elders and medicine people:

> Although a number of authors have commented on what mental health practitioners should be taught to be effective and appropriate with indigenous people, rarely have traditional healers been

asked for their views (Mehl-Madrona, 2009, p. 20).

One example of understanding the cultural aspect of Indigenous psychology comes from Duran (2006) who wrote that in some Native American groups a mental health diagnosis can be similar to a naming ceremony. Naming ceremonies are part of many cultures and traditions and are used to assign spiritual identities to the person receiving the name. A naming ceremony performed by a therapist or a healer has deep implications to the person and the community. This can mean that assigning a stereotypical diagnosis from the Diagnostic and Statistical Manuel of Mental Illness Volume V to Indigenous people in many instances can be problematic. None of the diagnoses considers the historical implications and factors of the naming ceremony, which are of critical importance in this process. When a person goes through the mental health diagnosis, they may perceive that they have been named for a particular pathological identity and may incorporate the symptoms of the diagnosis into their psychological makeup (Duran, 2006). Within the belief systems of some Indigenous people, there is the notion that once their identity has been crystallized through the naming ceremony, it remains until a more powerful ceremony occurs, like a later formal procedure to remove the negative name. One of the keys for therapists working with Indigenous people is decolonizing the individual from the ideologies of diagnosis and naming:

> Soul wounding of the land also can occur when there is a massacre of human beings on the land. Basically, the land needs to undergo assessment and treatment in order to restore balance. It is difficult to restore balance to the community of human beings if the land's soul has been wounded and left unhealed (Duran, 2006, p. 121).

Because we are the Indigenous people from a Place, healing the Place is just as critical as healing the community or the individual. The land has also been a victim of historical trauma; the lands, the waters, and the animals have swallowed the blood, bones, ashes, and screams of our ancestors. Healing the land, the animals, and the waters is crucial. We heal the Place that makes us who we are; we heal ourselves; we heal the soul wounds that were inflicted on many of the Indigenous people of the earth.

Countless community members find that mainstream therapists who work in Indigenous communities have no concept of these historical and underlying causes of problems, and these are usually left untreated. An understanding of the history of Native people is essential to deconstruct these problems seen daily in clinical practice. To understand how to heal the individual and collective identity of Indigenous people, we need to explore the colonial impact on identity. For example the loss of culture and language that resulted in forced assimilation into the boarding schools:

> The legacy of the policies of forced assimilation is also seen in the current relationship of Aboriginal peoples with the larger Canadian society. Images of the "savage" and stereotypes of the "drunken Indian" continue to recur in popular media. Racism is still widespread... [and] there is a continuing lack of historical awareness of the experience of Aboriginal peoples with colonization and the enduring impact on their well-being and social options (Kirmayer & Valaskakis, 2009, p. 19).

Barnes (2000) wrote that we [as Indigenous researchers and healers] need to recognize problems as belonging to communities instead of individuals and to address the needs and resources of communities instead of stigmatizing individuals as defective or inferior. Mainstream and Western trained psychologists have not yet begun to understand and accept the spiritual dimension of behaviors in Indigenous communities (Krippner & Welch, 1992).

The Native American participants in a study conducted by the UC Davis Center for Reducing Health Disparities (2009) indicated that drug and alcohol use was a major problem in their communities. Not only did drug and alcohol use affect the mental health of individuals, but also the presence of drugs was seen as contributing to the violence in communities. Violence and drug use were seen by participants as directly related to the disconnect that individuals feel from their community and their sense of isolation and depression. Additionally, forms of racism and discrimination were experienced in mental health services and were an area of significant concern to Native American communities.

Stigma and lack of awareness of what is culturally appropriate mental health care by mental health providers created barriers and discouraged Native Americans with mental illness from seeking treatment (anonymous participants, UC Davis Center for Reducing Health Disparities, 2009).

For scores of Native Americans (tribes not identified in the UC Davis Center for Reducing Health Disparities study, 2009), the problem lay in the absence of real listening or understanding on the part of the dominant society. Some participants in the study suggested that anti-stigma education is key to protect the community from discrimination, and that Native Americans should be proactive in educating non-Indian people about the needs of their communities (UC Davis Center for Reducing Health Disparities, 2009). For many, the impact of historical trauma on their communities was deeply felt. Historical trauma is the term used to express the legacy of social and cultural suffering related to harmful policies imposed on Native American communities by the United States government. Many participants mentioned one such policy—the forced removal of Native American children from their homes and placement in boarding schools—as a policy that has had a lasting impact on the mental health of Native American communities. The suffering that was caused by this policy has been transmitted through generations (Duran, 2006; Yellow Horse Brave Heart, 2003; UC Davis Center for Reducing Health Disparities, 2009).

The findings in the UC Davis Center for Reducing Health Disparities study (2009) are congruent with my findings in interviews with participants from the South Sea Island and Murri communities in Australia, the Sayisi Dene of Tadoule Lake, Manitoba, and the Flathead Indian Reservation in Montana.

Native Americans have been shown to suffer from disproportionately high degrees of psychological distress. Researchers and professionals have consistently associated this distress with Indigenous historical experiences of European colonization (Duran, 2006; Kirmayer, Simpson, & Cargo, 2003). Indeed, professional and community discourse regarding mental health in Native North America is distinguished by this emphasis on the impact of colonization on Indigenous communities (Gone & Alcantara, 2007). That Native people are at greater risk for experiencing traumatic events in their lives would be difficult to dispute. Research by Beals, et al. (2013) found that PTSD or post traumatic stress disorder has been found to be more common among American Indians than other populations. In contrast to personal experiences of a traumatic nature, however, historical trauma calls attention to the intergenerational accumulation of risk for poor mental health status among Native people, including Indigenous people of Australia and Canada. That risk ostensibly originates from the depredations of past colonial conquest, including ethnocidal policies and practices. Yellow Horse Brave Heart (2003) and Duran & Duran (1995) wrote that Native American historical trauma is modeled after logstanding clinical observations of the adverse psychological effects of the extermination of the Jews by Nazi Germany not just for Holocaust survivors, but also for their offspring. Conversely, the world continues to ignore the Native American Holocaust experience and this remains a stumbling block for the soul healing of Native people.

In the North American context, these researchers have assumed as fact a collective, cumulative, and intergenerational transmission of risk for adverse mental health outcomes that stem from the historical unresolved grief or "soul wound" inflicted by experiences of colonization. The pathological reactions are said to depart substantially from established categories of psychopathology, but nevertheless include many of the symptoms of complicated bereavement and complex post traumatic stress disorder (Baranowsky, Young, Johnson-Douglas, Williams-Keeler, & McCarrey, 1998).

At this point I want to address specifically the horrific experiences of our ancestors that led to historical trauma of later generations. Children were rounded up and sent to institutions run by churches under the auspices of governments. Their goal was to kill the Indian and save the man. These industrial schools subjected children as young as four years of age to rote learning, inadequate nutrition, manual labor, Christian indoctrination, cultural assimilation, military-style comportment, and brutal corporal punishment (Adams, 1995; Miller, 1996). Indeed, the Cariboo Tribal Council was involved in one study, which examined the impact of these schools on a First Nation community. They concluded:

> Residential school students were overloaded with activities more appropriate to a correctional institution than a school.. .[and] could not be considered appropriate for learning, growth, and personal fulfillment (Cariboo Tribal Council, 1991, p. 172).

Dr. Frank Oberklaid's (2013) data demonstrated that persistent stress on the brain increases cortisone levels and increases heart rate, which leads to shorter lives.

Mehl-Madrona (2011) wrote that Aboriginal people in Australia who experienced trauma in the residential schools or abuse at the hands of white Australians may have passed the effects of that abuse to their children. These effects have been shown to last at least four generations unless modified through corrective emotional experience, but healing is possible. However, "suffering cannot be resolved without healing the wound that underlies the suffering at the soul level" (Duran, 2006, p. 47):

> Historical trauma (HT) is cumulative emotional and psychological wounding over the lifespan and across generations, emanating from massive group trauma experiences; the historical trauma response (HTR) is the constellation of features in reaction to this trauma. The HTR often includes depression, self-destructive behavior, suicidal thoughts and gestures, anxiety, low self-esteem, anger, and difficulty recognizing and expressing emotions. It may include substance abuse, often an attempt to avoid painful feelings through self-medication. Historical unresolved grief is the associated affect that accompanies HTR; this grief may be considered fixated, impaired, delayed, and/or disenfranchised (Yellow Horse Brave Heart, 2003, p. 7).

In addition to the violence, widespread loss of Indigenous languages, cultures, and ceremonies, all have combined with multigenerational disruptions in parenting practices to yield a harrowing legacy of distress and disability for contemporary Native people. Evidence of the adverse psychosocial correlates of the boarding school experience has appeared routinely (Corrado & Cohen, 2003).

Luiggi (2012) wrote about the work of molecular biologist, Thomas Elbert, who has been exploring emotional memory—which deals with storage of emotionally traumatic events and highlights Elbert's work in the 1994 Rwanda genocide. Elbert's research participants were children from war torn areas of Somalia, Sudan, Afghanistan, Iraq, and northeast Sri Lanka, and their experiences have afforded him an opportunity to understand the effects of traumatic stress on populations: "Elbert's field observations are supported by research showing that traumatic experiences effect neuronal and epigenetic changes in the brain, particularly in regions such as the hippocampus and the amygdala" (Luiggi, 2012, p. 16).

Evidence of adverse psychosocial experiences correlates with the boarding school experiences, and has appeared routinely in psychological treatment (Corrado & Cohen, 2003). For example, one of the earliest systematic investigations of this legacy found that between one half and two thirds of respondents from a First Nation community assigned to the St. Joseph's Residential School in British Columbia reported childhood experiences of sexual abuse (Cariboo Tribal Council, 1991). There was increased stress on the children, and an absence of caring parents. Changes in brain physiology, as well as social determinants, destroyed resistance and increased risk factors for the children.

Brasfield (2001) has proposed diagnostic criteria for a "residential school syndrome" that essentially contextualizes and tailors the signs and symptoms of PTSD to the residential school experience of Native Americans across North America. In Canada, the call for national redress and reconciliation has largely run its course, resulting in a national apology and the creation of the Aboriginal Healing Foundation (AHF). The AHF through the government of Canada, has disbursed federal funds in the amount of $350 million to Aboriginal organizations and communities to "address the healing needs of First Nations, Inuit and Metis individuals, families and communities who suffer the legacy of physical and sexual abuse at residential schools, including intergenerational impacts" (Aboriginal Healing Foundation, 2002, p. 9).

Stories from children who attended the Kamoloops Residential School, British Columbia, Canada attest to the issues of severe discipline. Punishments included shaving the heads of children, diets of bread and water, public humiliation, and being beaten with a strap:

> Some people got punished; they got to lay down on the floor. Just pure bread and water to eat, laying on the floor...oh, I don't know how many days (Haig-Brown, 1988, p. 76).
> I was punished quite a bit because I spoke my language...I was put in a corner and punished

and sometimes, I was just given bread and water
...(Haig-Brown, 1988, p. 76).
[Children who ran away] always came back. They
got them back...Some got expelled; they got twenty lashes and then they got expelled...Father had a
strap; it was about an inch, inch and a half maybe.
And there was two doubled and they were rivetted
[sic] together. He used that. (Haig-Brown, 1988,
p. 99).

I was first sexually abused by a student when I
was six years old, and by a supervisor, an ex-Navy
homosexual, when I was eight. Homosexuality was
prevalent in the school. I learned to use sexuality
to my advantage, as did many other students...But
this had its long-term effects...including alcoholism, the inability to touch people, and an "I don't
care" attitude (Fred, 1988, p. 17).

These experiences endured by First Nations children in Canada
also caused personal trauma to native children in the United States,
Australia, and New Zealand:

The forced separation of parents and children was
traumatic for the children, and following that they
were thrown into a completely alien environment
where strangers (white ones at that) stripped away
all exterior indicators of tribal identity, even to the
point of changing names...the constant marching,
the regulation of every aspect of daily existence, the
humiliating punishments. It is hardly surprising
that in the first few days and weeks the tortured
sound of grieving children crying themselves to
sleep was a regular feature of institutional life (Adams, 1995, p. 223).

In America, Australia, and Canada, Indigenous people recognize historical trauma of early contact and subsequent treatment
justified by Social Darwinism, as contributing to many of the mental health disparities manifested in their populations generations
later and into the twenty-first century. Social Darwinism was used
to justify numerous exploits that are classified as of doubtful moral
value today. Colonialism was seen as natural and inevitable and was
given justification through Social Darwinian ethics. Society viewed

Native Americans as weak and unfit, therefore whites felt justified in seizing land and resources. Finally, it gave the ethical nod to brutal colonial governments that used oppressive tactics to control and eliminate Native people:

> ...it took little imagination to discern that the entire school program constituted an uncompromising hegemonic assault on their cultural identity. As already observed, many Indian parents were quick to see boarding schools as yet another attempt to destroy Indian lifeways (Adams, 1995, p. 223).

Mental health issues, poor self-esteem, devaluation of culture and language, substance abuse, incarceration, and poverty led to poor nutrition, housing, sanitation, and loss of parenting skills. These attitudes affect health access and health in general. When a population of people are brainwashed into believing that their lifeways and culture are devalued, of course there is going to be despondency, loss of self-esteem, and lack of motivation. Determinants of mental health are strongly linked to traditional cultural activities: What I mean by traditional cultural activities are activities done before contact that continue into the modern age: dancing at powwows (provides cardiovascular exercise), sweat lodge ceremonies (purge toxins from our bodies and maintain chemical balance), and hunting (makes possible a diet rich in traditional foods). For example, a traditional diet could include deer, moose, fish, kangaroo, lizard, barramundi, witchity grubs, buffalo, nuts, grains, and berries. To hunt and gather these foods helps social networking within the family and community as well. Climbing a mountain to gather berries is a wonderful form of exercise, as well as making it possible to commune with the natural, peaceful world. Playing active Native games provides social contacts and networks so individuals won't feel isolated and alone. Practicing Indigenous research with evidence based heath practice, steeped in the philosophy, language, culture, and ceremonies of Native communities, validates tribal knowledge and lifeways and reduces issues of colonization.

For Indigenous people in America, and from what I have learned speaking with Australian Indigenous people, determinants of mental health are also linked to the training of mental health care providers and researchers. Researchers should speak the language, understand and respect the culture, and relate to

Indigenous people with explanations of mental health procedures and interventions in language that is easily understood by the people. Moreover, Gone (2013) indicated, in a presentation at Montana State University, Bozeman, Montana, that in Indigenous communities, psychotherapy needs to hybridize and integrate therapies to fit the needs and culture of the community. Although very little evidence-based practice or research is available in this area, Gone hypothesizes that implementing cultural experiences, which encourage youth and adults to gain knowledge of their ceremonies, language, and arts, helps to heal addictions. Having a traditional healer or medicine person who combines treatments with Western psychotherapy is far more effective than psychotherapy alone. He is attracted to combining Western healing practices with community ceremonies and practices to determine if these hybridizations are more effective than Western psychotherapy alone. But finding funding for such projects is always a concern.

American Indian tribes federally recognized by the Bureau of Indian Affairs and the Department of the Interior are the only population in the United States born with the legal right to health care. Under the various treaties, the tribes exchanged vast amounts of land and natural resources for certain social services, including housing, education, and health care. That's why the Bureau of Indian Affairs and the Indian Health Service (IHS) exists to carry out the federal government's trust responsibility to provide these services (Warne, 2008). However, having said that, there are major funding disparities that contribute to determinants of mental health for American Indians.

The IHS per capita funding in 2005 was $2,100 per person. Medicare funding (for people over 65) was $7,200, and the Veterans Administration was $5,600. Even in prisons nearly $4,000 was spent per person on health care per year—almost double that of IHS. And who was born with a right to health care? Only American Indians do through treaty rights (Warne, 2008).

Warne, an Oglala Lakota medical doctor wrote, "the federal government has a trust responsibility to provide health care to American Indians." Warne quoted a tribal leader who said, "If you want to get rid of the Indian Health Service, that's fine. Just give us our land back" (Warne, 2008, pp. 1-2). American Indians who live on reservations and those who live in urban areas, are more inclined to come into the IHS clinics if the mental health therapist

or councilor has shared their Indigenous experiences and understands a shared culture. If we are to intervene early in mental health
problems, we need to find ways to bring Indigenous people into
the clinics, and they will come if there are Indigenous doctors or
nurses there.

Durie wrote (2001) that access to quality health services is an
important determinant of health for Indigenous people. American
Indians have the Indian Health Service on each of the 550 reservations. Australian Indigenous people have Aboriginal and Torres
Strait Island Health Service. In New Zealand, as well as in the high
Arctic of Canada, Indigenous health workers are often employed
as cultural or community aides. They have a first hand knowledge
of the community and a capacity to engage reluctant patients. But
if clients can't get to or won't go to the clinic, we need strategies to
help them.

Indigenous Concepts of Psychology:
The Murri People of Queensland

The Murris are the Indigenous people from the state of
Queensland, Australia; they are comprised of many groups such
as the Gungalu people from the Dawson and Callide Valley, and
Darumbal people. Over the years, since the early 1800s when Britain invaded their lands, they have undergone traumatic relocation
experiences which include loss of culture, loss of history, and language loss (personal communication, Robert Toby, Rockhampton,
Queensland, 1999). One can perceive how integrative psychological
treatments that combine Western methodologies and Indigenous
treatments would reduce this historical trauma:

> The discipline and practice of psychology
> have historically had a fraught relationship with
> Indigenous Australians. The colonisers brought
> with them the prevailing Western worldview
> of their day, that the Indigenous people were
> inferior, and, according to the principles of social
> Darwinism, would die out within a few generations.
> As psychology emerged as a profession in the
> 20th Century, psychological research was used to
> confirm the prevailing stereotypes of inferiority
> in multiple domains, and as agents of the state
> psychologists were instrumental in the removal of

Aboriginal children from their families. Even today
psychology is viewed with suspicion and mistrust by
many if not most Indigenous Australians (Ranzijn,
McConnochie, & Nolan, 2008, p. 9).
In fact, Aboriginal grandmothers and aunties recall with sadness
how their ancestors were treated:

> ...people had been hunted from their tribal coun-
> try "like animals"....Women and children were
> exploited like slaves by whites who were "respon-
> sible to no authority"; local groups were seduced
> by white men "of position and reputation" who
> used opium to snare servile workers and submissive
> sexual partners (Kidd, 1997, p. 44).

It was in these horrific times that the Queensland Black Police
began slaughtering the Murris. If they were not killed for defend-
ing their homelands and their families, they were relocated to
missions, operated by various churches. Here they had to interact
with enemy tribes. Relocation of people from their traditional territories has caused grief, and soul wounds, and these issues have
been handed down to their descendants (Duran, 2006).

Many Murri communities have no definition of mental health
as a potential area for sickness. However, medical professionals may
diagnose it as such because of a misunderstanding of the Murri
culture: "The question concerning Aboriginal mental health is embedded in a larger set of questions relating to culture and cultural
differences, historical events, social and cultural change and coping
mechanisms" (Bailey, 2005, p. 1).

It includes the health and welfare of all family members and addresses issues of grief, loss, sorrow, health, housing, socioeconomic
status, employment, and community. All of these issues are seen as
interwoven together in the fabric of community and family. However, many agencies and professionals treat the individual's needs
separately (White, Warren, & Hickey, 2008).

For Aboriginal people, the concept of health means "not just
the physical wellbeing of an individual but the social, emotional
and cultural well-being of the whole Community..." (Aboriginal
Health and Medical Research Council of New South Wales, 2013,
p. 7).

In many communities sadness, grief, and loss are a constant
presence. This sadness may originate from the historical loss of

children to missions and boarding schools where death, genocide, ill health, loss of language and culture, and suicide continue to impact the children several generations later (White, Warren, & Hickey, 2008). These children today are known as known as the *Stolen Generation* (McCarthy, 2000).

It is especially difficult for the men in Murri communities. They are angry and frustrated because their identity and role in society has been lost due to relocation and cultural devaluation. Since contact, customs and rituals have been lost, especially regarding sexual behavior and aggression. They often show anger and explosive behavior when talking about their situation. They are often victims of violent abuse, and, with the addition of alcohol, the abusive behavior escalates (Day, Nakata, & Howells, 2008).

Cries for help through harmful behaviors such as substance abuse and violence against self are all historical forms of anger. Some elders link the source of anger and hurt to the absence of a parent or caregiver who was responsible for that young person. In her paper, "You're not listening to me! Aboriginal Mental Health is different—Don't you Understand?," Jenine Bailey (2005) of James Cook University, Australia, describes Aboriginal poor mental health as not necessarily a sickness or disease, although it is mis-diagnosed as such by medical professionals. This is largely due to poor understanding of aspects pertaining to the culture of Aboriginal people. Questions concerning Aboriginal mental health are embedded in a larger set of questions relating to culture, cultural differences, historical events, social and cultural change, and coping mechanisms.

Bailey believes that mental health care providers need to move beyond the current "welfare/disadvantage" to a "rights/entitlements" approach in mental health. She believes that mental health professionals must understand the culture and history of the people they are treating:

> It can be said that the majority of health problems Aboriginal communities face today stem from colonisation....One could imply that we are still grieving for the past traumas....There is confusion about roles within family groups, breaking down of cultural values and beliefs, alcohol and drugs abuses, family violence, high rates of chronic diseases, suicides and high rates of morbidity and mortality.

All have had a negative impact on the spirit that is family, albeit, our culture (Bailey, 2005, p. 6).

Chapter 6
Research Through Decolonizing Eyes

Decolonization eliminates settler property rights and settler sovereignty. It requires the abolition of land as property and upholds the sovereignty of Native land and people (Tuck & Yang, 2012, p. 26.)

As I have said before, multiple generations of American Indian people, and other Indigenous people, have survived violent massacres, colonization, pandemic diseases, forced relocation, genocidal policies, removal of children to boarding schools, and the assault on culture and language. These impacts had far reaching effects on adult individuals as well as the mental health of children. The history of Indigenous people over the past 500 years is one rife with documented historical traumas. Even after centuries of attacks, our people have endured. Wilson (2008) and others (hooks, 1981; Yellow Horse Brave Heart, 2003; Martin, 2003) argue that decolonization provided an opportunity to unlearn internalized attitudes reflecting inferiority, but also a way to reject being the victim. Embracing traditional philosophies, practices, and values can positively energize Indigenous communities and restore health and prosperity.

Recently, my Cheyenne-South Sea-Aboriginal tribal brother, Mark Warcon, sent me the *Community Guide to the UN Declaration on the Rights of Indigenous Peoples* (Australian Human Rights Commission, 2010). This document was printed especially for Aboriginal communities in Australia, but it is important for all people to understand that the rights of Indigenous people are protected by the United Nations. Self-determination and recognizing rights to education, country, culture, language, free speech, ideas, and lifeways can help with overcoming historical trauma and negative environmental impacts. Reclaiming our self-respect and acknowledging the contributions Indigenous people have made in realms of traditional knowledge and western science strengthens the mental health of people. As the wave of Europeans swept across the North American, Australian, and Asian continents, the colonizers trivialized Indigenous knowledge, research, and lifeways. Today, emerging Indigenous scholars are reclaiming these lifeways:

> Tuhiwai Smith's book challenges traditional Western ways of knowing and researching and calls for the "decolonization" of methodologies, and for a new agenda of indigenous research. According to Tuhiwai Smith, "decolonization" is concerned with having "a more critical understanding of the underlying assumptions, motivations and values that inform research practices" (C. Wilson, 2001, p. 214).

Since then, others such as Kovach, 2009; Wilson, 2008; Walters, et al., 2009; and Chilisa, 2012, have added to Smith's work:

> For indigenous peoples, therefore, decolonizing research methods include deconstructing and externalizing the myth of the intellectually inferior Indian, while simultaneously privileging and centering indigenous worldviews and knowledge to promote revitalization of indigenous epistemologies, research practices, and ultimately, indigenous wellness practices (Walters, et al., 2009, p. 148).

In Native communities, the research must move the community forward past historical trauma and into self-determination. Generations later, residents of Native communities continue to experience the mental health effects of boarding schools, reservations, and land and culture loss—victims of *The Stolen Generation*. To forget these past atrocities, or to dull the pain, Indigenous people have turned to alcohol, substance abuse, child and spousal abuse, and suicide (Elder, 1998; Kidd, 1997; Duran, 2006). The people in these communities recognize these negative coping behaviors:

> ...the elevated rates of suicide, alcoholism, and domestic violence and the pervasive demoralization seen in many Aboriginal communities can be readily

understood as both direct and indirect consequences of this history of colonization, cultural oppression, loss of autonomy, dislocations and disruptions of traditional life-ways, and disconnection from the land" (Kirmayer & Valaskakis, 2009, p. 27).

In contrast to personal experiences of a traumatic nature, however, historical trauma calls attention to the intergenerational accumulation of risk for poor mental health status among Native people. This trauma purportedly originates from the depredations of past colonial subjugation, including ethnocidal policies and practices. Yellow Horse Brave Heart (2003) compares Native American historical trauma to longstanding clinical observations of the adverse psychological effects of the extermination of the Jews by Nazi Germany, not just for Holocaust survivors, but also for their offspring.

Fanon (1965) wrote that colonization is not only the occupation of territory, but it results in a relationship in which the colonized is seen as inferior, savage, primitive, and uncivilized. In the contemporary university it is no longer non-Western people who are inferior, but also their systems of knowledge and perceptions of the world.

Epistemology is knowledge. Reclaiming cultural knowledge is fundamental to deconstructing ideas of the superiority of Western knowledge. This process of deconstruction is an essential element in decolonization movements among Indigenous people (Wilson, 2008; Smith, 1999). Indigenous knowledge and local knowledge have become important in the emerging global economy, with observers stating that, "The basic component of any country's knowledge system is its local knowledge. This encompasses the skills, experiences and insights of people, applied to maintain or improve their livelihood" (United Nations Food and Agriculture Organization, 2005, p. 9). It is important to listen to the voices of historically silenced groups to learn about their epistemologies and ways of knowing (Chilisa, 2012).

Laenui (2009) suggests that the following five phases are important in the process of decolonization: (1) Rediscovery and recovery of history, language, culture, and identity. In this way the colonized can define in their own terms what can be known, what can be spoken about, written about, how when and where. (2) Mourning is an important part of the healing process and moving on to dreaming about what the future could be. (3) Dreaming is the phase in recovery where the colonized explore their cultures, invoke their histories, worldviews, and Indigenous knowledge systems to theorize and imagine other possibilities. (4) Commitment is the stage following dreaming in which the researcher defines the role of research in the community and becomes a political activist for the responsibility of scholarship and research in the community. The last stage is (5) action where dreams and commitment translate into strategies for social transformation. The researcher has a moral obligation to support the community in their belief that their collective experiences, knowledge, and history are valuable (Laenui, 2009):

> To dream is to invoke indigenous knowledge systems, literatures, languages, worldviews, and collective experiences of the colonized Other to theorize and facilitate a research process that gives voice and is indigenous to the communities you research (Chilisa, 2012, p. 16).

Historically, American Indian people have been one of the most neglected groups of people in the country in education, medicine, mental health, and economic development. The insignificant amount of ethical research and program funding in mental health, in a population that clearly has been in dire need, is indicative of this neglect (Duran, 2006). This must change.

Finally, a decolonized research processes, with outcomes that provide value to a community, also help to build the capacity of those communities to conduct their own research and to develop relationships with institutions and agencies for future collaborative research efforts. Focusing on the relevance of the research creates space to allow the community to struggle with knowledge paradigms, their own research priorities, and data dissemination. This struggle is key to building capacities for research among community members otherwise not trained in this area, and it also allows the community to speak back to the institutions and curricula that train Indigenous researchers (Johnston-Goodstar, 2012).

Chapter 7
Centering Tribal Culture Within the Research

Indigenous peoples have the responsibility and right to restore, maintain, and develop their own civilization in accordance with their own traditions and ceremonies (Battiste, 2000, p. 286).

As has been said previously, countless researchers in the past and even today enter Indigenous communities and view the community and community members negatively through the eyes of their own cultural biases (Castellano, 2004; Kuokkanen, 2010). This is known as Social Darwinism. Some older community members from the Mi'kmaq and Salish tribes understood this and told me that they often gave inaccurate information because they felt they were being taken advantage of (personal communications with anonymous elders, 1994-2011). In their interviews, members of the Joskeleigh community in Queensland, reiterated this. Principles of ethics for Indigenous researchers are simply stated: kindness, caring, sharing, and respect. These ethical values govern our relationships with all other living beings and forms of life. A fifth principle that is sometimes added is service to community and others.

Axiology defines the ethics (making a good decision about right and wrong behavior) and aesthetics (the beauty) of something. Indigenous axiology is built on accountability. Ethics in Indigenous communities is more than human subject protection. It is protection of the cultural ways, ceremonies, language, and relationships with the data, which go back to time immemorial in our history (Castellano, 2004; Wilson, 2008). This is similar to the process of crafting the Mi'kmaq potato basket, where the artist would never think of stealing the designs from another tribe or basket maker. Wilson (2008) indicates that researchers who work

in Indigenous communities need to continually self-reflect. They
need to question themselves: Does the research agenda emanate
from within the community itself? How does it move the community closer to self-determination? Does the research move the
community toward survival and recovery from historical trauma
and colonization? Does the research topic come from the members
of the community? Is there cooperation and coordination with the
community participants? When we understand the culture of the
community, and when the community tells the researcher what it
needs, these questions can be answered.

We must ask ourselves questions. According to Wilson (2008)
and Kovach (2009): Does the community collaborate with the
researcher? Not the researcher's agenda, but the agenda of the community is important. It is not what the community can do for
you...to write the dissertation; but what does your research do for
the community? How does the research empower the community?
Our research must be a respectful collaboration with members of
each community:

> The research needs to be meaningful to the commu-
> nity and the research "question" comes from within
> the community and not one from the outside look-
> ing in. The decision about which methodologies
> [method] are appropriate is determined by going
> first to the community to verify that the research
> topic is relevant and beneficial and to seek the com-
> munity's approval before proceeding any further in
> the development of a research proposal (Moeke-
> Pickering, et al., 2006, p. 5).

Methodologies for Indigenous Research

> *Ethnography is about telling a credible, rigorous,*
> *and authentic story....gives voice to people in their*
> *own local context... [and] The story is told through*
> *the eyes of local people (Fetterman, 2010, p. 1).*

Lavallée (2009) described sharing circles and how they are a
healing approach in which all participants (including the facilitator)
are seen as equal partners. In a sharing circle, intellectual information, spiritual values, and emotional issues, are shared. Sharing
circles are a technique that is well known and consoling for many
Indigenous people. They are increasingly used by Indigenous re-

searchers (Baskin, 2005; Restoule, 2004; Stevenson, 1999). In a research setting, the principles behind a sharing circle are quite different from the Western focus group. In some Indigenous sharing circles, elders are present and food is served. Spirits from the past are honored. As I researched for this work, some information was gathered through sharing circle stories and through individual visits. Gifts are always given. In Australia, for example because of time constraints and scheduling issues, much of the information was gathered through sharing circles.

Working with the community, culture, ethics

These are methods that can stand alone and work well to lead researchers and community co-researchers down many paths of knowledge acquisition and creation. Whenever any researcher works with Indigenous communities, there is a protocol that must be followed, and that is usually controlled by the tribe or community. I have spoken to Indigenous researchers who do research in their own communities in Queensland. We all agree on the following: The research agenda should intentionally build community capacity, respect values of the tribe or community, lead to self-determination, and build a relationship with the tribe or community that is long term. It is important to not just collect the data, write the paper or the book, and never go back.

In 2013, I had the opportunity to return to Churchill, Manitoba, Canada, to revisit with two of my partners from the Sayisi Dene community. I gave them a copy of the manuscript that I am editing and asked them to make any changes. Caroline said to me, "You are the only person who has come back to visit with me, after all the interviews I have done." We had a wonderful lunch at Gypsy's restaurant and renewed old friendships with her daughter Rachel.

As Indigenous researchers we are obliged to take care that the community owns the research data; that we get permissions from leading elders to share knowledge and culture; and that the research empowers the community. The research must not contribute to marginalization of that community, or contribute to stereotypes. Too many Indigenous people all over the world have been marginalized through the efforts of others (Kuokkanan, 2010).

Another central principle of Indigenous research methods and methodologies is giving back to the community and the participants.

This forms the foundation of our current research. Giving back can be accomplished by reporting back, sharing the benefits, bringing back new knowledge to the community, or taking the needs of the people into focus when formulating the research agenda. These activities insure that the academic research we do is not used as a tool of colonialism, or as a way of exploiting the community (Kuokkanen, 2010; Smith, 1999).

An important central element of Indigenous research includes distribution of the research results in an appropriate and meaningful way so the community can understand the results. This must mean more than just sending a copy of the final report to the community (Kuokkanen, 2010; Smith, 1999; Kovach, 2009).

There is a difference between sharing knowledge and sharing surface information. This points out the necessity of sharing "the theories and analyses which inform the way knowledge and information are constructed" (Smith, 1999, p. 16). This aspect of "giving back" should be a major concern for researchers as they question, "How will community members learn what we have learned?" Perhaps the people in the community may not understand academic and technical jargon. One must consider that there may be no Internet access, so reading websites may not be possible, although many communities are connected to radio and television. For those communities that are unconnected, posters or brochures written in language that the community understands are effective. Another successful method is to gather the community for a community meeting and present the data in a map of the community or a creative art piece, shared in a way that the total community can understand what has been learned.

Who owns the data? Many of my partners from Australia told me that the researchers, the university, or the funders own the data. In many of our communities in the United States, I would venture to say that very few Indigenous communities own the data, and in many communities the researcher never returns to the community to ask for clarification. As well, the community's axiology or ethics, protocols, and epistemology or knowledge should be involved in the dissemination of the data and how it is to be used. I believe that this conceptual framework model differs from Community Based Participatory Research (CBPR). CBPR is applied research in which the community collaborates on equal partnership with the researcher and shares data. In Indigenous research methodologies, the culture, needs of the community, and the researcher's passion for the knowledge are central to the project.

Processes of decolonizing research

Do no harm to culture, language, or individuals. Do not exploit the research data. The research must move the community forward by asking a positive and strengthening research question. When the research question focuses on the positive aspects and resilience of a community, the affirmative aspects will be the outcome. For example, the problem statement is the excessive numbers of families in a community that are abusing drugs. A pessimistic research questions would be focused on the negative aspects of the community, "What are the factors in this family that cause the children to abuse drugs?" Rather than a question that focuses on the resilience described in this question, "What are the factors in this family that prevent substance abuse?" This demonstrates strength, a positive aspect of families in the community.

And so I return to the epistemologies of the Mi'kmaq and of my Mi'kmaq elder, Albert Marshall who tells us: "Knowledge is not a tool but rather it is a spirit. It transforms the holder. It also reminds us that we have responsibilities to the spirit of that knowledge. We must pass it on" (Albert Marshall, personal communication, 2009).

In our research journey we must be reflective and look back on our research experience. How can we do this better? What did we do right? How did the research change us?

The Academy

> We [as Indigenous peoples] have always carried a fire within us; a fire that has never gone out despite the hardships we have endured in our historical journey. When we take our fire into the foreign environment of an academic institution it tends to be smothered...As Indigenous peoples we have the responsibility to keep our fire alive no matter what environment we are in (Moeke-Pickering, et al., 2006, p. 2).

In the global environment, the academy, steeped in Euro-androcentric roots and foundations, must examine and take its responsibilities seriously regarding who can create knowledge and whose knowledge can be bought. Academic imperialism is the term that refers to the counter productive tendency to quash alternative perspectives and theories, [methods] and methodologies (Chilisa, 2012). Chilisa (2012) further argues that colonized people should be the center for the production and storage of knowledge produced about their own people. A key issue in Indigenous scholarship is research ethics—or conducting research so that it adheres to Indigenous protocols for culturally appropriate research (Kuokkanen, 2010).

For our knowledge to survive, it must live in many places including Western academies. Kovach (2009) wrote that if mainstream universities continue to resist Indigenous knowledge and research methodologies, they will be trapped in the homogeneity of their Western and Eurocentric positions. If on the other hand, they move beyond these ideals, to create and accept Indigenous forms of creating knowledge and theories, they can reduce methodological discrimination. According to Moeke-Pickering, et al. (2006) attempting to bring Indigenous worldviews into academia is a complex process. It may be apparent to the Indigenous students in academia that their discourses are allowed to exist in the university, but are relegated to marginalized places, such as in Native studies programs, or Indigenous studies, where they are hidden from other academic majors. Many tribal college graduates who seek advanced degrees in mainstream universities echo these sentiments. They find it difficult to speak from a position of their own epistemology and be understood by their classmates. As well, I have had mainstream university professors ask me, "How can we best serve the research needs of the Indigenous students if we don't understand how to supervise their research methodologies?" Kovach wrote that they must trust the student. The academy must be willing to change their mindset to a new way of conceptualizing knowledge and pedagogy to include the "Other" rather then emulating the neocolonial pedagogy and just paying lip service to the research methodologies of Indigenous students.

Some institutions highlight their Indigenous studies curriculum as a means of giving credit to themselves rather than the Indigenous people who are engaged in the meaningful work of Indigenous education. For example,

> Australian universities recognise cultural competency as an essential attribute for graduates. Within this context, the Australian Psychology

Accreditation Committee (APAC) has enforced requirements for students within psychology programmes to have access to Indigenous content. Though Indigenous participation rates are low, the inclusion of Indigenous content or what is often labeled "Indigenous psychology" acts at least as a symbolic gesture and important step forward in reconciling the massively disadvantaged position of Indigenous Australians. However there is little to date in that way of guides to help develop appropriate teaching methods to include such content more substantially in programmes (Guilfoyle, 2008, p. 201).

It is in the best interest of us as Indigenous scholars to insist that our academies examine their role in the decolonization of Indigenous people, and accept and emulate the diversity that permeates mainstream universities. Academies also should be doing their homework with regard to their own students' and scholars' cultural orientations and research methodologies. This issue could be a major stumbling block for us as Indigenous researchers or it can move our agendas forward. Indigenous researchers, who work and teach in mainstream institutions, must be true to our Indigenous values, culture, and ways of knowing and gathering data. Additionally, we must identify our research methodology in the scope of western research: "Indigenist research occurs through centring [sic] Aboriginal Ways of Knowing, Ways of Being and Ways of Doing in alignment with aspects of western qualitative research frameworks" (Martin, 2003, p. 211). Kuokkanen (2010) wrote that the academy is loath to expand its limited vision of Western-European epistemic foundations and accordingly its accountability in expanding knowledge. However, in spite of the academy's position, these are exciting times for Indigenous people. As we have seen, Indigenous methodologies can invigorate and stimulate scholarship. These methodologies strengthen Indigenous people' identities, and support the efforts to achieve intellectual self-determination (Louis, 2007). Indigenous knowledge, voices, and research methodologies and methods are important to integrate into mainstream academies:

> ….the voices of indigenous and other non-Western peoples become increasingly vital, not because such

peoples categorically possess any kind of magical, mystical power to fix countless generations of abuse and neglect, but because non-Western peoples and nations exist as living critiques of the dominant culture, providing critique-al knowledge and potentially transformative paradigms (Grande, 2004, p. 65).

Regardless of academic challenges, Indigenous research will continue to grow and Indigenous people will find the ways and means necessary to honor their Indigenous values, worldviews, and epistemologies. When people feel valued and honored, the search and quest for new knowledge becomes exciting, and the world benefits from the "wisdom" that is created (Moeke-Pickering, et al., 2006). Indigenous people tell the world: "When we honor our customs, and when we perform ceremonies, and when we listen to our ancestors, then we have everything we need to heal ourselves within ourselves" (Olowan Thunder Hawk Martinez quoted in Fuller, 2012, p. 52).

On the next few pages, you will read the sentiments of Indigenous people from four distinctly different Indigenous communities. Their stories and their ideas of Indigenous research are similar. We begin in Australia.

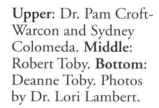

Upper: Dr. Pam Croft-Warcon and Sydney Colomeda. **Middle:** Robert Toby. **Bottom:** Deanne Toby. Photos by Dr. Lori Lambert.

Dr. Lori Lambert and Mark Warcon,
photo by Dr. Carol Baldwin.

Rockhampton •

Australia

Chapter 8
Steps Along the Journey: Voices from Australia

I have known Robert Toby since 1999 when I met him in Rockhampton, Queensland. I consider him a tribal brother and a friend. He is the cultural preservation leader of the Gungalu people of the Dawson and Callide River Valleys in Queensland, Australia. Robert has taught me much about his culture, his tribal stories and, the history of Murri people in Queensland. The following story of the Rainbow Serpent is one that I have been allowed to tell:

> In the Dreaming, the world was flat, bare, and cold. The Rainbow Serpent slept under the ground with all the animal tribes in her belly waiting to be born. When it was time, she pushed up, calling to the animals to come from their sleep. She threw the land out, making mountains and hills and spilled water over the land, making rivers and lakes. She made the sun, the fire, and all the colours. When she traveled the land, sleeping when she tired, and left behind her winding tracks and the imprint of her sleeping body. When she had travelled the earth, she returned and called to the frogs to come out, but they were very slow because their bellies were full of water. The Rainbow Serpent tickled their stomachs and when the frogs laughed, the water flowed out of their mouths and filled the tracks and hollows left by the Rainbow Serpent, creating the rivers and lakes. This woke all of the animals and plants, who then followed the Rainbow Serpent across the land (permission from Robert Toby, Gungalu cultural leader, Queensland).

Our story is in the land...it is written in those sacred places...My children will look after those places. That's the law (Bill, Neidjie, Kakadu[8] elder).

The Australian Aboriginal people themselves know that their culture has survived on the land for over 50,000 years. In that time, the varied groups of people have learned to survive in the diverse biomes of deserts, oceans, rainforests, mountains, and forests. According to Robert Toby (1999), cultural preservationist from the Gungalu-Murri people of the Dawson and Callide Valleys, there are over 500 tribes or groups of Aboriginal Australians each with their own language, culture, laws, and ceremonies.

The European invaders in Australia alleged that Indigenous civilizations were at a primitive stage of evolution. Europeans commonly enslaved the Native inhabitants they encountered to serve the invaders. Australia, Canada, America, and New Zealand were colonized at a time when European countries were constructing extensive empires all over the world. The invaders brought with them the prevailing idea that their ways—the Western-European ways—were far superior to all other ways and that the people they encountered were primitive, inferior savages. Kidd (1997) wrote that Australian land was declared empty or *Terra Nullius* and the Australian Aboriginal men and women, who had been living on the lands for over 50,000 years, were counted not as people but among the fauna/animals of the country. Cattle ranches in Australia, commonly known as stations, began expanding in the 1800s and Aboriginal people were enslaved and trained as maids, cattle drovers, and workers for the white landowners. Aboriginal women were taken, raped, and abused. Their half white and half black children, called half-castes by the invaders, were forcibly removed from their mothers' care and placed in institutions or missions. Today they are known as "The Stolen Generation." The Queensland Black Police were equally tortuous to their own people.

The stories told by Murri participants expose the mental health disparities that they face on a daily basis. To understand the mental health of a community one must have lived in the community and understand the culture, the lifeways, and the disparities in housing, education, and economics, and to know what it is like to be considered a marginalized person in your own country. To be an effective researcher in Indigenous communities, one must understand their history:

Few White psychologists challenged the idea that taking Aboriginal children away from their families was in their best interests and, indeed, practicing psychologists working for welfare agencies after 1950 probably had a complicit role in many such cases....Psychology and psychologists could have used their disciplinary knowledge and social standing to act as advocates for Aboriginal children, but did not do so (Bretherton & Mellor, 2006, pp. 92-93).

As a result of that trauma, many Indigenous Australians even today are fearful of going to the psychologist because they may be labeled "crazy" or incompetent to look after their children. They could be taken away themselves and placed in an institution or have their children taken from them (Ranzijn, et al., 2008).

There are a number of national and community based ethical guidelines, protocols, and principles of practice available for practitioners working with Aboriginal and Torres Strait Islander people and communities. It is important that practitioners be aware of these and put into practice such guidelines particularly as they may relate specifically to the communities they may come into contact with and to whom they provide services. It is necessary for all practitioners prior to working with Aboriginal and Torres Strait Islander communities to be familiar with local history, customs, and ways of doing business, as well as the local mental health issues. In addition, a local orientation and cultural awareness program may be necessary before engaging with the community. Every Aboriginal and Torres Strait Islander person and community is unique and there is no one rule when it comes to interacting with individuals or communities. Be mindful that the approach the researcher takes will and should be different depending on the individual's or community's location, and their cultural beliefs and practices, and their history and experiences, especially with mental health services. Even within a small geographical area, there may be several distinct cultural and language groups that require consideration.

The Murri Community in Queensland
Dr. Pamela Croft-Warcon

Dr. Pamela Croft-Warcon is my friend and a casualty of The Stolen Generation. She was the first Aboriginal woman in Australia to earn a Ph.D. in Visual Arts. Today she talks about how her stories and art healed her. We meet at her beautiful farm nestled near the sea just outside of Rockhampton in a place called the Sand Hills. Her dog, Wundarra, sits at her feet enjoying the cold air conditioner of her office. Outside, in the sweltering heat of a Queensland summer, the Rosella parakeets' calls fill the valley with a cacophony of sounds as they call one another to the feast of seeds in Pam's garden.

I thought that telling my story would be my way of being part of reconciliation for my ancestors who've gone, for the family that's still here, and for my future family. I recognized in telling my story, that family was the only thing that I ever wanted in my life. I hope people understand that telling my story wasn't easy. I did it for me, for [my] family and for Australia—for Australians, and for our future. I told my story so that children are never hurt in this way in this country again. I wanted it for myself and for my children and my grandchildren. I had lived my whole life to the point of doing this interview without all of my identity and my experiences. When I met my partner, who I have since married, I saw him with his family, living their identity [Northern Cheyenne, South Sea Islander, and Aboriginal], living within and with their stories and experiences. I wanted to consolidate mine, for me and also for my partner, my sons, my birth mother, my in-laws, and any grandchildren that I might be gifted with in the future.

With reconciliation being talked about, I kept thinking that you couldn't reconcile without knowing and understanding history and what you were or are trying to reconcile from that history. I knew my story was part of that history just like the other stories were and are part of history. When I told my story, it wasn't only about what happened to me, Pamela, but something that happened to other people, something that Australia had denied—its past—its history.

In the past I was frightened about being put away in a place, a home for people that were suffering with acute mental illness. I thought that if I told my story that other people would think I was mentally ill. For years I asked myself, did it really happen? I at times didn't believe my own story. I had such a turbulent and traumatic life story that I questioned if it really happened, how could it have happened, how could other people let that happen to me when I was a little girl, or a young woman? I was worried that other people would also deny my story. People like my adopted parents, the people from the Fundamentalist Brethren Church in which I was raised, my ex-husband and others. I knew I also didn't want people to feel sorry for me. I didn't want to be put in that victim place or to be victimized.

When I began to think about telling my story, I weighed all of this up. When my adopted parents passed on and were no longer alive, this gave me power to voice my story. I didn't want to hurt them in any way. I thought about the people from the Brethren Church and others. Many of them were now older people, just as I was older and they no longer had the hold over me that they once did. Before I told my story, people were contacting me about my artwork titled *Matters of Her Heart,* and I would talk to them a little, but I never revealed too much. *Matters of Her Heart* was a major art installation that I produced in 1993 and I'll explain this a little bit later.

I began to think that maybe I needed to go to a counselor. My early life experiences were really impacting on my adult life. That's when I heard that the Bidgerdii Aboriginal and Torres Strait Islander Community Health Service in Rockhampton gained some funding for counseling the members of The Stolen Generation and for people affected by separations. I decided to access the counseling. I went every week for over a year starting in 1998. The counseling gave me the confidence to begin telling my story to my partner, children, family, and friends. It also gave me the confidence to actually want to be a part of the oral history project when the opportunity arose in 2000.

It is now six years since I recorded my story and I still haven't listened to the tapes. I have only read my story once. That was when I did the editing. One day I might listen to the tapes. The important thing for me is that I told my story. I found my voice. Maybe it isn't important to listen to the tapes. What would it achieve? I don't know. Working as an artist, I have been working on identity issues for as long as I can remember. I was always challenging myself, but the biggest challenge I needed to place ahead of me, in terms of myself, was to speak my story. I did this through the Oral History Project. I don't know how other people, who didn't have access to counseling, or didn't have the path I had in terms of gradually building up to tell my story, managed the challenge of telling their story. It may have been equally as scary and as hard as it was for me, it may have even been harder. I have wondered about them. Telling my story has provided a lot of healing. It was a healing tool, which led to me finding my voice. I am pleased that I found the courage to do it. I now see myself as a wise and peaceful woman. My voice is much stronger. Before I held back, on opinions, decisions, group discussions, on all sorts of issues. I no longer do this. I have stopped being a pleaser to others. I have learned to love myself and please myself. I come first in my life now. I can give greater depth to the artwork I do and I can understand my artwork more. Telling my story has allowed me to articulate my artwork. It has allowed me to complete my doctorate in visual arts. If I didn't tell my story, I don't think I would have completed it as some of the content was about my story and how it has connected and is connected to my artwork. I think I probably would not have been prepared to delve too deeply into my life, my experiences and the artwork I have produced and produce. I am now presenting my story and my artwork internationally. I am talking about The Stolen Generation.

I believe that research that is done in Aboriginal communities must be done from the cultural values of that community. The research must be to move the community forward, to heal issues of historical trauma, to promote self-determination, and to make visible the issues in those communities so we can come together as a community and make a plan to remedy the issues. Our stories belong in the community. They do not belong to the university or the government. They are ours—our data—and they belong to the Aboriginal community where the research is being carried out.

Kevin McNulty

As we sit at a moss covered picnic table in the Rockhampton Botanical Gardens, dappled sunlight finds its way through thick leaves of the rainforest canopy. It is a causal meeting of friends, as well as a conversation about research. The meeting style is familiar and congruent with Indigenous research methodologies (Kovach, 2009, Smith 1999, Wilson, 2008). We speak of research and researchers in the Aboriginal community near Rockhampton. Kevin McNulty, is a Murri/Aboriginal man from Botany Bay where contact first happened between Europeans and Australia's Aboriginal people. Kevin McNulty allowed their names and words to be used in this work. I am grateful. Kevin shares that he "was a former athlete, grown up hard, done prison time, and learned to read late in life." He is a university graduate working in Aboriginal and Torres Island

Affairs in Queensland. He has done research and understands the needs for guidelines and ethics. He also understands what Indigenous communities need from researchers. We talk briefly about research in Worrabinda[9] and Botany Bay communities.

Scholars who come into our community may know nothing about our culture. They may know generally but nothing specific. They may have some competency. The elders did try to set the agenda for the researchers. There is a committee to deal with the researchers, but their first point of contact is the council and they will be given the protocol there. Researchers learn about our community of Worrabinda. They come and ask. Whoever is paying for the research to be done owns the research, the researcher or the university. It [the research results] is rarely shared with the community. Sometimes the researcher comes back to the community for clarification, but they rarely do. It is not a common practice. In Australia they have research guidelines and an ethics board in Canberra and researchers have to realize that they have to go there before they go into the community. Some never go through Canberra before they go to the community. The researchers write up reports and send it to where it needs to go, but I never see any good come from it. But there are some good people.

It is the historical stuff. The stories that community people give to the researcher are always open for interpretation. If it is a non-Indigenous person, they will interpret it from their worldview as opposed to an Aboriginal worldview.

If I could make changes, they would be to always make sure that the researchers go to council and to make sure they are allowed to come into the community. The researchers should go straight to council to make sure they are allowed into the community. There should be a research board set up that includes traditional owners, council, and relevant people, and someone with academic skills. I wouldn't want a male researcher talking to young girls about women's business. Also I would make the researcher hire a cultural guide as part of the process.

When people had mental health problems in our community, they would put them in dormitories. Removal from country is one of the biggest reasons that people have mental health problems. They are depressed and go to prescription drugs. It is not only your mind, it is your spirit as well. I never delved into mental health issues.

Cultural property rights are non-existent at this point and the researcher can own the information. But this needs to be included now in Native title. The researcher gives the community food and feast in order to come into the community to do the work. The community has the right to determine if the research can benefit the community. If it does not, the researcher cannot do the research; sometimes the community will give the researcher false information if they do not trust the researcher.

Mental health issues include depression, low self-esteem, language and cultural loss; loss of warrior status when men go on the dole, in that event it causes depression. Dissemination takes place through working groups, written papers, and community groups. Men versus women have different roles in each community and perhaps a male researcher cannot speak with a female member of the community.

Graeme White, Stella Ware, Emma Jeffrey, from the Darumbal Mob [Clan]

Graeme White is a 43-year-old Aboriginal man from the Darumbal in Central Queensland area now living in Rockhampton who works for the Social and Well Being Group for Bidgerdii. He is the father of two and is married. Stella Ware is a 28-year-old woman from the Darumbal Region and currently living with her partner and child in Rockhampton. Emma Jeffery is 24 years old. She lives in Rockhampton with her partner and also works for Bidgerdii.

Graeme: I met a few people that come through and try to get a grasp on our culture and cultural identity and how we discipline. We have had a number of people who try to discipline kids when their kids are in the program. We have a lot of problems trying to keep kids involved. So they [researchers] come in and observe and try to integrate and try get a grasp on what is our culture; a lot of them do well and the successful ones are the ones with bubbly personalities and are with outgoing personalities. People [in the community] warm to them differently. They [the researchers] sit and watch then learn and learn, and others are more wary of them.

Emma: We've got two communities; we've got an urban community where people are brought up in the mainstream and then there is a rural one, Worrabinda, and these people [from Worrabinda] are entirely different. The Rockhampton group people come in and introduce themselves.

Graeme: A more successful [researcher] person has an outgoing personality and is familiar with the history of Australia and Stolen Generations. [Others] are more guarded with their personalities and Aboriginal people have a harder time trusting them in that sense and are more guarded in that they question whether they may have a hidden agenda.

Stella: I get a negative reaction when I hear the word "research" or "researcher." I think they failed to hit the mark in a number of studies they completed. We have a lot of people in jail and other demographics, poor housing…and we are always trying to fix it and most researchers are in there trying to fix it and don't actually sit with the people instead of working with the people and asking, "How would you like to see this fixed?" They go in and do it their way. "Do it our way and do what you are told." They never really come back.

Graeme: An important fact is they don't know our learning styles and how we go about things; we never know what the actual research is going to achieve. It is the way people come in and how they understand our culture. For us sitting down and having a yarn is more important than someone sitting there and them asking questions. When I hear the word "researcher," I automatically think negatively. I think from my own experience it is the white man coming in to help the "poor black fellas." So I like to know what is in it for me and what is in it for them, and what the outcome is and why they are doing it. I have a lot of apprehension about researchers coming into our community to learn about mental health issues.

Emma: As far as mental health issues, we are getting misdiagnosed or over diagnosed or under diagnosed. They are not taking on cultural issues. People don't like to hear the word "mad." An aboriginal word for the word "mad" is "Womba." No one likes to be branded with the word "Womba." There is a big stigma about that. I have an apprehension that most people get it wrong. I have only seen one person be successful and they were Indigenous in nature [understanding the lifeways], and they went through a psychology degree and they had no problem mixing both cultures with western understanding of treatment, [using] a mixture of both [cultural ways of treatment]. I have apprehension.

Graeme: It is important for researchers entering the community that they touch base with the right community members or the right community organizations and social groups, especially in terms of mental health. Mental health is usually referred to in Indigenous communities as being Womba. And with that is the under diagnosis and the mis-diagnosis. We also need to take into account our spiritual beliefs and our culture. Because these are contributing to our mental health or can be contributing to our mental health but others may not see it that way. Researchers at first may be quite clinical in their approach and how they approach us. And that never works because of our culture and our way of learning and our way of absorbing information. It doesn't collate with the non-Indigenous community, and that may make it quite difficult for researchers. They have to give respect to the culture.

Stella: They never consult the elders for advice. The researchers come into the community with a certain idea in their head. In a perfect world they would consult with the elders. But if they tried to contact an elder, the elder would be very standoffish and ask a lot of questions about why they were doing the research and what the research was for. And that again comes back to Indigenous history with government bodies and Stolen Generations and how the government has failed.

Graeme: In Worrabinda there is no official protocol for researchers to follow; it is more word of mouth and the experience of other people that you have to rely on [for how they should behave]. Translators may give an introduction process and explain protocols and about the traditional owners and the names of the locations. Worrabinda is a Dog Community where many tribes were brought in and that led to a problem with identity. There was no one really from that area as traditional owners. They have different totems and memories. There is no one protocol. It can be disjointed when different tribes are all in one place. In those communities you have things like alcohol. Again it is around respect and learning about someone's culture. If a researcher wants a successful outcome for all parties, they would go to find out about the protocols and have a successful outcome. It should be written into mainstream organizations that they go and pay [their] respects to the local people. It is all about respect.

Stella: Researchers also need to participate and live in the community and not just watch. People will accept them better if they participate. They are bringing something to the community. They are not standoffish. They may have a picture in their head about Aboriginal people. Everyone who contributes information needs to have some form of ownership of the data. Whether they are being researched or doing the research. The people need to have some form of ownership of the information that is being provided. And that comes down to researchers sharing with the community.

Emma: We recently had an intoxication program where a researcher came out and interviewed us about people who were intoxicated in parks or not conforming to the norms of society. During the study the researcher sent us emails about what she was writing and at the end of it she came back and invited us to a meeting where she presented her recommendations to us and to the government, so hopefully they can act on these recommendations that are found. There needs to be more community involvement and it [the project outcome] is not successful unless someone acts on them. Sometimes that is a struggle in itself.

Graeme: The clinical people in mental heath are not asking advice from the community. They are using the booklet. They are using what they were taught and not from the community. They use their clinical jargon or terminology and people don't know what they are doing, and they have to ask around to find out what people are doing. When they introduce themselves, Western people don't tell you their life story like we do. We tell what is your mob and family lands and try to find ways to know your identity.

When they are looking at mental health issues or psychology issues in a community, a lot of researchers tend to have the assumption in their head that because you have a mental health issue, that you don't have that capacity to understand or be in the know, so to speak. However, for me working in mental health, [those in] a mental health facility have lived experiences of dealing with mental health issues [and] are quite intelligent, but their thought patterns are just different and they interpret things differently.

Emma: When a researcher brings up the whole alcohol and drug thing that brings up the whole shame thing of having mental health issues or psychological issues. What we value is more important than cars and material things. It is family, my grandparents and parents and what they taught me. And when disaster happens, family can be there.

Stella: Another thing that researchers in Australia need to understand is that there are two groups of Indigenous peoples, the Aboriginals who live off the lands and the Torres Strait Islanders who live off the sea. Even though we are all under one banner, we are two separate groups and we have different customs and spirituality and culture.

Graeme: We don't really know what the government does with the information. It all comes back to authority and who actually pays for the research and who holds the research data and what they want to do with it. The government owns the research here and they have implemented changes without telling anybody. Also the researcher owns the information. We often see the results of it, but we don't know where they keep it. Coming back to the community for the researcher depends on how successful they want to be with their outcomes. They will come back to make sure the information is correct. Whereas if they are doing the research for their own hidden agenda so to speak then they won't come back, they won't care what we think.

Emma: One outcome for people going through the court system is that the Queensland police can look up in the database to see if a person has a mental health issue and has committed a crime and the police know exactly what diagnosis that person has, what meds they are on and who is the contact person for that person. And that has all come about in the Model of Care.

Graeme: A researcher will interpret a person's story on an analytical level given that they are looking for information based on that topic. If it was another person depending on what learning method they have or what their vocabulary perception is like, they may interpret things differently. The researcher may interpret things very positively but an Indigenous person may see things negatively, like the history of Indigenous people is negative [to us]. It all comes back to the culture and the spirituality and how you interpret. It is important for the researcher to have good listening skills. It all comes down to jargon—language and street talk—and about not judging that person on a personal level and not judging the book by its cover. Information can be swayed to build a case depending on how it is used positive or negative cases.

Judy Tatow: Worrabina, Queensland

I am going to use my traditional name of Bunjinga. I am a clan from the Woorabinda area. I work for Angelcare in Central Queensland and the program that I work for is Winnebarra, which I am the coordinator of. It is an outreach service and most of the people that we deal with are from Queensland.

I don't care who the researchers or scholars are but most people [in Queensland] have grown up with Murri people and they went to school with us, or those who come in from someplace. Some of them do a bit of background work to find out about our culture, but they still don't really understand what our culture is all about.

Worrabinda is probably the most researched community in the world. They come in [to] dig up the past and help the future. Hopefully, it is all going to be a positive thing and it is not going to be tucked away in someone's drawer and someone else comes in twenty years tine and researchers what has already been done.

When researchers want to come in and find out about the issues in our community…and I am not a drug and alcohol counselor or a psychologist, they get in contact with our managers and maybe they ask if they can come. Or maybe they have to ask the elders. I have not been involved in mental health issues directly. We do like to include some of the elders, but we are an organization that is not really involved in a community. But I like to do that with people [on] account of my age, because I am an elder, depending on the situation of what researchers want to know. Sometimes we have to include elders depending on what the issues are. Researchers have to make the connection first so we can know what they are on about. If it is something that our organization is associated with, it also has to go through the board. Our elders are on the board, and we need to know what the researchers really want. We want to know what they are going to do with it [the data]. Is it going to sit on someone's desk? Is it going to be a big encyclopedia, or is it going to be a one-page paper?

Researchers learn about our community through their networks. They don't come in with a closed mind. Some of them get in contact with a particular organization, or they may go through a funding body. The people who give the information should own the research or at least part of it. But we sort of don't know what the researchers are going to do with it. So from there the researchers own it, but I feel the community should own part of it.

If the results are in a DVD or a paper, there is usually a "launch" to share the findings with the community. We recently had a launch regarding suicide. The whole community was invited to go to view a DVD. That is a better way because a lot of our people can't read, so it is better to have something visual. They [researchers] have their own ethical board to guide the research and their own agenda.

"Womba" means mental health, sick in the head. People don't like to use the words mental health. Researchers who look into these issues have to understand that we have a lot of alcohol FAS [fetal alcohol] syndrome and they don't get any treatment. That is where a lot of our mental health issues come about. Babies who are affected look different. They have a different looking face. And they need to be trained to be pick up the syndrome. The mother and father go through the shame game, they think, "There is nothing wrong with my child." There are shame issues that go along with it.

I really don't know what the researchers do with the information. They come and take all this information, and then they take it all away. But then you don't hear of anything. They may be getting distinctions and all that at the uni [university] for what they have done, but then it doesn't come back to us grass-roots people. Most of it is not shared with the community. It is best if it comes back to the community in a picture form because most of us can't read. Very few of the researchers come back to the community for clarification of the information. They ride off into the sunset but it would be nice if they came back and asked for clarification.

I think when people tell the researcher stories the meaning gets caught up in the trap of interpretation. What I may hear and what you may hear is different unless the researcher gets back to you before they print the whole lot up to determine what you really mean.

It is good for all of us to be all on the same road. Sometime some Murries may say, "Well, you shouldn't have said that." But it is not what I said, it is what the researcher interpreted. It can cause conflict in the community.

Before researchers do any writing or taping [tape recording] or anything, I would like them to come into the community to get to know the community to give them a bit of a grounding and speak with the community people. Back in the day, because we are a caring community people [who were thought to have mental problems] would have been taken care of in our way. Maybe go out and get "gumbi gumbi"[10] and see if that was going to work, and traditional medicine. And the thing about it too, is that we would not let people make fun of the people who had Womba. You got to keep watch over the people to make sure they were not going to hurt themselves. We tried very hard not to let them go away to places, because they were going to be with strangers and when you go to hospital in those days, there were no Murri people. They didn't want them there. Today, we have our own people working there and they are quite skilled people. Sometimes if it [mental illness] got to out of hand, [back in the day] their family would have had to put them away.

I work with people who are alcohol dependent, but one of the things it isn't only the alcohol that can steal you mind. Of course when you have an alcohol problem you are going to have other things like kidney problems, liver, all of those things are going to tell on you later on in life. The alcohol affects down in your body but also in the mind as well. That is the mental health side of it. Not everybody who drinks alcohol has a mental illness but in the area where I deal, that is what I see. And FAS as well. It goes right back from us being divided from our families, and some of us were taken from Palm [Island] to Worrabinda, and that breaks people's spirits and you don't know where you come from and that is hard mentally. There may be a young adult who is madly in love with a man, we don't know if that man is a blood relation. You can't have that man because he is your mob [family]. Doing things like that can cause grief, because you don't know where you come from. You gotta go back to where you come from, not Rockhampton, but your land, your heart.

Womba for us really puts the idea of mental health in a nutshell. It is not that somebody is going to come in and stab you with a knife five or six times a day. It is people coming in very quiet and don't say anything and they pull their hair and maybe cross their legs. These behaviors are part of their illness. And we send them to people who are better qualified [to help them].

Laurie Armstrong: Rockhampton, Australia

As a descendant of the Kulilli Aboriginal Nation, Laurie Armstrong is passionate about the social wellbeing and advancement of Australian Aboriginals and Torres Strait Islanders.

Culture is an interesting word. I'm sure that most people research a little bit on what Aboriginal culture is, but most of them don't really grasp what is going on here in Australia. When we talk about culture we can talk about the way things were [before contact] and another thing about how things are today. And the reason why we are in the situation we are in today. They can break that barrier by introducing themselves and telling about their family and where they come from.

Scholars don't really understand what I see as our culture. Anybody who doesn't understand about the diversity of Aboriginal Australia...Some people may know what it is like in different parts of Australia or the Northern Territory, but they certainly don't grasp the complexity of what has happened here in Queensland as a result of dispossession and everything that's happened to our people here. It is a complex thing. Researchers who come into communities, and they don't know anything about our culture, need to live in our community for a few months to find out what our culture is all about. As far as the ethics committee is concerned....

The first thing that comes to my mind when I hear the word "research" or "researcher" is that they are trying to find out what is going on, trying to get an idea, an understanding or learning about stuff. It depends on what people are doing the research for and why they are doing it. Some people are just doing research because they want to get a degree at a university like a postgraduate degree or a doctorate. That is more of a benefit for them rather than the community. So as long as they tick the boxes and gather some information and the people that mark their papers are happy, then their research is done. It doesn't really go anywhere. Then there are people who do research with the desire to really find out the truth and [implement] something to add value to things.

What they do to come into the community, they probably use their networks and where they come from and who they know. The problem with that is, it depends on their networks, and the people who are in their networks dictate the value of their research. If they are not getting to the right people in their networks, then the research isn't really covering the amount that it needs to. That dependency on networks can be a flaw in their research then. Then it depends on how long they want to take to build up respect because our people, especially if we go to a little community like Worrabinda. Those people are so used to researchers coming in and asking questions that if the researchers don't do their job properly in the first place and gain the proper respect that is required, and go through the right protocols that are informal and unwritten, then the researchers are not likely to be told anything.

I think researchers would like to talk to elders, but this is a problem of who is an elder, just any old person? But if you talk with community people, an elder to the person may not be an elder to somebody else, so it depends on the respect that the elder's got. I don't think that there is any protocol written down about any elder setting any agenda. And if they do approach an elder, do they get someone who is just an old person or do they get someone who is actually respected as an elder of a particular group. It goes back to what we were talking about culture. There are so many Aboriginal people from different groups here in Queensland that to get an elder to ask the right questions would not be very easy. It is something that has to be looked at very carefully for researchers [in Rockhampton, Queensland]. There are no formal protocols for people wanting to research in this community. I have never seen any written protocols. There are [informal] protocols, but it is up to the researcher to find out what they are. Finding the protocols comes down to respect and finding the right people who they are talking to. And so there are unwritten protocols that **we** know and if they were not abided by, then even people like myself would not take their research very seriously. I've been involved in bits of research over time, not a lot but a bit. So two key points here are gaining respect and talking to the right people.

Researchers learn about the community by having a general idea. I have never seen a researcher come in and really learn about our community. I guess what a researcher needs to do to learn about any community is to go and live in that community for a while to know the people, and I think the dilemma here is that most researchers don't have the time or the resources to do that properly. But I think they use their general knowledge about Aboriginal Australia and Aboriginal culture, then they use their networks.

I think the question about who owns the research is cut and dry. It is the person who pays the researcher. If it is an organization, then that organization is likely to be the owner. If the researcher is doing an education qualification then I expect that the institution would own it. It is an interesting question because there are not a lot of times that the Murris end up owning it. Murris get frustrated with that. Aboriginal people get frustrated with that, having people come in and get their information and take it away. Sometimes we see a book has been written and all the stuff that they have been telling the researcher is in the book and the community gets nothing out of it. They get no compensation at all for it. Then when other researchers come in and want to ask questions, the people just clam up.

What research I've been involved in around the university and all is mostly there is a clause in the introduction that the research findings will be shared with the participants of the research, but I haven't seen any researchers come back and have a seminar and say, "Well, look, we did all this research two years ago and this is what we found out." Although, now and then it does happen. There have been a couple of publications here and there. And at one time there was a function put on in Rocky to launch a publication of their research. But it doesn't happen too often where we get to see the results of the research.

The universities have an ethical board. They have Aboriginal and Torres Strait Island representatives on the board. But again it is a question of who those people are. So at this stage we've got an Aboriginal representative on the board at Central Queensland University who is not even recognized in the community as an Aboriginal person. So I question that. They do have an ethics board and there are some well-meaning people on it. They keep a very close eye on how evidence is collected. Also government departments have one as well, like the Department of Aboriginal Communities. Some of the research I had been working on had to wait for ethical clearance from the university and the Department of Communities, so there is an ethical board set up. So there is an attempt to do it right. But there are questions of who they get to put on the board. That is an issue with government appointees.

This community of Rockhampton has been wracked by mental health issues shown by the huge suicide rate in the town and some of the surrounding communities as well. If researchers do not understand our culture, they are not going to understand why we have the mental health issues that we do. The researchers can collect the data, but I am not sure that they understand why it is happening and what are the solutions. Generally researchers use the data to write papers for their university qualification or if they want to get published in a journal or get personal recognition for stuff. The information doesn't always get back to the community or if it does, the community members might not know where to find it even though it may be out there, unless there is a launch and people are told about it. I have never seen researchers that bring the research back to the community to clarify points, but I am sure that some researchers do. It depends on how much integrity the researcher has, but once they get their article, they move on then.

How the researcher interprets the story depends on their own experience and their own life and how they think of First Nations peoples. If I could make any changes the way researchers come into the community, I think the researchers should take the time to get to know the community properly. For example, when over in the Pannawonica, the mining companies paid a lot of money to this anthropologist and they wanted him to come over to do some work and they wanted him that bad and he told them, "I will only do the job if I can spend the first twelve months living in the community, in Jigalong." That is what a good researcher must do…spend time in the community to really get to know the people, the community and to know what is going on. There also needs to be lots of community consultation. Again that word "respect" is important. Their research is going to be useless unless they give respect [to the community members] and they have to get the knowledge of the community; another important point is who is on the ethics committee.

Back in the day, before our culture was torn apart, I don't think there were as many mental health issues. Because of the way the family was structured and the way that everybody nurtured each other in the family, I think that would be taken care of. I think if it was noticeable that someone had a mental illness then families would gather around and it would be worked out, and that would be okay. It is a bit different today and the reason why we have so many mental health issues is because of what's happened in this country [with the Australian government and assimilation of Indigenous peoples]. And people's identity is being torn apart and all their cultures and the structures of their families has been snuffed out, and you mix that loss of identity with the amount of addictions of gambling, alcohol, and the like, and that is why we see so many mental health problems that we've got today. The guts of all of it comes down to identity and connection with land, connections with ancestors. That's where it really comes from. That affects peoples' minds and spirits.

When I think of mental health I think of things like depression and anxiety and high stress levels and things like that. One of my kids has mental health problems and he suffers from severe depression at times. So I really see mental illness as a disease. It is something that needs to be taken seriously, and in the past we haven't taken it seriously as what we need to, and in some professions it is not taken as seriously as what it should be.

If I could make changes in how research is done I would make them live in the community and not let them come in just straight up. They will find that with Rockhampton—it is quite guarded to access for research purposes. People need to identify with their own culture and put a land claim in and they are with the wrong mob. Researchers need to be more relaxed and not think they are going to change the world, and they need to enjoy the experience. We don't want them to document the negative stuff so much but look at some of the positive things.

Our mob takes care of people with Womba. There was an old gentleman who grew up with limited capacity, who was having Womba and he lived on Creek Street. And he knocked [punched] a seven year old and a ten-year-old boy. We [the Aboriginal community] have seminars for caretakers just to learn how to manage resources. We are used to looking after our own people.

If researchers want to get into the Aboriginal community they have to tap on doors and say, "Okay we are here and we want to help you." The biggest mental health issues we have are alcohol, fetal alcohol syndrome, young people with drug abuse, racial discrimination…a lot of that.

We don't ask our Indigenous people if they have a mental health issue. They won't know what we mean. But if we ask, "Do you have Womba?" and they will say, "Well, ya." It all comes back to street talk and jargon and terminology. It comes down to how they learned to survive. Ideally for my health would be a holistic approach to mental health. We aren't talking about mental illness, but sometimes people with Womba function quite well, but they don't want that stigma. We all need to have a level of ownership of how we feel and how we understand what it is we have.

The South Sea Island Community of Queensland

In 1876, in the New Hebrides, now called Vanuatu, people were hunted like animals. They called it "Blackbirding," collecting South Sea Islanders to work in the sugarcane fields of northern Queensland, Australia. Over 60,000 men, women, and children were taken from Fiji, Vanuatu, and even the Solomon Islands. The Europeans who settled in Australia sailed to the islands in schooners and set siege to the people with axes, muskets, and cannons. Sometimes they were offered a pleasure cruise from which they never returned. Once aboard the ships, we can only imagine their lives in the dark, stinking holds. Fights would break out among the people from the various islands acting out old tribal rivalries. When fighting did break out, the fighters were chained. When the survivors of the journey arrived in Queensland, they worked in the hot sugarcane fields on the white man's property. Overseers, who rode on horses and were armed with stock whips, always guarded them. They were treated worse than animals.

By the 1900s the Australian government decided that European-Australians had acclimatized enough to work in the heat of the cane fields and the officials deported the South Sea Islanders to the islands of Vanuatu. But what is unknown is that many of the people were dumped anywhere without regard from which island they came. In addition, many had been born in Australia. Fifteen hundred to two thousand South Sea Islanders stayed in Australia and lived a subsistence lifestyle, hiding in small groups around the Sand Hills. Their descendents still fish and live in these historical places and listen to the stories the old people from Vanuatu tell of their plight:

> Most of the Australian South Sea Islander people who were brought to Queensland between 1863 and 1904 followed their own traditional religions, believing in the power of spirits, ancestors and one or more gods. By the time recruitment to sugarcane and cotton farms had ended in 1904, most

Australian South Sea Islander people had converted
to Christianity (Abatto, 2011, p. 8).

According to conversations with Mark Warcon, and Deanne
Toby, South Sea Islanders are not considered Indigenous people
of Australia. The South Sea Islanders in Australia have been completely disenfranchised from their lands, their culture, and their
language. Without the land, they suffer from greater marginalization than other Indigenous groups in Australia. Historian Abatto
documents Mark and Deanne's story:

> Australian South Sea Islander people have low ac-
> cess to health services. Reasons include limited
> knowledge of the services to which they are en-
> titled, lack of transport in rural areas, and being
> mistaken for Indigenous people and consequently
> referred to services to which they are not entitled
> (Abatto, 2011, p. 10).

In 1942, the bloody battle for the Pacific in World War II raged
on. In distant lands, from isolated villages of New Guinea to the se-
cluded barrios of the Philippines, Japan was winning the war. The
area surrounding Rockhampton was ideal jungle training ground
for the soldiers with local sand hills, jungle, open country, and
beaches (Shortal, 1987). During World War II thousands of American soldiers came into the community of Joskeleigh, then called
The Sand Hills. They were preparing for jungle warfare. Some of
these soldiers met and fell in love with South Sea Islander women.
The children and grandchildren of these unions make up several of
the families in Joskeleigh.

Ben Parter, an elder in the Joskeleigh-Sand Hills community,
tells how the Americans trained:

> The American soldiers arrived in the Sand Hills
> on July 12, 1942. The old people from Joskeleigh
> who remember this story tell of how the soldiers
> trained for jungle warfare by marching from Mount
> Hedlow to the Sand Hills with salt water in their
> canteens. The soldiers trained at night. People said,
> "You could hear them running around the houses;
> no one went out at night in those times" (personal
> communication, Ben Parter, 2002).

During the 1940s, Rockhampton was a city of about thirty-five
thousand. Today it has mushroomed into a population of sixty-

five thousand. It is located in the valley of the Fitzroy River on the Tropic of Capricorn where the climate is mostly tropical. Rockhampton was a prefect place to train for jungle warfare in New Guinea:

> The camp at [Sand Hills] Rockhampton was made up of tents pitched among trees on the outskirts of town. Each tent held six canvas army cots furnished with mosquito netting that hung from wooden racks built over the bunks....Everything seemed to be twenty years behind the times. The cars were small and had right-hand drive, the streets were narrow and the pace was slow.... it seemed that everything [was] either "bloomin" or "bloody." Everyone was a "mate" (Catanzaro, 2002, pp. 30-31).

Then, as now, the land around Rockhampton was settled in cattle and sheep grazing country. The city's major industry is the meat processing plant, affectionately known as "the meat works" by the locals. During World War II and today, hard working South Sea Island people staff the meat works. When the 41st Division moved into camp nearby, the men were given a warm welcome and were seen as the protectors of the community (Shortal, 1987).

Today, archeological evidence exists of the World War II army base, which is now protected by the government as an historic site as it is surrounded by new housing developments. One can also can walk along the beach and see the old mango trees that were planted by the first South Sea Island captives to Australia and listen to the laughing calls of Kookaburras and Rosellas. It is in this community, that we see the beauty of the culture, the lands and learn of their horrific history.

In Australian history books, this story of how a people were taken by force and deception is never told. The price the South Sea Islanders paid has been immense. Their cultures have been distorted, their lands lost, and they continue to be subjects of discrimination. We also unearth issues of mental health disparities emanating from their historical trauma: low self-esteem, alcohol and drug abuse. It is here that we listen to the stories of how they crave an Indigenous way of [mental health] treatment and [their objections to] how research is carried out in their community.

Deanne Toby

My name is Deanne Toby and my maiden name is Warcon. I am a South Sea Islander and Northern Cheyenne. [Deanne's grandfather was a soldier in World War II and he was from the Northern Cheyenne Indian Reservation in Montana]. My Island heritage is in Bank and Ambrum. I am speaking as one of the two Peak Presidents of the community of Joskeleigh, originally known as the Sand Hills. We are not Indigenous to Australia, and I think that is important for you to understand. Our people have a slave trade history known as Blackbirding. Our people were brought here to work as cheap labor in a number of industries but predominantly in the sugar and cattle industry. Over 60,000 people were forcibly brought here. We were not allowed to speak our language and were made to work pretty much from sunup to sundown for six days [a week] and in 1906-1908 the Queensland government made a decision to deport the majority of the 60,000 people. It was absolute chaos as Islanders would face certain death for marrying across islands, or they would have been separated. There was the fear of being dumped at any island, again this would have resulted in certain death. So the Queensland government set criteria to allow you to stay in Queensland. And some of the islanders met that criteria and that's why we have Joskeleigh today. And that's how that community got established and has grown. I would just like to say we are not Indigenous to Australia.

I explained that the Joskeleigh community is made up of [people from] different islands and different island families and some people are from Ambrum [Island] and some from Pentecost [Island]; some are from Banks [Island] and so on. Now before [Constitutional] Recognition in the year 2000, a lot of researchers saw us as just Islanders. But after [Constitutional] Recognition, the Queensland government included us as a disadvantaged minority group and we were publicly recognized in ceremony and included in service delivery and programs for health, education, housing, employment, culture, and arts. So researchers quickly learned about who we were.

When I heard the word "researcher" before the year 2000, I thought researchers came in and stole information. People didn't report back to the community and people were very untrustworthy. And after 2000 researchers came into Joskeleigh for different reasons. If they are after history though, they are still perceived as robbers of information. If they were doing a community project, however, where the community benefited, the researchers were seen as helping to get positive outcomes for the community.

No research has been done in our community around mental health, but my general knowledge of mental illnesses is that there are still unmet needs not only in Joskeleigh but in the general community.

In South Sea culture it is the senior people that set the agenda. Having said that though, we still take counsel from the elders on everything. Traditionally it was the men who did the decision-making, but we women do that now. We are better leaders. We are good listeners. We have good careers. We are good planners. We are good at recording things when we see the importance of that. And we are good organizers. We are not gunners. And we hook in and get the job done and the elder women have taught us to do that.

Since 2000 there is a standard protocol where the researchers have to contact the Peak Body [a volunteer organization of citizens who have the same interests, who may engage in activities such as lobbying the government]. One of the Peak Bodies is JCA [Joskeleigh Community Association] and we set the research up and allow the researchers to talk to the community [about] what they want to do. And then it is up to the people then if they want to be involved with the project.

Researchers learn about our community because after 2000 all levels of government, that is state government, local government, and federal government, use a standard communications protocol whereby researchers or consultants or project officers….must contact the Peak Bodies, as in our case, Victor or JCA. And both those bodies hold combined forums where people attend the session to hear what the researchers actually want, and that is the best opportunity for the people to talk about their needs and concerns…in that forum.

The law in this country, in Australia, about who owns the research is [that] once it is published by the researchers, it becomes their property, and any court in the land will see the researcher as the expert, hence there is that mistrust and that unwillingness to tell personal stories or cultural knowledge or cultural protocol; it has to be something pretty important for people to actually give that information over.

In the case of sharing research, the case is in the hands of the local council, and they were supposed to devise a strategic plan with the community and publish the research and get it out to us, and also support us taking that document to all the different government departments to get us on their agendas. Before recognition in the year 2000 there was a project and the Islanders did all the planning. They wrote it up, they published it, and printed the thing at their expense. There was no money paid to that community for all that work, so that was a bit disappointing. But they [government agencies] wouldn't get away with that now.

About who owns the research: I am going to use an example of a big project that we did as a community. It wasn't on mental health but what the researchers did they worked collaboratively with the Peak Bodies to achieve positive outcomes for that community. They wrote the project up and worked with the community to actually do the project. They were good researchers and they returned six months later to see how things were going. Since 2000 researchers have always come back to the community to check that they are right. I get the sense that this [incumbent] government wants to achieve positive outcomes for our people, but we have a Labor government and since the year 2000 we have only had a Labor government; I guess things might change if the Nash-ows get in and the funds might dry up and we might not get those people coming into our community. [The Nash-ows are the National Party, personal communication Robert Toby, 2013.]

The Labor government is the same as the Democrats in the U.S. and the Nash-ows is the same as the Republicans. Actually all the projects that I have undertaken in my capacity as the President of the community have been on a voluntary basis. So researchers have always been very patient, because I am time poor. When they come back for clarification, it might have to be done after hours, or shared among a few people to make the decisions or clarifications. Most of the Peak Bodies are voluntary so they don't get paid for their work.

When researchers ask people to tell stories or experiences, they assume that people are going to trust them, and they come out with all this information that the researcher might need. Unless the message is written down the right way, they [person telling the story] won't tell them [the researcher]. And that is how our people are. They are not going to give out all this information just because someone comes to town and they have a nice golden egg to give them. I have seen in my time a lot of stories would have been told if the researcher asked them [the person telling the story] the right way, or did it the right way. Most stories will go untold because those people are gone now. And there is this other thing called the hidden agenda...I'll tell a story to the researcher and Aunty Mary will tell a story to the researcher. Is that story going to be used against the people or that community and not be used for their benefit? And that has happened. The whole thing is trust. The researchers may take just parts of the story depending on what their agenda is ...what the purpose is. Researchers will get different meanings from the same story. If I could make any changes when researchers come into the community, they would have to do a cross-cultural training course...delivered by our people and not someone else. They should travel with the community health workers and visit the community before, during, and after the project.

Before we had all the programs for mental health, these issues were dealt with depending on what Black Rights [land rights or Indigenous rights] you were coming from, whether you were Murri, South Sea Islander, or Torres Straight. [Today], we have all been subjected to the same laws. We all been affected [by the laws of] colonization, to racism, and from all of that pain has been inflicted. Some of us have been very fortunate because we are strong spiritually and our families are very well bonded. In our Islander community it has always been the family that provides the support because that is where the trust lies. But having said that these families are under resourced. They are not well off and so there is alcohol involved—sometimes drugs, and unfortunately mothers go to sleep at night crying because they cannot help their children.

Given the South Sea Islanders history, we know today our generation and my daughter's generation, have been told stories of how we come to be here [in Australia]. It is not been a glossy story and they were told how the women were kidnapped when they were only teenagers. And the person who is important to my family on my mother's side is Bena. She is a very well known character here in our community. Well known across the broader sense of the Islander community; Bena had a terrible start. She was kidnapped. She came to Australia. She jumped ship twice and the white sailors brought her back. She married Johnny and they had my great grandfather, well actually they had twins and poor Bena and Charles. Bena could have been killed because you aren't supposed to have a girl child when you have twins. But she had to give that baby away. But the thing is somehow, all of that pain, even though it was there and granddad Eddie learned about it, he was able to get over that and get by that pain....that major barrier of his mother being Blackbirded and his sister being given away and in fact that community at that time was very young and healthy, and their minds were very healthy because they were like a big family. And so if there was any type of illness, and I am talking about mental illness as well as physical illness, it was that community that they all helped one another and it is different now because it is a different environment now in the present day. Another thing, if you are subjected to racism day after day in a job; if you are separated from your family and you want to live in another city and send money home to your family or not just having enough money. A lot of things in our work today can make us unwell. And just because you are a professional working in a good job doesn't mean that you might not become unwell psychologically because we all have points in our lives where we become so burdened; and ya, we have some ways of managing that. Some of us go whoosh; some of us go to church and some of us go sit somewhere and pray, others go to men's group, youth groups.

Mark Little Sun Warcon

Mark embraces his many cultures from the Northern Cheyenne in Montana, to the South Sea Islands of the New Hebrides, to Aboriginal (Murri). He is a trained mental health professional. At the time of this interview, Mark was the director of an Aboriginal mental health facility in Queensland. I have known him since 1999.

I don't think people who come into my community understand the South Sea Island culture. Our relatives were brought here from the islands of Vanuatu and New Hebrides, to work on the sugarcane fields in the 1880s. They were kidnapped much like the Black African slaves were kidnapped to work the cotton fields in the American South.

Researchers who want to do research in our community have to approach our communities through the government body because of funding policy. Students or individuals, who are doing a Ph.D. or Master's program and want to research here, have to contact someone in the community [and ask] to be allowed to come into the community if they are [already] known in the community. This may need a visual of the person. If they are not known, they have to approach an organization like an Aboriginal, Torres Strait Island, or South Sea Island organization and set up a meeting or an interview with the organization. They would be given a name of a person in the community to speak with....what to say and when to talk with people. They would have to be aware of protocols of when and how to talk to people. Contact an aboriginal entity or committee in the community. Depending on what the research is about, the elders can set the agenda for the researcher...they can tell the researcher what to do. Contact with elders is important and they shouldn't be left out of the group at all. Sometimes in their wisdom they may set the agenda. The elders may not want to talk about some of the questions that a researcher wants to know about, but they would go about answering the questions in another way. The elders need to be there to interpret what was told the researcher. Some researchers do come back to let the elders see what they have written.

If it is a government project, they [the researchers] generally provide a report, especially if it is a government researcher, so people in the community can understand what was found and provide feedback. Someone who has knowledge or experience at a particular level in the area that is being researched reads the report.

There is no written protocol [for researching in a South Sea Island community] in the community that I know of. It is generally someone who has knowledge or experience at a certain level that may ask to do research in the community. It is dangerous not to have a written protocol. It is something we need to develop throughout all the areas where South Sea Islanders' communities are researched. We need to have it as a standard for....South Sea Island populations.

South Sea Islanders are not on the political agenda and our issues are usually on the back burner regarding research. We are not there on the political agenda like the Torres Strait Islanders and Aboriginal people, [who are the original peoples of Australia]. The less we are heard of, the less embarrassment Australia will have about the history of the Blackbirders and how the South Sea Islanders were captured and what they did to create the sugarcane industry in Australia. The government says it was the Italians. It wasn't the Italians. It was us!

Researchers learn about South Sea Island communities and their mental health issues in a number of ways. There is a number

South Sea Island organizations on the east coast that they can get hold of. The Bureau of Ethnic Affairs will have all the numbers to get in touch with the community.

In my time [as a mental health professional] I have not read any research papers regarding mental health or psychology issues in Australian South Sea Islander communities. We get tied in with the Torres Strait Islanders. No one has done any research on this in our communities. No one is specifically studying South Sea Islanders. As far as we are aware we do not suffer from mental health issues. The only papers that have been written are on the Torres Strait Island and Aboriginal Murri people. When people in South Sea Island communities like Joskeleigh have mental health issues, the people in the community, like their family, tell them that they need to go to church. They tell them that there is nothing wrong with the person; the best option for the family is to send the person to church. They contact one of their relatives who is a minister and that person tells them that they have to go to church [to be cured]. There is a big idea of Christianity there.

Most of the mental health issues or behavioral issues stem from access to alcohol and tobacco, especially if you are pregnant. That makes changes in the baby and that is exactly what is happening. But to say that a mental health issue can be saved by going to church, I don't believe it. Sure you can come in and say a prayer, but, if the people are suffering from manic depression or schizophrenia, a prayer isn't going to do them any good. The family thinks that the only way mental health can be improved is to come in and say a prayer with them. It is a shock to me to think that the only way for them [to heal mental illness] is that you can say a prayer, or have the person go to church to make a difference in their stability. I don't believe a word of it. That is just kafuffle. But you see this is the Christian way in these communities. But sure you can sit down and say a prayer for them but if they are suffering from a real mental illness that is not going to do any good in my opinion. It is Christian research gone bad. I was quite shocked to see this.

I would have support for the person through our local medical center and make a referral and have the mental health worker and Indigenous mental health worker come in and have a talk with that person. Or have mental health worker go out to the community. Joskeleigh is just tucked away out of sight, out of mind. There are just enough people there to make it livable. People are seeking a se-cluded isolated spot. There is no housing in town or employment in town, so they just live in isolation out there—a quiet peaceful way in that community, looking up at the stars…living alone. They need to talk with people, to go out for tea, go to the theater and be with people, to talk with people. Some of our mob don't talk to people. Some are just quite happy sitting out there alone.

The people who are funding the researcher own the research, not the community. They set up a series of workshops to let the community know what was found. Mental health is only one area that needs to be researched…There are all these other issues that create good mental health…It is housing, unemployment, education, relationships, transportation. It is all these areas that people put in boxes, but it is more than that…All of these lead up to healthy people.

What is normal behavior out there anyway? There is no normal in that community. If they want to go out to the paddocks and have a conversation with themselves then good on 'em, they are busy. If you are going around doing housework and talk to yourself, good for you. If you go into town and have a good time singing to themselves, sing to yourself then good for them.

If someone acts out a bizarre situation then that is not normal. If someone has a psychosis or severe depression, and they are not doing anything wrong, no one does anything. But as soon as that person throws a chair through the window, then people say, "Let's call the ambulance," not the mental health worker.

They [the family] may be worried about the embarrassment. And especially in small communities, and the rest of the relatives avoid them [the mentally ill person], and they stay the hell away from them.…especially if that person has had a couple of beers, which is not good either. I think we need a much more political push for mental health issues. South Sea Islanders need to be put on the agenda for mental health issues. I have never seen anything for mental health, skin infections, heart disease, diabetes, social diseases. I have never seen anything specific for Australian South Sea Islanders. That's where it has to get identified health positions specifically for Australian South Sea Islanders. We need research for education. We have been on the back burner for years. We need a South Sea Islander liaison in the hospitals; we need South Sea Islanders mental health positions; we need some of those Indigenous health workers. There is an organization that will **not** fund or service

South Sea Islanders, only Aboriginal and Torres Strait Islanders. The funding body in the agreement needs to say, "You will service South Sea Islanders."

In the old times some people believed that someone put Black Magic on them and that is why they act the way they do [make them go to church]. They got a spell put on them. Someone picked up their hair and put a spell on them. Sometimes it is good and keeps the status quo and keeps people behaving.

Back in the day, people were able to heal mental health. There must have been a medicine person that would have participated to help that person, but I do not know for sure. The people who were brought here from Vanuatu would have had their own medicine people. They may have not even had a category of mental health, but they picked up Black Magic and they probably had them go through a ceremony.

Imagine the people who came over and they lost their lands and medicine plants. There was a lot of stress on them. If a medicine person didn't come with them, they would have suffered and gone mad. They worked all day in the heat cutting sugarcane and they may never ever have seen their grandmother or grandfather or family again. And not even being able to go to the salt water, because they were island people, must have been very traumatic.

We, as island people, never got any compensation like The Stolen Generations got. We have to make changes ourselves. We want the government to acknowledge what we've been through as well. A clear understanding of what we have been through and not putting us into the same categories as the Aboriginals and Torres Strait Islanders. It is unfair for them and for us [for funding issues]. And some people have a very hard time seeing the difference between a Torres Strait Islander and a South Sea Islander. If they see three Black Fellas standing on the street, could they tell which one is the South Sea Islander? It is like they think all Malaysians or all Indians are the same too.

We would like to have researchers help us research our own specific issues as South Sea Islanders. We can't be put in the same category as Aboriginals and Torres Strait Islanders. Somewhere along the line, the government has to come to acknowledge the hard work that we have done [South Sea Islanders] to create an industry here in Australia, the Blackbirding issue, and give us some political backing and support and not just "breed us out." We shouldn't be a burden on our other brothers and sisters. There is a lot of work for South Sea Islander researchers in our community, but it comes back to the government body. We definitely need researchers. Who is going to pay for them? What are they going to research and that comes back to creating opportunities for education. There aren't enough of us. And what are we going to research?

I was glad Lori [Lambert] found my grandfather in America. It healed a hole in my identity. In high school they asked me, "Okay Mark, what is it going to be French or German?" I said, "I want to do English. I speak English and I want to learn how to write. I want to know about my people. I want to know who I am."

Evan Sirris

Evan Sirris is an Australian South Sea Islander living in Rock-hampton, Queensland.

I am a descendent of Banks Island Johnny who is one of the first Blackbirders who was brought out to Australia, to Joskeleigh. She was originally from Banks Island, New Hebrides.

When scholars come into our community, I think they have done their homework [to learn about our culture] or had a bit of a think about the community. They come in with pretty general broad understanding of what Australian South Seas Islanders are.

Researchers are a personal group of people who want to investigate a problem in the society, in the culture, and understand what impact it has, whether it is positive or negative on the community. Hopefully with enough research and understanding of the problem provide some sort of outcome to help improve the situation or understand the situation.

Most people are hesitant to give out information to the researchers. I don't think the elders set the agenda for the researchers, but I think they have some input because of their knowledge and that. They have been around the community a fair bit and they can help have some input. The elders will speak up even when it comes to white researchers coming into the community. The elders in the island setting are usually males or females. I am not sure if there are protocols in South Sea Island communities, but from experiences I have had with researchers in other places, from working in Mount Isa, in mental health, and we had researchers coming into the community up there who had to go through certain processes up there to make sure they were doing the right thing.

Researchers learn about our community by coming up to study, as had been previously done. That supplements what they have researched from the government. For example suicides is one thing that came up, and that was due to high deaths in our community, and they wanted to know what was going on there and to come up with some ideas as to how to stop it.

When the researchers finish and write up their report they give a report form directly to the community. It includes certain things around services and what they can do is part of that report as well. The researchers own the data and the research. They own the information, but any stories that are put in, like from the community, they reference the names of the person who told the story. Any psychologist and sociologist are bound by ethical standards. The researchers write up their reports and make recommendations and how to best address the problem...small steps not large steps to address the problem.

Upper left: Evelyn Matt Hernandez, photo by Frank Tyro. **Upper right**: Virgil Braverock, photo by Frank Tyro. **Lower left**: Whisper Camel Means. **Lower right: Leslie Camel.**

Frank Finley, photo by Dr. Lori Lambert.

Flathead Indian Reservation, Montana

Chapter 9
Steps Along the Journey: Voices from the Flathead Indian Reservation, Montana

I have had the privilege of living for over twenty years on the Flathead Indian Reservation in Montana. The following are some of the images I have gathered over the years:

The land is rich with the lives of our kin. The bones of our ancestors blend with the soils to share new life with plants and animals. Women's curves contour the surrounding hills like a brown skinned girl lying on her side. In contrast, hills like brown, rippled, and muscular buffalo, run along side her. Long prairie grasses playing in the wind give a sense of shadow and movement. Overhead, Red Tail Hawks and Harriers circle effortlessly in search of mice or voles. Winter snows blow down from Canada staining the brown skinned girl and buffalo hills a milky brown. Coyote and family announce their hunting presence with a chorus of yips and barks that blend with the soft moans of young calves.

In spring, songs of returning Meadowlarks fill the landscape. At last the sun has returned and days are longer. Swallows follow clouds of insects plowed up by potato farmers. Young calves, older now, frolic about while their "nursemaids" keep watch. The air smells sweet.

Time to a mountain is but a whisper. Everything is understood as living, as being alive, in the teachings of my own tribe, and in the beliefs of the Salish:

> Each living thing has a specific role as a teacher and family member. Everything on Earth whether stone, tree, creature, cloud, sun, moon, or human being, is one of our relatives (Sams, 1994, p. vii).

In the shadows of the landscape there is a suffering of generations—soul wounds. The people are chained to historical trauma, low self-esteem, alcohol, methamphetamines, and prescription drugs. Like many other tribes in America, the people were forced from their traditional homelands, put into boarding schools, and mandated to live on reservations far from the healing plants and the ashes of their ancestors.

The Salish Creation Story[11]

According to Salish legend, our story began when the Creator, the Maker, put the animal people on this earth. The world was not yet fit for mankind because of many evils, so the Creator sent Coyote first—with his brother Fox—to this big island (as the elders call this land) to free it of evils. The brothers were responsible for creating many geological formations and for providing special skills and knowledge for mankind to use. However, Coyote—being Coyote—left many faults such as greed, jealousy, hunger, envy, anger, and many other imperfections that we know today.

At the core of this story is the fact that we are all made by the Creator, and we must respect and love each other. Creation consists not only of mankind, but of the animal world, the mineral world, and the plant world—all elements and forces of nature. Each has a spirit that lives and must be respected and loved.

The elders tell us that Coyote and his brother are at the edge of this island, this land, waiting. When Coyote and Fox come back through here, it will be the end of our time. It will be the end of the universe, if we do not live as one creation—all part of one big circle. We must always work for a time when there will be no evil, no racial prejudice, no pollution, when once again everything will be clean and all will be beautiful for the eye to behold—a time when spiritual, physical, mental, and social values are interconnected to form a complete circle.   —Salish Culture Committee

The creation story of the Salish and Pend d'Oreille people begins with Coyote who made the world safe for the people. He killed the monsters. He prepared the land and made it good with clean air, clean water, and clean earth. The stories teach many things including relationships with animals, traditional ways to hunt, medicine plants, and how men and women should behave in their relationships toward one another. On the Flathead Indian Reservation and within the wide expanse of what was the aboriginal homeland of the Salish and Pend d'Oreille people, Coyote stories have given place names to many of the land formations: "It was good! Their home life was good, they were growing up in a good way, the children of the long-ago people" (Mitch Smallsalmon, quoted in Salish-Pend d'Orielle Culture Committee, 2005, p. 4). The people still have memories and stories of how life used to be:

> Prior to the intrusion of whites into Flathead territories, tribal life had been ordered by the traditional hunting and gathering subsistence patterns common to the Plateau region. According to elders of the Salish and Pend d'Oreilles tribes, the quest for food was an uninterrupted task starting in early spring and ending in late fall…(O'Nell, 1996, p. 25).

All of this changed in 1855 when Isaac Stevens pressured the people to sign the Hellgate Treaty. The treaty forced the people out of their Bitterroot Valley homeland onto the lands of the Lower Flathead Valley, now known as the Flathead Indian Reservation, where in 1910 the Dawes Act opened up the "surplus" lands of the reservation to white settlers (U.S. Statutes at Large, 1887).

The Genesis of the Flathead Indian Reservation

> *On July 16, 1855, eighteen leaders of the Flathead, Kootenai, and Upper Pend d'Oreilles Indians hesitantly signed an agreement with the United States Government….It provided the legal foundation for the relationship between the Confederated Salish and Kootenai Tribes and the federal government and established the Flathead Indian Reservation (Bigart, & Woodcock, 1996, p. 1).*

The Dawes Act also known as the General Allotment Act, provided for the allotment of lands in severalty to Indians on the various reservations. What the Dawes Act did was to remove lands held in common by the tribes and divide the lands so that each tribal member received 80 or 160 acres. The rest was open to white homesteaders in 1910.

In the film, *The Place of Falling Waters* (Bigcrane & Smith, 1991), Joe Eneas echoed much of what all tribal members were feeling at the time: "We got 80 acres, all rocks. We got no plow. The government did this and they know we got all these kids to feed." The Dawes Act stole away the lifestyle from a people whose needs were met by plants and animals in their environment and forced them to become farmers. Because they were hunter–gatherer people, they had no idea, until years later, how to plant corn beans and squash together as the Three Sisters of the agrarian tribes. Against the legalities of the Hellgate Treaty, which set aside the Flathead Reservation for the sole use of the Salish, Pend d'Orielles, and Kootenai people, a binding treaty between two sovereign nations, the members of the Confederated Salish and Kootenai Tribes are a minority on their own reservation.

Today the tribes are using monies from economic development enterprises to buy back the lands that were given away under the Dawes Act. One of the most recent purchases is 18,000 acres along the Highway 93 (Tom McDonald, personal communication, 2011).

Every tribe has its own ceremonies, histories, and languages. Generally they share a similar history of oppression and colonialism that has led to mental health issues. In a 2009 study on unnamed tribes by UC Davis Center for Reducing Health Disparities, their focus groups discussed what happens when culture is lost. The Salish people are no exception to culture loss:

> ….disconnection with cultural values and tradition was seen as a key factor contributing to the fragmentation of their communities. They suggested that the disconnection with their culture and heritage contributes to the high rates of drug and alcohol use, family violence, and school dropout seen in their communities. Many felt that the lack of a sense of community built on traditions, values, and cultural pride was at the root of the mental health difficulties experienced by both youth and adults (UC Davis Center for Reducing Health Disparities, 2009, p. 4).

I interviewed Salish partners on the campus of Salish Kootenai College to discover what tribal members think of researchers, the scarcity of social science graduates, Indigenous cultural research methodologies in psychology, and how their stories and words will make a difference in the lives of other Indigenous people.

Roy Bigcrane's Words

Roy Bigcrane is a member of the Confederated Salish and Kootenai Tribes. He told me that he is Pend d'Oreille on his mother's side and Salish on his father's side. For the past twenty years or more, Roy has been the valuable assistant to the director of the Salish Kootenai College Media Department and public television station. I value his friendship and his wise words. He is the person I approach with gifts of tobacco when I need advice. Over the years, he has been a close friend who is willing to share his cultural beliefs over long talks and discussions over philosophical values.

[Speaking of the culture] There are differences with the Salish and the Pend d'Oreille even though we are related. There may be a few word differences but probably not a lot of deep ones. But I know because I've been around, because ever since I started knowing things and expanding from when I was a kid, I always liked to learn about Indian people and maybe I didn't learn as much about our own people as a lot of people do when they start learning culture. Usually they learn their own culture right away. When I started getting smart enough to understand things, I wasn't living here on this Rez. I was living on the Yakima Rez. So I knew some things about ours, but not the stuff that I know now. But there are a lot of similarities, but there are differences too. I heard a lot of things pertaining to the cultural things, "You do it this way." And then someone else will say, "You don't do it that way, you do it this way." I don't know if that comes from Christianity getting into our deep cultural beliefs, because if you know Christianity each one of them say that their way is the true way to God and Jesus. You know that. I know that. We all know that, except the Christians. They don't know that.

I think our people used to be so accepting of learning. We are all trying to get closer to God, get closer to the Spirit. It seems like a way long time ago that if somebody had something to say, "This is a vision I had," or "This is something that came to talk to God, to ask for help." And this is what I learned from people. They were smart enough. There wasn't too many fake people in them days, because they just knew if you or somebody, "Oh ya I had this big vision and was told to do this or that," and they were medicine people, they could sense it in you. They don't have any power. Not like nowadays where there is this charismatic people. I'm not talking about Indian people of all kinds where they're these people who are willing to drop everything and sell everything and go follow these so-called spiritual people and all they've got is the great gift of gab. I don't know what else, except the great gift of gab, where every one of these people will follow them to their death. Like I said there is a lot of similarities [among tribes] and I think it is because of our teachers, the earth, the spirits, teachers like the elderly people and the spirits. We are part of this land and we are part of this life and we are part of it when we leave our bodies. When we leave our bodies we can't argue with ourselves that we are separate from this earth. Our minds, our parents' public school teachings, maybe they don't keep that door open on our relationship with the land, with the animals and with the earth, the sky, and the stars. Whereas if we are taught right, we know we are part of it. Our medicines, our names, our spiritual knowledge all come from these things. Maybe God won't talk to us directly in our ears. Maybe so, and maybe not. So these other things will be their mouthpiece because they live, and there is only one way to live, and they will teach us how to live according to God's laws, the natural laws.

So when we have that, then we know that there is a lot of similarities. It is one of those paradoxes or rules of life, the yin and yang. Some things are pretty much the same. The tribes all over the country live according to their land area so maybe their animals will teach them one thing and we over here will have some of that same knowledge. There's a lot of similarities like the sharing of food, the use of tobacco for our elders and maybe more older religions, and the role of women in society and the cultural and spiritual life. Some things are different like the white people refusing to deal with the women back in the days when the white people first came over here because their culture didn't have the power of women. So some things are the same and some are different, just like life.

When I hear the word "researcher," I guess I think of somebody from the city...somebody who is smart, apparently. Maybe they are smart in the world of academia, but not smart in dealing with people, the human beings. Things change all the time. So researchers...it just depends. There are the vision seekers and academia researchers. When I hear [the word] "researcher," I don't usually think of our people being researchers, but that is what we do. The cloud formations tell that this is going to happen because this is what we knew. Our personal research, we know how to read signs; we know how to read trails; we know how to read the land. My first instinct is to think about academia and white researchers. So there are two different thoughts on it.

Our tribe has a pretty good mental health department in those areas [of mental health and psychology]. Since I don't deal with them a lot, I don't know how well versed they are in the cultural things. So I think these researchers go through them, which is a good thing. They have to, if they want our blessings. I think they also go to the council and say this is what I would like to do and this and that. So that is something that is done, but there is also a protocol, a traditional protocol that you do that I know of and that I understand and maybe our tribe has some of those same things. Some of these things are universal like the offering of tobacco. It is used pretty strong here. But in other places, I know you approach them and ask them for some knowledge or you ask them for some help, or you want to hear some sacred talk, then tobacco is offered. Tobacco is offered because then the people who know, they understand where you are coming from. They understand you because you know something. You know that you have a little bit of knowledge to offer that tobacco to you and in front of the Creator. So that is one of the instances. I don't know what the mental health department people do if they say, "Let's go talk to these old people." But this is how you should approach them. What you should do because if they are talking to older people, there are just ways that they do, how they answer. They have their own ways as opposed to young people who want this knowledge right now. Whereas, if you go to older people, you are on their clock [the elders]. You don't expect to go in, "I have 30 minutes. I'm going to get this info and then I'm going to head out." It is not necessary that way. First they might offer you some drink or some food and this is some of the differences we have. If you don't know the cultural things, if you are from a western society, you may say, "No I don't want any." If you are in Indian country, most of the time you don't decline.

I haven't met a lot of researchers who come in. I would guess that it is somebody outside to do the research [as opposed to the elders setting the agenda for researchers]. I don't know if our mental health department goes out and seeks that knowledge. I would think that the researchers out there are looking for something. I don't know why they would come here as opposed to Blackfeet or Cheyenne. Maybe they do, but if I read the tribal council minutes asking permission, I don't know if they went to the mental health department first, or if they talked to someone else.

It used to be that the researchers came in and they thought they were god and they could come in and do anything. I think a lot of times they did come in. They did just what they wanted to do. I think a lot of times some of that research…well they thought they knew about Indian people.…Or lies, or things wouldn't come in as a favorable light. Or they couldn't interpret what was being told to them because of cultural differences because of right brain, left brain type of thing, or if our elderly people are telling them something in a spiritual context about the animals or the winds and you got somebody whose brain is on the logical side and [the elder] wants to talk about some high spiritual thing. Well, the researcher can't comprehend that deep knowledge, most of them because they don't think like that. So some things get misinterpreted, miscommunication.

What little I know, the tribe requests to look at the data when the researcher is done. I don't think they ask to store it. I don't really know that protocol. I don't think that researchers share the data. They don't publish it. I think it is one of those things where they say they will share it, but unless you know they're going to share, I don't know how you are going to know unless you ask the right people. Some of them I've seen they want to share it and say they want to share it, but, over time, you don't even know when they are done…us common citizens out here. We might read the [tribal council] minutes and see that they finished it and completed it [their project] and came up to the council and to give it to them and people like me might read [the minutes] and go seek the information, but there are a lot of people who don't. It seems like a lot of Western researchers are figuring it out other than going to blast in and blast out, "My research is to help you." Especially misinterpretation…it is so easy [for research to be misinterpreted]. I think a lot of tribes these days have an IRB [Institutional Review Board]. Tribes are getting smarter. We couldn't even control our own way of life for a long time. The BIA [Bureau of Indian Affairs] told us what to do…bossing Indians around.

Researchers got rich off of us. It is way different now. I am kinda old and I kinda know some things because of past researchers that came in. I want to have knowledge, but people came in at the turn of the [twentieth] century and took knowledge and information and robbed graves to get information, got people drunk to get information, and take things. Up until the mid 1900s, until our people started to know we could control our own lives and not have BIA or government assume that they have our best interest, as our people became smarter in dealing with those academia people.

Me, I think mental health is your head, your brain. Ya, interpretation when I hear the words "Medicine Wheel," I have this imagery in my head just of the book learning of the Medicine Wheel. They show you the Medicine Wheel and they have these words that say, "This is that and this is that." But if I live the life that I say I do or try to do, you have an understanding of life and of balance without the word "Medicine Wheel." I guess it is just an understanding. Maybe in an instance it could be "of God," or something big, huge, beyond words, God. But because of Western thought when you hear the word God you have the imagery of an old white man with a white beard and white robe. That is just what we were taught. But maybe in some of the Native language words for God is something that you really can't describe. Human words are pitiful to describe something that is beyond comprehension. How to encapsulate something so incredible into a three letter word or the imagery of an old man? Maybe he is, or maybe she is, or they are. I don't know it is something that people seek out, the Mother Earth, our teacher, the Creator.

I just think of academia people who have training in institutions because that is what it [mental health] is anymore. I guess the mental health on that side, run by the government, funded through dollars. Maybe mental health places on different reservations, maybe there are a lot of cultural people who do have cultural knowledge who do the Sun Dances, sweats, who are sincere and humble and who do have MSW [Master's of Social Work] or LCSW [Licensed Clinical Social Worker]. I know there are people like that on this reservation who have that degree. I think nowadays that mental health…well, I think of academia but since I don't deal with that, but if there are people who have their roots in traditions [they] can deal with mental health things. How to explain things like psychology: if people are psychologists, they learn the academia part of psychology, but if they don't know the psychology of our people…we are not white people.

The things I think of that affect people's spirits and minds are PTSD [Post Traumatic Stress Disorder] or people who have been in wars or violent relations or how they grew up like kids being around drinking parents, or they have seen abuse. It affects them. Maybe they don't even know it, because it is deep back [in history], some of those things like all that Christianity. Our people being told they were not talking to God. They were talking to the devil. If we were smoking the pipe and something tells something that we can't see, we were told that it was the devil, or, if we listened to some Methodist people talking to us, and the Catholics would say, "Oh you are talking to the devil"…all that, and historical trauma. Boy, we are kind of a messed up people. We're fighting our way back to stability. We're fighting our way back, but it is still pretty tough because some people don't even know they are traumatized. They think, "Well, I'll beat up the old lady, and kick the dog, and smack around the kids, and drink in front of them, and have parties here." How many of them do really understand that this isn't right? It isn't right. My kids should be first. Talking to God should be first and say, "Help me, help us. Thank you for this day. Thank you for this night." A lot of them have bad luck and they think that is the only kind of luck there is. "My car is died and I don't have any food and I'm sick, and that's life and that is just the way it is." That is not just the way it is. There is something you can do about it, but they don't.

Our traditional spiritual practices teach us so many things, like to endure. Things get tough. You get tough. What is that saying, "If it doesn't kill you, it makes you stronger." But sitting in the sweats, Sun Dancing, fasting, those things make you tougher, but when things get tougher, you pray hard. When you pray hard, the spirits hear you and they help you. If you are smart, you understand that you may not get help as soon as you finish your prayer, but you will. Sometimes they might see if you are sincere and they let things go a day or two, a week or something, [then] you will see something happening. And you know they are helping you now. But we know that alcohol and the drugs are strong, powerful, because you get that instant gratification. Seek the spirit. To seek the fulfillment of the spirit, you have to work at it. But when you are a child, most kids you can remember life; you can remember the joy of life. Most kids, if they wasn't starving for food or seen dysfunction in the family from drinking or things like that, they can remember the joy of life. They can remember the feeling of a spirit when they think they are by themselves being by creeks, or the water, wherever. And they knew they wasn't alone. But as a kid when they get older, that door almost closes for some people. Public schools, or maybe because their parents aren't teaching them the spiritual things that keep that door open.

Communication with words and I don't know, like maybe two Indian people speaking together in Native language could have that deeper understanding but English [the meaning of the story] might be different depending on the spiritual level of the two people talking. If somebody understands these things, they will get it, but left brain, right brain, raised academia style…because there are some white people who live around us who probably even think they're Indian in some ways, but you see something happen. Something they said or did, shows that they don't really understand. But we all make mistakes. An Indian researcher could be just as bad. Maybe they were raised in Denver or someplace and knew they were Indian but it might be hard for them to understand nature and nature things, ceremonial things because our ceremonies come from the land and from nature. That's how our ceremonies are, from the land, our songs, our pipes. Maybe they are living in Denver and they have book knowledge and if I come to tell them my experiences in my research of life. That I communicate with the spirits, and I'm telling them something that the spirits have shown me, if I would even tell them that anyway. Maybe I sense a different connection in them that they don't even know about. I can sense a quest for knowledge, and I tell them something, maybe they don't understand it right then and there but maybe there is such a person who will run it through their mind, and maybe it reaches their heart too, because to believe it comes from the heart.

All our beliefs come from the heart. That is just the way it is, Babe. The hummingbird comes to me and talks to me and you say, "Ya, Right." It did talk to me too when I took five hits of acid and some mescaline and then somebody might think, "Hmmm ya, I believe that even though I was raised in Denver." Because of the way I explained it to them the analogy of their pets, people, and their dogs. People do anything for their dogs. They jump into scalding water in Yellowstone National Park to save their dog and die from it. People do that. And if I say, "This hummingbird and this chickadees, or bugs or whatever, told me something," then they believe that. So I know that some people have that connection even though they were raised in Seattle or what. Our people in our ceremonials are all nature based—the natural laws. So you just don't know until you talk with someone. They may say, "I have a Ph.D. or MA and MSW or MFA [Master's of Fine Arts] and blah, blah, blah yadda, yadda, yadda and I went and seen the Dali Llama," and this and all that. I hear your words but all I can say is that your force tells me that you don't know Jack Shit. You have a lot of knowledge in your head but your heart is still kind of cold, not accepting. Sometimes it's like that and sometimes it's not. Our old people were all Ph.D.s in a lot of ways and they were all in medicine or psychology. I heard someone introducing someone and they said they were a lawyer without a degree, or a doctor without a degree, or a psychologist without a degree, because they were a medicine person, because they understood human beings. They understood the life, the laws of the land, the natural laws. When they do these things, they have understanding without going through the sacred halls of Harvard or Yale or the University of Montana. Some of these old people have that knowledge. So the researchers some of them I think understand them [the elders' stories] and some of them don't. Some of them are just so busy writing down what they [the elders] are saying that they …unless they read their notes later what they write down and what somebody said. They're not necessarily true because you see all the time in a newspaper report. You tell them something and you read it, "That ain't what I said."

What would I change when researchers come in? Since I don't deal with them enough…if we could have them make this information more accessible. Some of it is our fault as well. Maybe we should ask them, "What about that research that you did?" But maybe they come in and we don't get to know them. But some of them I do get to know like that German woman. I used to see her around and we used to chitchat around and I kept up with her and she sent me her work that she did and she also sent it to the SKC [Salish Kootenai College] library. But I know some of them that are doing things within the tribe. They say that it [the findings] is open for people to read but unless you know about it, unless you read it in the council minutes like me and some other people or are involved in that certain field. I would like it to be somehow made accessible for people to read. There are a lot of people who like to read. Maybe they are not academia college people, like my Mom. My Mom read a lot. She only went to eighth grade, but she read a lot. She read the newspaper a lot. She read. She knew things that were going on in the world. There's a lot of people like that who read a lot but they don't know what is going on in this academia research world and they would like to read it also for their enjoyment of reading and knowledge. So I don't know how it could be done, maybe DVDs, poster, and programs on TV.

Evelyn Matt Hernandez's Words

I am proud to call Evelyn Matt Hernandez one of my former students at Salish Kootenai College. She graduated with a Bachelor's Degree in Human Services and went on to get her Master's of Social Work. She is a great grandmother who dances in the sacred circle with her great grandchildren. A role model for her family, Evelyn has worked hard to break the cycle of alcoholism. I am proud to know her.

I was born to a family of 15. My mother was a full-blooded Salish and my father was Mexican. I grew up in Dixon. I am not the oldest and not the youngest. I am not the middle. But I am between the middle and the youngest child. Growing up I always wondered why my mother only talked about her people just a little bit. I remember my grandfather lived at the Indian Agency, and he had a tiny house. But I didn't find out a lot about him until I got a little older. Actually it was my oldest sisters who told me, because I was still a little girl when he died, about six or seven years old. And he died of diabetes and I never knew that until I was a little older in my life. But what I did find out about my grampa [Henry] Matt was that he was a people person. He helped Indian people. He went to school at Carlisle Indian School in Pennsylvania. And he ran away from that school and he walked all the way back to the reservation in Montana. He was friends with Mike Mansfield and he used to go into Missoula to see him. Mike was attending the university at that time and he would borrow law books from Mike. At that time we didn't have Indian attorneys, but what he did was to go into the tribal courts and defend Indian people. I am not sure if he got paid, but from what I heard, I don't think he got paid. But he traveled all over the Flathead Indian Reservation. So people knew him from Evaro all the way to Elmo because he also helped Kootenai people even though he was Salish/Pend d' Oreille. I can't remember much about my grandfather except he walked with a cane, and he was old. And of course my parents were alcoholics. He would come down, and we lived in a three-room railroad house, and he would come down when my parents would start drinking, and he would come down and take care of us. All I remember is that he was a jolly old man, and he used to put us on his leg and bounce us on the end of his leg all the time and say, "Tiddley dee Tiddley dee," and those are really fond memories of him. I wish that he could have lived longer than he did. Like many of us Indian people we die of a disease called diabetes.

But we also die of another disease called alcoholism. So I grew up and I am a recovering alcoholic. And I have been sober about 25 years. I sobered up and moved back to the Flathead Indian Reservation, attended school at Salish Kootenai College. I got two associate degrees, two bachelor's degrees and a Master's Degree in Social Work. I am the only one in my family who has ever got that education. I am sure my parents and my grampa Matt would be proud of that. By following in the footsteps of my grampa, my goal for getting that education, I could help my Indian people, the Salish and Kootenai people.

And in my job right now, I work for the Native Wellness Program and that's exactly what I'm doing. What me and my coworker are trying to do is to bring back some of the traditions. Some of the ways we used to heal ourselves. Some of the ways we know that worked for our people but got lost and most of the things we do on the reservation are from the non-Native people, but, when we took a look at the past and the historical trauma, we found how important it is for Native people to go back to our roots and that alcohol and drugs and suicide or family violence was never part of our traditions. That it never was. And we worked together as Indian communities. We helped each other. We just knew when we had to help each other like my grandfather Matt. He traveled all across the reservation even to the Kootenai people. He helped them and he listened to their problems and their concerns. So I guess I can say that I am following in my grandfather Henry Matt's footsteps. He is guiding me. I just really feel that through my grandfather and Creator, I was given this gift to help my Indian people and not to do it in a selfish way. Yes, I went to school and got this education, but when I'm working with my people I don't talk about this education that I have, because I don't want to brag and make them feel that I am better than them. So when I am working with those people I try to keep a low key so they can just be themselves, and by being themselves they can tell me the things that are happening in their lives, and I can give them advice on things they can do to change. But not just things, cultural things that have been in the Salish and Kootenai tribes for generations and that we need to really take a look at those traditions in our culture and use those traditions to heal ourselves versus going to a psychiatrist, going through counseling.

We have to learn how to have pride and become who we were born to be, and that is members of the Salish and Kootenai tribes. And through that, we can help our people heal themselves and that the families can get healed, and, when the families are healed, the children get healed and they no longer have to carry that shame of historical trauma. That they can finally let that go and be who they are, which are Indian people who bring back some of their ways of healing themselves like the sweat lodge and Jump Dances and the different ceremonies that we use that our ancestors passed down to us, but we weren't allowed to practice once the coming of the white man, and, when you look at it now, it is beautiful. We had it the right way thousands and thousands of years ago. Until the coming of the whites, who took it away from us, and now what we are trying to do is bring back that feeling that we are here and not be selfish. We are here to use our minds and our hearts. And the heart is really important because if you are working with Indian people, you need to have that Red Heart to reach out to them and understand them, especially with the problems that they have with alcohol, drugs, and suicide affecting our whole tribe. If one person commits suicide or dies from drugs or alcohol, it doesn't just effect that family on the reservation, it affects every Indian and every Indian community down to the littlest child.

In order for us to win this so called war, we just have to go back into the past and learn our traditional ways of healing ourselves and being who we are and not being ashamed of who we are, and finally being able to walk around with our heads up instead of looking at the ground. That part was really hard for me growing up. No wonder I became an alcoholic. I was ashamed of being an Indian. I don't say that in a mean way or I don't say it in a bad way or in a way that I want someone to feel sorry for me. But during that time of growing up, it wasn't good to be an Indian in an all-white school, where you are abused physically and verbally by white teachers. Then listening to my mother. They called her Daisy, but her name was Margaret Dorsey Matt. She grew up in the Ursulines, the boarding school run by the Ursulines order of Catholic nuns. And I thought, "Well, that is good because all the Indian people grew up in the Catholic faith." But what I didn't see was what was behind those scenes. What was behind those scenes and how my mother lost the ability that my grandmother and my grandfather had to raise her Indian children. So since she lost that [parenting skills] at the Ursulines and what she learned was to be physically and verbally abusive to her kids because of the Catholic church, the nuns, and the priests who took that away from her and many other Salish and Kootenai people.

She is not to blame because we lost our traditions. We lost the ability to raise our kids in the Native way. So now we have people now dying of suicide, dying of drug addiction…and young people and really young people dying of these diseases. And the mental health and the substance abuse programs, those are the ones that are going to help our people, by bringing back the old ways that grampa Matt used to talk about that they are important. We went to these white schools and we lost all of that. We lost the ways to heal ourselves. It is just not how to heal our physical selves. It is how to heal spiritually. Us Indian people, we are born with that spirituality. It is there in us. It is a gift from the Creator that he gave us. He gave it to us so we could pass it down to our children. And they can pass it down to their children and on and on. After the coming of the Jesuits, we learned different. My mom talked about Indian children being beaten. Indian children being shamed. Indian children having kerosene poured over the top of their head. When I think about that now, I think, "Oh my God." I am so thankful that my mom survived that and I didn't have to go through that. But I went through other prejudice on this reservation by the white people, the suyapi. Never thinking that because I was Indian I was never going to make it. And I was destined to become an alcoholic and die of that disease.

But I learned to go back to my Native ways from other people in the tribe. And I learned how to heal myself and to heal my spirit that had been wounded by my mom's spirit. I always thought I was okay, but I wasn't. And, like many Indian people, I turned to alcohol to get me through and to make me feel okay. But I really thank Creator, but I am not there yet, because I can never be perfect. I still make mistakes and when I make those mistakes, I need to apologize for them, because I am not perfect. But I need to apologize. It is the Indian way. You apologize and say, "I am sorry." Growing up around mostly white people and stuff, no matter what happened with the teachers, my mother's teachers, the nuns and priests in the Ursulines were very abusive of them [Indian children who were at the boarding school] and the [Catholic] Church never apologized.

They never apologized until today and it is 2011. And my mother has already passed away. She wasn't here to hear that apology, just her children, her grandchildren, and her great grandchildren.

Now it is up to me as a yaya and a tupia to pass that down, about what happened, our history and what we are doing today to bring our traditions and our cultures back to heal ourselves, because we still have that sickness that was brought into us. And we need to heal our families and ourselves. And I am really trying to focus on that because I have twenty grandchildren, two great grandchildren and two more great grandchildren who will be born before summer is over. So Creator tells me that I need to pass this stuff down that Creator gave us so that it doesn't get lost, so my children and grandchildren can keep passing it down, so that we will remain tribal people who we are and be proud of who we are and walk around with our heads up and not with our heads down as if we were nothing. We don't need the white people to tell us how to live, how to think, and what we need to do, because we already know that. Creator gave us that gift a long, long, long time ago before my grandfather and before his father and grandfather. He passed that down from generation to generation, and now it is really important to bring that back to our children and our grandchildren.

To be honest, I do not think that scholars or researchers who come into the reservation understand the culture here. Not all of them, but the majority of them. I feel like we are in a lab being looked at. And this is my own personal opinion. And it makes me feel like I am not normal, that I am something to be studied and neither are my children, or my grandchildren or my tupias. You know we are not here to be studied. We are a unique people. I get really, really defensive sometimes. If researchers come from another Indigenous community they have similar ways of looking at the world and they know how to respect other Indian people. They know how to be respectful. And the other Indian people, who are speaking with them and sharing things about themselves and their tribe, feel more comfortable. When I hear the word "research," I think of a lab that has those little mice in cages. When researchers want to learn about my community, and this is my opinion, but they need to come in and introduce themselves and tell why they are here. We have elders in the tribes, and the elders are the highest in the tribe, and they need to introduce themselves to the elders first. And they need to speak to the elders and have them tell the researchers what they need to do when they are doing this research and how to be respectful and to honor our traditions instead of coming in and listening and not writing the real truth about our people because they [the researchers] don't know the real truth. The only ones who know the real truth are the elders and the tribal people.

I think the researchers come in with their own agenda and what I understand about the Salish elders, and I can't speak for the Kootenai elders, but the Salish elders are real strong, traditional elders. If they are asked questions about our people or our tribe, and if it is asked in the wrong way, or said in the wrong way, the elders will speak up. So the researchers need to know that and when they are speaking to our people, they can't speak to us as if we are people who they are going to write about or put on TV like a documentary. They need to sit down with our people and they need to share some of our traditional foods. I say some of our traditions because some of our traditions are sacred. And researchers should understand the parts that are sacred and they should not try to get into them because if someone is telling them that, they are not traditional and they may tell something that is going to harm our tribe or harm what our elders say to us.

We don't have a protocol to come to talk to us. If you are coming to talk with us, just be yourself. Treat us people to people, regardless of the color of our skin, and if the researcher is able to do that in a meeting with our people or elders, our tribal people will open up. And the researcher has to listen to them, and that is a big skill in Native American communities. So many times non-Indians don't listen or they interrupt and that is not our way. When someone is speaking, you shut up, and you listen, and you don't interrupt them, and that is not the time to ask questions. You do that after the person has stopped speaking. I think the researcher needs to go before council and not only the before council, but before the Salish and Kootenai elders as well. Those elders are protecting their people and they need to know what is going on before they start. Like if someone comes to me I have…sure I am Native, but I don't know everything, and that is what the elders are there for. If I have questions and I am not sure if I am doing it right or wrong I can go to the elders too.

I don't know how researchers learn about our community, but in the age we are living in now with computers, pictures, history books—but in history books, they won't be getting the right information. You have to remember that those history books were written by non-Indians and sometimes they have a tendency to make us glamorous. You know, like they do in the movies. And we are not. We are just people like them. We have different skin color and we may speak in our Salish language. We may dress different. But we are people just like them. Our clothes may be different, but we are [the same] people. Treat us like people.

When the researcher writes up the paper, I am not sure who owns the information. But in our tribe we really got educated and with that education we can keep our tribe's traditions and know what we can give out and what we can't. There are some things that we will never give out to any researcher. And they have no business having it and they have no business trying to get some tribal member to give them that information. If it is sacred and you cross that sacred line, something will happen. When we say that is only for us Indian people, they mean it. It is only for Indian people, and we don't want it exploited or put out to the public where they are making money off of it.

Once the research project is finished, and this is only my opinion, sometimes when the researchers come the one thing they have to do is go before the tribal council, and the council will tell them that they also have to go before the cultural committees because they need to know what the research is. They need to know what questions the research is going to ask. There are some things that we will never share with the researchers and they will never know. There have been a few researchers who have come back to share, but I am always really suspicious of researchers because Indian people are so great, and some of the researchers come in here and take that stuff, information, in order to make money and that is totally wrong. Our traditions and our belief—no money in the world can buy it. It is given to us freely by our Creator and no money in the world can buy it. Researchers need to be accountable to the Salish and Kootenai people, the elders. And if the elders say, "I will tell you this, but I don't want it written down," and when they tell you that they mean it. Instead of the researchers coming in and thinking, "Oh well, you know what this elder told me something, and I'm going to put it down because it will help me sell more magazines or sell more books or videos or whatever." And that is wrong. And the researchers need to respect us, as tribal people and what we believe in.

Researchers look at mental health issues the same way that people who teach about psychology or mental health in the white universities. I believe you are either born an Indian or not born an Indian no matter how many ceremonies or how many things you do, you'll never be an Indian. And that really bothers me because those researchers will say, "Oh, I like this Indian way of life and I'm going to stay here and do everything the Indians do." But they are still suyapis, still white people, and I have to live in this world. I had to get educated. I had to go to white schools. I had to do all this, not because I wanted to, or because my parents wanted me to, but because the white man said we had to. When I look back on it, I'm kinda glad, but we lost a lot in that process. But I am kinda glad, because now I can live in both worlds. I'm learning more about my people and I always talking more to the elders.

I don't think that the researchers come back to clarify the information or let us see the transcripts of the interviews. That is why I have a lot of respect for your research and I am open to talking to you because no matter what words come out of my mouth you honor those words and they are important. They [the interviewees] don't want you to just think, "Oh, I am going to sit and listen to you and record you." Indian people are not about themselves. It is about their Indian people and what they do for their tribes. I hope this project will be passed on to researchers who come to our reservation.

For the idea of mental health, I have never really thought about it, but I have my own mental health problem. I thought about all this stuff that we had to endure that was passed on from our grandmothers and grandfathers, that is historical trauma. And I feel like even with my education, I am still healing from that historical trauma. And in order to heal from that historical trauma, I have to continue to go to the elders and the people who kept our traditions and listen to what they say. To be able to do it and be able to pass it down, I have to do that. Our Salish elders are getting older and older. And I am a grandma now and a tupia now and a qene now, but I don't consider myself an elder because I don't understand all the traditions and all that I need to understand before I can say that I am an elder. It is not about age, like the white man senior citizen, but for us it is not about reaching a certain age, it is "What do you know about your traditions? What do you know about your language? What do you know about traditional child rearing?" And I came back to the reservation educated, and I am still learning. And it is okay. Sometimes I have to learn. And the people may not be educated university style, but they are richly educated in their culture. We have to remember that today, right now this minute; we have to pass it down to our children and not be ashamed at what we are passing down to them. To be able to stand tall and raise their heads up like Indian people used to, and know that this is our way, not the white man's way, but our way. This affected my whole family. I was from a family of fifteen. I had the disease of alcoholism. I went through treatment. I went to addictions counseling and was a member of AA [Alcoholics Anonymous]. And I came back to the reservation and what really helped me was to be involved in my people's ways, going to the sweats. You go into the sweat lodge and it is not about yourself or how you look to people or anything. It is between you and the Creator. And you do it for yourself, your family, and your Indian community.

I don't really know the ways of my mother's sister. One of her older sisters died of a mental health issue. Her Indian husband left her for another woman. During those times that was never traditional [for Salish people]. You didn't switch partners. When you took a partner, you took that partner for life. When he left her with all those tiny little kids and stuff, she went into a state of depression...not eating, not talking, and she died of it. They never put a word to it during that time. But that is what she had. She died of a mental health problem. From what I learned in school, mental health problems can be passed down from generation to generation. Sometimes it can skip generations, but it is there.

When a researcher hears a story from someone, I do not think that the researcher hears the story in the same way it was told. It doesn't have the same meaning. When the elders tell you something, their words are sacred when they come out of their mouth. A lot of them may not be educated; I just heard a tape of my grandfather. You wouldn't call him educated today, but at that time, he was one of the educated Indians. When they are speaking to you, and they are sharing with you these sacred words and stuff, we need to write it or record it exactly how they say it. Because if you take that research and you give it back to the family, the person you are doing the research on, then you are passing on that generational knowledge of the person you are researching. Then the family can say they have a tape of their grandfather who has been dead for sixty years. When I miss my grampa I can put that tape on and I can get the history of my grandfather who has been dead for so long. I got the tape from Frank Tyro, and Bob Bigart found it, and they made sure I got it. So why can't researchers do that and let us listen to it or let us read it so we can know the researcher is telling the truth. And don't make it into a Hollywood thing. We don't want to be glamorized. That isn't what Indian people are all about. We are about our families, our communities, and our tribes. It is not about what is going on in Hollywood or Washington, D.C. It is the three strands of the braid when we braid our hair [each strand represents something].

I would like to see researchers spend a month with the elders so they can really get a feel for tribal people rather than just spending and hour or two with the elders. Just like taking a class at Salish Kootenai College, you just don't go in a couple of times and think you know everything about that class. You need to spend some time with the instructor. Those elders, they have all the knowledge of everything. Use it. Become part of it. Sit down and eat some fry bread and stew or chili. Eat some of the tribal foods with them. Help them go out and dig bitterroot. I said that researchers should spend a year with the elders, and they should ask questions and quote exactly what they say, and in the way they say it to make it look glamorous. Indian people are not about being glamorous. We don't care. We are not out to be movie stars. The only time we are glamorous is when we dress for powwow and we can say, "This is my buckskin and I turn my head and see all my people out there and I dance for my people." I dance for my family and I dance for my tribe. It is not about winning the dance contest.

My advice to young researchers is that you come to our communities and you live in our communities and you spend time with the elders and do what we do and maybe, just maybe, you will understand Indian people. And when we say something, every word that comes out of our mouth and given to the researcher is sacred. You take those words and write it exactly the way we say it. Don't change those words because it loses the meaning to the person who is telling. Respect their words. Honor their words. And before you even start asking those research questions, spend some time in the community, so you can feel it. You can feel that strong Indian spirit that we have in our community. We kept that generation after generation because they couldn't take that Indian spirit away, and they still can't take it away. I'm going to hold on to that until the day I die, and I am going to pass it on to our grandchildren.

Thank you for asking me to be part of this project.

Virgil Braverock

I am originally from Alberta, Canada. That is where my family is from. I came here [to the Flathead] in 1993 pursuing a degree in social work. I worked in the field of social work, but could never get advances because I lacked the degree. In most of the programs I was working with, I worked with adolescents and so because I didn't have the proper credentials, I couldn't get advancement. When I moved up here in 1993, I moved up with my three daughters. My youngest was three months and my oldest was six. I started a whole new life as a single parent. I started pursuing my education in the social work program and graduated from this program at Salish Kootenai College in 1997. My whole journey here was part of life changing. I went to some universities in the United States and Canada and this was a fit for what I was doing. After I graduated from SKC, I moved on to Eastern Washington University, I got my Master's [Degree] in Social Work.

After graduating from there, I came back to the Flathead where my wife was from and Job Corps hired me up there to help develop a base program that had emphasis on retention, cultural awareness. So I developed that program. And that was in 1999. I was the cultural coordinator. I worked out there for five years in developing that program. And at the time they had students from tribes all across the United States. My emphasis was to have the students use their cultural awareness and their background to face the struggles of being in Job Corps and being far from their homes. The students were from all over the state of Montana and across the United States so we brought the cultural awareness to them. It had a big impact on the center and the students to use their culture and what they learned from their family to help them. For me it was the beginning of using the cultural knowledge I might have had and to share that with the students. Because I had so many students from different cultures, the way that I did it was to have the students research and bring their own knowledge in [to the class]. Once they brought that knowledge in the class to share, we did so many things to make them aware of being in their culture. Because food is such a big part of culture, and one year we had a fry bread cook off and we had all the different tribes represented there. We had all the students talk to their families and each day we had a different tribe's fry bread. We bought all the flour and whatever they needed to make the fry bread. Every day for each meal we would have a score sheet and we scored the fry bread. And at the end of two weeks, the Navajo students came out on top. They are from New Mexico and Arizona. The ones who ended up winning were from the Flagstaff area. It was really something for those Navajo students to be recognized for their culture. There were many other events that we had, trying to incorporate the culture and the knowledge. I was not the only one involved in that. There were many other staff that saw the effect of it. A lot of the other staff tried to come up with ideas of how we could share culture. It was a lot of fun doing it, and a whole new experience for me. The main emphasis behind it was retention. We changed the whole institution around to be culturally based. For me, it was learning and applying my own culture to it.

The students we had in culinary arts at the time were preparing for careers in the casinos as cooks, so they were allowed to attend these activities. They also cooked for the ceremonies in the sweat lodge. The whole institution bought into it and they learned about the different cultures.

When I look at culture and scholars who come here, I look at it from the college here. There are many tribes at this college, when visitors come here they are in awe. They are inspired at the program here and what the Salish and Kootenai people have done to incorporate culture into the programs here. They want to take that back to their communities. There is a great need for cultural awareness. When students come here they may be looking to find about their own culture and even if they are non-Native they may be looking to find out about cultures.

Right now researchers learn about our community because there is a lot of technology and the world is smaller. SKC is well renowned around the country and this institution has done a good job of its public relations. Right now our Bachelor's Degree in Social Work is the only one at a tribal college. Other reservations are becoming aware of our program. We hold high standards for our students. Universities are looking at our students [for graduate studies] as very much prepared with a lot of skill. The faculty in social work is doing a really good job of preparing our students to go on to graduate school.

When I look at the word "research," there can't be enough research done. The more research we do as a faculty in methodologies and the more we share, the more the students can have the tool boxes for their skills. The more research the students do, it gives them the tools to go back to their communities to do research such as research policy, it will improve better delivery of programs. Research is very important.

When researchers approach this community, I would give some advice [to] not go into the community with a set agenda but be open-minded. Indian communities are a lot different from other communities. They are set in their ways and each one is different. Each tribe has a different protocol as far as how much research can be done. You have to be very culturally sensitive about what you are doing. You talk about methodology and what the tribes themselves will allow. The researcher has to be prepared to understand about how much the tribes are willing to share. When you talk about psychology, the tribes have their own psychological kinds of issues. Many tribes are very close knit spiritually and through family. If they try to break into those issues, that is where cultural understanding comes in. You have to prepare the questions. When the researchers go into a community they need to be aware of sensitive issues. The ones to approach are the elders. The elders are the ones who will guide them. Elders are recognized by so many tribes as the ones having the most information.

I don't think the elders will set the agenda for the researchers, but they will help guide us in what not to do. If the researchers asked the wrong question that would quell the research, because, once the door is closed, the community themselves may not open the door. They may not allow the research. If they have an elder that is involved with research and guides the type of questions of what can and should be asked and how it is asked and where they can find the research. That would be a door for the researcher to come in: "What do we have to do? Who do I have to know? Who do I go to? Who knows the protocol?" Tribal members are very suspicious of researchers and what kind of information they want to share. They will ask, "Who is going to see it? How will it be used? And where is this going?" Because they have seen what past research has done. The researchers have gone in and used that information for their own gains. We want to make sure the research is helping the tribes. That by sharing culturally sensitive information, the elders will come in and most likely tell the researcher that this is not the right question. The protocol for this community is probably the same for this tribe. The elders are the historical outlet. If anyone wants to find the true meaning for their research, I think the elders will give them the true meaning behind tribal histories, politics. Many tribes are trying to catalogue their information, so even then, the elders are key.

It's about relationships with family. Our community is a family. The ethics board is the elders committee and they are very involved in what information is released and how it is released. They are cautious about what is released. The Salish and Kootenai Culture Committees are very much involved. Even for us, what information we share, has to go through that committee. They are always involved in some way or another. When I worked at Kicking Horse, I had the culture committees involved all the way through. We brought our students down and they cooked for funerals and other activities; they cleaned the elders' yards, painted, because many of those students didn't have elders at home so we wanted to give them that connection. The relationship with the elders is very valuable. Since I came to SKC, I continue to keep my connection to the elders. I really don't know what researchers do with the information they gather in our community. My thought is about the elders.

I heard the tribes are being more involved with that information and where it goes and who is being approached. I think that researchers who research in the college come back to clarify the information and what is being shared.

About owning the information for example, water rights research. That information was shared with the tribe. The ones who gathered that information gave it to the tribal Department of Natural Resources. Once it was shared with the people here, they were more aware of what was happening with the water rights and what was being done. That research was done by an outside researcher and they looked at run off, water flow, and rainfall. The tribes keep the information that researchers do.

The tribe would never be involved with a researcher who wanted to own the research information, because of researchers who have come in and never shared their findings. In the Social Work Department we look at the social issues that affect people's minds and spirits. One of the things we are trying to address is the new social issues. For example one of the major leading addictions in Indian communities right now is meth. It is a huge drug and has a huge effect on our services. Not only the services we give to families. Right behind meth is prescription drugs. Over the counter and prescription drugs is causing a lot of social issues. And right behind prescription drugs is alcohol. Alcohol is having the impact it always had on our people. After that is huffing and that has become highly addictive. It is impacting our youth in many isolated communities, cannabis is way behind. So when we see what is affecting people's minds; it is also affecting a lot of our youth. As far as social issues with families, it affects suicide rates, deaths, prisons. Tribes are try-ing to find ways to address these issues. Where do the elders come in on all of this? There has been a huge shift not only in social issues, but in population shifts to the city. Tribes are trying to maintain their culture in the face of these social issues. All tribes are being affected. A lot of tribes don't have the resources to deal with it. They don't have the financial; they don't have the institutions or technology available to them.

When I look at mental health I guess in a cultural perspective, I would have to say that mental health for Indian people is mind, spirit, body. Once we start looking at ourselves if any one of those are affected by alcohol or anything else, this is where our own cul-tural awareness comes in to guide us. The importance of spirituality, community, supporting one another helps…even our own tribal people we want to hold each other and they don't share with oth-ers in the tribes. Many tribal people need to know where to go for different things. The outcome would be different. The information needs to be shared with others.

I lost a daughter a year ago but without my elders being there to give me support and guidance and what protocol, I couldn't face that issue by myself. I have been talking with others who were in the same situation. I had a friend who lost a son, and she wanted to find information how to deal with it. And so when I started sharing my situation, it made her feel like she wanted to go to the elders and share her story. Even my elders who live hundreds of miles away came here to support me. And I have gone back for ceremonies. So it is really looking at community, and it has to start with what is in that community and whatever strength that got us this far in his-tory. That information and that knowledge has to be shared.

Researchers aren't going to know that. They want to come in and look at mental health issues or psychology in the communi-ty. When researchers come in to look at anything, they need to do their research before they come into the tribe. That prior research of being aware of where they are going and the protocols, and who the tribe trusts. If they go to the wrong sources, that tribe is going to be offended. Have the tribes themselves get involved with the research. The more the tribes are involved with that research, the more they will own it. If they are going to share things with you like their philosophy and history, they will take you to those sites and show you. If you are out there by yourself, you will never find the true meaning of the history or philosophy. The tribe will help you to find it. It is a matter of being culturally sensitive. Even though it is very old information, it is all based on ancient history, like child rearing and our philosophy....behind child rearing and the connections to the land, the importance of land and the importance of certain sites and the connectedness to the oral history which is so rich. That land which is traditionally where the people come from. Even though it was hundreds of years ago, we still feel ownership to that land. The people go there and that is theirs. That is the connection to their children and the young ones, and this is where we live. This is our land and part of our history. All tribes have their center of the universe and the place that makes them strong. For our tribe, the Bloods, it is the Sweet Grass Hills. For the Blackfeet it is Chief Mountain. For all tribes we have our landmarks and the modern significance of those places.

Back in traditional times, depending on the sickness there were, even though what was referred to in the dominant society as shamans, in our Native American ways we had ceremonies and ceremony leaders...each one in the traditional way. There were many different people who did different ceremonies. There were societies where each tribal member had different roles. There were medicines that helped the different sicknesses. We had Sun Dance ceremonies that dealt with the different sicknesses that individuals had. There were a lot of rituals that were done for whatever ailment the person had. So they had different people who dealt with stomach ailments or other things. That continues today. When researchers come into our communities, they are looking for, "How was it done?" Many of the rituals are still here. Many of our tribal people still go to Sun Dances. It is for the same purpose that it was done back in the day.

Those ceremonies are an integral part of our culture. The art of the ceremony like the Sun Dance ceremony, the sweat lodge, the name giving ceremony all those are still here, maybe in different formats, but they are still here. They haven't been lost. Researchers can be very helpful to tribes, but they have to come in and be very culturally aware in how they phrase their questions. The language is still there for tribal members. It is like how many people claim to be German or German descent, or Dutch, or Mexican, and they don't know their language. I commend our elders for keeping our language because of assimilation practices. When it comes to research, the researchers have to take into consideration who we are today. We are still very cultural.

When a researcher comes in to gather information, and this is where the elders come in, it is important to have the elders agree on it. The researcher has to make sure that the information they are receiving is accurate. Without having the guidance from the culture committee or whatever, the tribe knows the information is accurate. If they go to an individual who is an elder, but that individual is not recognized by that tribe as an elder who has actually gained that respect to share their information, they may be talking to an elder, but that other elders may question the validity of the information. By having an involvement of an elder they have to make sure that the source is accurate and they will have information that is accurate enough based on other people who will say, "Well, that individual is okay." Versus if they did an interview with anybody [someone who is not knowledgeable] and it is not accurate, and they go off with that information and they share it, then that can be disputed by the elders. And so the researcher could waste their time. There are protocols and there is the right way of doing research. They need to know who to go to who is involved, and give respect. Respect is very, very important. They have to be patient and not rush the information. It takes the protocol they have to go through to get accurate information. This is for the oral stories and the historical sites. But the researcher has to be patient to hear the story. They [the elders] are testing you to see if you are paying attention.

If I am a researcher and I come to them, I could be seen as suspicious because I have a education. They have seen both sides. I have a tool that is very powerful. They want to know if I am going to help them [with my research].

If I could make changes to the way researchers come into my community, I would like to see a protocol established. It may already be there but a protocol what is being researched; how is the information being disseminated; who is going to share it. Research should be shared with the community. For example in the water rights issues that I spoke about before. That gave the community an idea as to what was currently happening and it sparked interest in the community. It sparked interest that would otherwise not be there. It really helps the community and provides ownership to the community. They feel it belongs to them. In terms of the water, they want to keep it clean and not have oil lines here and the ecological damage that has created and the environmental damage. Now the tribes are involved in cultural sites and we don't want those oil lines going through. They impact the migration patterns. So the tribes having their own input into ecological research helps them to say, "This is our cultural ground and we own it. We don't want pipelines coming in." The researchers are coming in to help the tribes research why it should or should not be done or on the opposite side, how does it benefit them?

If I could give advice to a young researcher who comes into this community [it] is that they have to understand first who they are and what they have to do. Without their own understanding, they could conflict with that culture. I would hate to see someone come in and have that conflict. If they don't understand how things are done, their own protocol, and they have to be open minded to accept the way that things are done. If they don't they will run into their own personal conflict. The best advice is to come into the community with an open mind. That is my best advice.

Kiana

Kiana is a registered nurse. She works for the Confederated Salish and Kootenai Tribes Health Department and is about forty years old. She has three children and has been a member of an advisory board which guides environmental health research that is done on the Flathead Indian Reservation.

I don't think scholars who come into this community to do research understand the people here. They have to be exposed and learn as they go along. If they are from here or if they have read some books or talk to the people they may, but when they first initially come, I don't think they understand the people. To learn about the community, they have to go out there and talk to the people. I don't think they have to live in the community, but they have to function within the community. They can't just come in from outside and do what you want to do and leave again, because you are not seeing what you want to see. You are just seeing a small portion of it. So if you want to see what the community is about, come to some of the functions.

If they are from another Indigenous community, they bring with them what they have learned. If they come from North Dakota, South Dakota, or Arizona, it is not going to be the same as this reservation here. There are some things that are generally the same, but not everything. It is just like the Salish and Kootenai [who live on the reservation here] they are two separate peoples also. To bring in your own cultural awareness is good but you also have to learn what theirs [the people you are researching] is. I think there is some similarity, but not a whole lot....like historical stuff.

When I hear the word "research" or "researcher," I think that somebody is going to come in and identify what it is they want to research and that is what they are going to look at. I also know that there are some people who think they are going to pick and prod, and dissect, but they are going to come in and learn just what they want to learn and not look at the big picture. They won't see the big picture and they will just learn what their main objective is.

When researchers want to learn about mental health or psych on this reservation, they go to those departments at tribal health or departments outside of tribal health, because there are a lot of mental health places around this area.

I don't know how much the elders are involved in setting the research agenda. If the researchers involve the elders, then the elders would have something to say about it. I don't know if the researchers are involving the elders.

I am uncertain about the research protocols. I know they have to go through the tribal council and go through the IRB [Institutional Review Board] at the college. I don't really know how people learn about this community. Maybe they research it on the Internet or Google it.

I would like to say that the tribe has some say about what is being done with the results of the research and it has to go through council before they are allowed to print. I don't know what the researchers do with the information. I think there are some entities that do send it back to the council and follow the protocol, but I am not sure. The researchers own the data.

Some of the researchers share the information with the professional community by printing posters and informational training sessions like workshops, but with the regular people in the community, I am not sure. Maybe they print it in the paper or something like that. If people have an interest in the results, they will find it. We do have an ethics board called the IRB.

Researchers look at the issues in mental health and psych by picking and choosing what they want to look at...the different types of mental illness. You can have a whole lot of different ones depending on whether it is chemical based or psychological or mental health based....or genetic based. I think historical trauma has a lot to do with mental health issues today.

Researchers may come back to give the community a small rundown on what they are doing, but a full debriefing I don't think they do. As far as reading the transcript from the participants, I don't think so.

My definition of mental health is just that, mental health. I don't believe in using negative words like "looney" or things like that. If they are having a good day or a bad day....Good mental health is like yin and yang and all those spiritual things working together.

The things that can affect peoples' minds or spirits that can throw everything off...stress, death in the family, something going on in the community, and, even if it is not in your family, you are part of that community. Anything that is going to affect that balance that you have.

Back in the day I think people healed mental health issues and this is what my grandmother taught me...you have sweats, Sun Dances, ceremonies, Jump Dances, and prayers. The stories that are told to the researcher may not have the same meaning as to the one telling the stories. It all depends on your different beliefs. For example, if I say I go to church, to someone that may mean the steeple and the church, but to me I can pray and see God at home and don't need a structure to go to.

If I could make any changes in how research is done here, it should be done more publicly. I don't think it should be done in secret. I have never seen any professional papers written about this reservation on mental health. I would like to say to the researcher that every place is different and try to see the interest of the people at hand and let the people know where to go and find the results. I would like to see more positive research done on our reservation. There are a lot of good things happening here. People know that mental health issues are here, but they don't like to think about it.

But to heal, there are institutions, and counselors, and for some, they just need someone to talk with.

Stephanie Gillen

Stephanie has a Master's Degree in Wildlife Biology and works for the tribe. She has done a lot of different research projects on the animals and human interaction on the reservation. Her recent project involved animal right-of-way bridges and underpasses on the main highway running through the reservation.

I don't think that scholars who come into this community understand the culture necessarily. Depending on where they are from, they may understand culture, but a lot of them come with an open mind, so I think a lot of them are willing to learn. So if they come from another Indigenous community, I think they understand that Native American culture is somewhat similar but they understand that there are differences as well. So I think it is better if they come from an Indigenous community. When I hear the word "research" or "researchers," to me it is just pretty much a more in-depth study of different things. As a researcher, I understand that it is not always a bad thing. And my family, too, understands. Personally I do not have negative feelings about research, but my grandmother, my yaya who is 89, she tells us we need to get an education and her mind set has changed [about research].

When researchers want to learn about issues in psychology they need to visit the tribal mental health department. Like my brother, he is a psychologist and he had to do this. And the college offers a degree in psychology, and they should visit with instructors here.

I think researchers definitely come into the community with their own agenda. If they are not from this area,… they are told what they can do and what they cannot do. And for the most part, they are very respectful of that. There are certain things that are sacred and they are not to be told about and certain things that should not be looked into. It is very powerful. Here the researchers have to go through council, and generally the council will direct you to the culture committee to make sure it is okay with them. And you give a presentation to the council and the culture committees. They like to be informed and they can ask questions about what you are looking for, and they can tell you what [information] you can use and what you can't use. And to be respectful of our culture and our community.

Researchers learn about the community by the great books that have been published. I know that Thompson Smith through the Salish Culture Committee have put out some great stuff. In the past ten years, it has been improved greatly about what can be learned about our community. There is lots of good literature out there finally. We also have web sites that tell little snippets.

I don't think the researchers own the information. They are allowed to use it, but they don't own it. I think the tribe owns the information. When it comes to culture, no one is allowed to own the information. When it comes to sharing the information with others, they need permission to share and publish. I don't know if outside research about our community ever comes back to the regular community. I think they are supposed to provide their final documents, but that is a far as it goes. For the most part because of that, there is still quite a bit of negativity regarding researchers and research, because it is not shared. They could share by coming back to do community presentations. That would be great.

The researchers have to follow the recommendations of the ethics committee or the IRB at the college, but I am unsure if there is any other ethics committee. Researchers look at mental health issues and psychology issues through historical trauma. We have a lot of depression, suicides. There have never been professional papers that I have seen about the mental health of this community. There are a lot of mental health issues here that can be researched.

It seems like researchers come in, write the book and their dissertation, and then leave and that is the negative part. Maybe also the lack of wanting to participate in a research project is also part of an issue here because of the negative stuff. Researchers need to research the positive resilience of why others don't participate in, say, drug abuse or alcohol abuse. That is a more positive area. The resilience. That strengthens the community.

I doubt if researchers come back to clarify the information that they have gathered from the participants. I am sure they are told they have to, because we don't want anything published that is not correct, but once their project is over, it is over. When you think mental health you try not to think negatively. It is a negative, hurtful and destructive, very sad thing. There are people who choose to use drugs and those who rise above it. Addiction is sad. I am very afraid of addiction because of my grandfather's history, what we learn from bad examples, we rise above and want better for our kids and our family. So you choose a better path. Education and our generation is breaking that cycle.

The sicknesses that can affect people's minds are drugs, alcohol, [and] prescription pills [which] have been very bad, and here in Montana prescription drugs are the drugs of choice. Suicide is another one. Depression associated with drugs and alcohol. It is all ages. The biggest thing is what the elders have been told in the past that their culture was no good, not to speak the language. My yaya is very fluent, but my dad went to the Ursulines and he can't speak Salish, but both my mom and I are taking language class to try to learn. One generation and the language is almost lost.

The elders sadly, I don't think that there was a lot of things they could do after contact to heal, but they would go to the sweat house, Jump Dances, medicine dances, ceremonies. But that is where lots of people don't understand why we do that. When I went to school in St. Ignatius, it was living two different lifestyles. I had my family, which was very cultural and my friends who were not. I don't know if they knew how to heal themselves back in the day. My aunts and uncles are still carrying the weight of the boarding schools, and they never got the help that they needed. My dad never knew why he had to go to that school [Ursulines boarding school] [to live] because he could see his house from there. He ran away many times. That had a big impact on him. Sadly the help may be available for them, but they choose not to take advantage of it.

We are all Catholic but we also have our own spiritual beliefs, which are separate, but we have blended our Catholic religion with our cultural practices.

When the story is told to the researcher, I think there is a loss of communication. Elders have a different way to telling stories and how the story should be told. So that is why it is so important to give a copy of the interview to the person so they can add or clarify. A lot of people are not willing to let the elder tell the whole story with the point of the story at the end. They want the point made now. I love how the elders tell the story. Society has changed us a lot and we are not as patient as we once were.

If I could make changes in the way researchers do research here, I would like to see more respect. We respect our elders and the researchers having enough respect to do the research. And have them sit in on council meetings to see how our community operates. For the most part, you need to be accepted. If they are not accepted, they won't get anywhere. But I think the most important thing is respect. Having respect to learn about what you are coming into. Because not all Indigenous communities are the same, some are way more advanced [Westernized?], and you can write on anything. They are very open with all their information. They are not like we are where you can't write or publish certain things. They are not meant to be told.

For young Native researchers I would tell them to learn about each culture they go into. What is accepted here may not be accepted there. So definitely learning about each culture they are visiting. Just like if you go to a foreign country, you would learn about their culture and speak their language a little. You won't go anywhere if you don't know how that community works. You will get very negative feedback if you don't know how that community works. So understanding the culture is key. And coming from a cultural background they will accept you. And being respectful.

Whisper Camel Means

Whisper is a tribal wildlife biologist who has researched many projects for the tribe. She teaches and is a guest speaker for the Biology Department at Salish Kootenai College.

Sometimes I think that scholars who come to the reservation don't understand our culture. I am thinking of things that I have seen. I am a wildlife biologist and one time as I was driving up around St. Mary's Lake and I saw people from the University [of Montana] doing some sampling in some of the streams. And I know that we have permits that the tribe puts out for these people, that we have our own protocol if they are doing any kind of sampling or any kind of research. I went back [to the tribe] and asked them and no one ever heard of these guys or given any permits or anything. So I think there are people who come here unbeknownst to us and do work, which I don't think is right. It is our land and we are supposed to be co-owners and the majority of things where we say you can go ahead and take data from us. We are the people of this land. And so I see where they don't understand the people and how things are done. I definitely think that people don't think there is a different culture here. It is surprising to me that when I hear people from

Polson or people who visit Polson don't even realize that they are on an Indian reservation. That blows my mind. So yes, I don't think they actually realize where they are.

I think that if Indigenous scholars from other reservations come here, they do have similar lifeways. They have that cultural sensitivity and societal sensitivity where they understand how things work and how to go through the proper channels. They don't just come in and do whatever they want. I think tribal people from other places do have an idea of what is going on, even if they are not exactly the same. I think we are a little different here. There is a lot of non-tribal culture assimilated into what is going on here compared to some other places.

When I hear the word "researcher" or "research," because for me as a scientist, I think about animal research and I think about somebody going out and looking at plants, animals, or water or fish or something like that. It can encompass people as well but I guess that is what directly draws my brain when I hear "research."

When researchers want to learn about issues of mental health I am not sure how they are reaching us. I have never been asked about that. I think it is important and I think there are people here whose needs are not being met, and so I am not sure how they are reaching us. I think they might try speaking with groups, or with Dr. Lori Lambert over at SKC because she has her finger on the pulse of what is going on with environmental research, and she is part of that board [IRB] and the link between the medical part and seeing that people have to go through a process. I guess touching base with tribal health. There is a tribal health mental health clinic. That would be one way, but also I think there are a lot of people who have a need for mental health attention, whether it be emotional or straight mental illness, that they don't get the help that they need to get. Maybe they are scared, or I don't know. Those people need to get those things out of their heads. Just talking. I don't know if people know that that kind of help is easily available. Maybe people with those problems need public information, maybe a billboard, or an ad in the paper or a radio spot.

I'm not sure if the elders set the agenda for the researchers or tell them what they want researched as far as my experience. I think for the kind of work I do, the elders are consulted, but I don't think at this point they are setting the standards. I think they could be asked, but I think if they are asked, but if we are talking about mental illness, they may need that kind of help as well, because there are elders that don't really have a grasp of what people need. The may be consulted, but not at the center of designing the projects. They definitely should be consulted, but there are people who are more aware of what the community's needs are [and they] should be the ones to design the projects.

There are protocols in place for researchers who want to come into the reservation and do research. For us we have to get permits and tell somebody that you are going to do something. You need to be in contact with the proper channels. So there is that. People don't appreciate when researchers come onto the reservation and do research without contacting someone. Someone related to that field of study that can direct that person to the people who could use that service or might have a concern about them doing the research. I think there should be a protocol on the tribal website for researchers. In this day and age, if people are doing Internet searches and they are scholarly, they would be looking for information that they would hit the website. It could say, "If you are looking to do research of any kind on the reservation, here is the protocol." Maybe add the name of a contact person. I am not sure who that would be, maybe someone in that field. Those offices would know the protocol to give the permit to allow these individuals to do research. We have animal protection protocol so animals won't be harmed unnecessarily and not to abuse them and to keep things respectfully. Respect is really important. You can't be killing everything off.

I think researchers learn about our community through the Internet, mostly, maybe some books, maybe speaking with other people or coming to a talk. I think SKC does a really good job of service to the community, like the things going on at the theater where there the public can come and see a movie or a video documentary or hearing people talk. I wish there was even more going on than right now. I have attended a lot of those programs as much as I can. We are kind of separated from other people, but there is that social media that brings it back to us.

When the researcher writes up that paper, if they have a grant, it is partially the person who paid for the research, partially the researchers, and the tribe has to have some ownership in that. We are not charging to get that information, but we own part of it. If protocols were ever to be established, that should definitely be in there, because people should realize that we are not just giving our information away. We don't even share some of our data with the state. That is ours and we paid for it, and the people who are above us feel it is not free for anyone to find out what is going on around here. They can request it from us and we might go through our channels and give it to them, but it is not just sitting on our website to say how many grizzly bears there are, or how many elk there are, or how many moose there are. That is our topic and our information.

When people do research here from outside, it is shared with our community on our website and so people can go there and read it; talks like over at the Arlee-Charlo theater, that is a great way to share information. I don't know if we ask the researchers to bring the findings back to the community. I wish that it would. With things that I have control of, I try to do that, but I don't know if it is really occurring. Maybe our people don't know the venues of the theater, but researchers have the knowledge to do a PowerPoint and people can come there and have a little reception. I think it is important. There are other places where they can share their findings, like community centers and such, but, as far as a scholarly place, I think that the theater is best. It is kind of new so as more people know about that place, they will realize it is a place where they can give the information back to people. We own that information and it shouldn't be locked up in a file cabinet and never see it. We should own it in a way that people can hear it.

I don't think there is an ethics board. But I know there is an Environmental Health Advisory Board that I have been part of with Lori, and we have looked at a few things, but overall, I don't think there is a governing ethics board. But I think we would benefit from that. There needs to be those protocols and the information in place so there is someone doing the oversight to say, "Yes, you can do this or do that." So it can be dealt with if people are abusing the tribe and the community could benefit from that. I've done a few interviews with students from the University of Montana on nature and culture and that, and they don't put it all out there, but where does that document go?

Researchers think that we have issues in mental health and psychology. People think that we are still a lot of alcoholics and people who have issues. But I don't know if we are respected as much as we could be. There is an aspect of damage that people feel and when people cannot express how they feel. Even people I have talked with like grandparents and parents. My grandparents went to the boarding schools and they were silenced for who they were, silenced for their culture, silenced for their language, silenced for being a person, and that totally gets passed down. I don't think that is a cycle that is easily broken from the home. And so my father's generation has issues where they can't talk about things. They won't talk about things. They won't acknowledge things, and it is just broke down. I think that, whether they realize it or not, there are still issues that weren't historically there and that have been created because of history, and I am just not sure that people realize how damaging a lot of that really was even for people now, years later.

I am not sure what the researchers do with information they gather in my community. I don't hear about it. Hopefully they are using [it] not to just get a degree and move on, or to fulfill a grant and move on. I hope they would come back. And I wanted to start this for a while. I think there is great value in talking circles. I just wanted to start one and I talked to the lady in psychology, and just have a women's talking circle where women can come together in confidentiality and speak freely and not be judged by the group and then leave in two hours and have that out of yourself and have confidence that these people in the group will not go gossip about what you just said, because that is not the trust that you just said. People may realize that that is something useful and cleansing.

If there were someone in the community that has the same interest, but you wouldn't know. It would create a sense of community and exchange information. In the interviews that I have done, people have sent me the transcripts of what I have said to make sure that that was correct before they published it. In my opinion, the researchers do come back to clarify the information. But that is only in my case. I don't know what other people do. I have not heard of any other researchers coming back to clarify. I am not sure how I would define mental health. I think it is your own ability to deal with situations in life and to have clarity in what you yourself need to do.

Things that affect people's mental health are chemicals, whether it was something you ingested yourself or if it was environmental that you are not aware of, but also mental illness in the sense of having a mental defect that due to it, you would not be able to rationalize correctly, or to think things through, or to react properly. There are things like classic types of depression, schizophrenia, or any of those issues. I have known people who have those mental illnesses, some of them untreated. They walk around without being able to feel things and not getting any help. So I acknowledge that there are people out there, and I acknowledge that there are many ways that they deal with it, but I also think that drugs can affect people's mental health like a brain on meth.

I wonder even if mental health problems were really an issue back in the day. I wonder if mental health issues were a product of maybe increased knowledge about the human brain. Maybe someone was just a little off and maybe people just let them be, and they didn't address that issue, but, if it was more pronounced, maybe they would say here take this root or go into the sweat and cleanse yourself. They probably just accepted people. I don't know if it was something that was treated, or if chemical abuse has led to more issues, dysfunction, depression, so I don't think there was alcohol abuse because that wasn't there. The loss of culture, the loss of identity and family structure, I think probably was the cause of mental issues. So I don't think there was mental issues in the way we know them today back then, at all. And if there was something that was a little bit off it wasn't something that was publicized. I think the emphasis was on life and surviving and not micromanaging what every little thing that every single person does every day. As technology increases and medical knowledge increases then we start picking and start looking at every single little thing we do.

I think that stories can be different from the one telling the story to the researcher hearing the story. They might strike from something that they experienced in their own life or something that they heard from someone else previously, that they heard and they did some research on it. I think the gist of it might be there, but there are personal biases whenever anyone hears a story. If I hear a story, and you hear a story, and we go retell that story, it will be different because we are going to focus on different aspects of it. I think that is just oral knowledge that things are fluid and change.

If I could make changes in the way researchers come into the community, I would make sure that researchers of any type know the policy that this is our stance, and we are willing to share knowledge, but you have to follow the protocol. People need to have council approval, which should include a board that would keep an eye on the ethics and other issues that might come up whether it is wildlife or mental health. Those things need to be evaluated because it is still research and other people coming in here, and there needs to be a give back of that information to the community so people know what is going on, whether it is a talk or a paper and have it made available so the people can go look at it. It could be shared at a booth at a health fair or pamphlets or posters. Something that gives back for the giving of ourselves and our land and have food to draw people in. If you have something and there is no food, people won't come, but if you say there is food, people will come. I think it is a really good idea to have the grant findings to develop a tribal protocol for researchers. Different aspects of research should be considered when putting together the board. So some representative of that discipline should come and share a little bit and be part of the decision. I would look into our tribal government and employees and go that way.

Maybe get a group of people together that you know could pull ideas together and say, "Okay this is how we want to look at fish, wildlife, water." Other types of medical research that could occur they could look at cancer and other types of things and those types of people could come together and they could suggest people who could be on this overall committee. Or they could take that information to the people that they know to get just a little bit more idea. Then there might be some protocol set up. So that everybody could know what is being considered. And that research in general is looking to have that baseline protocol. I think that people like streamlined, defined protocol, but I think we don't have it for as many as we could around here.

Frank Finley

Frank is my former student and an amazing multi-talented individual. Son of the last War Dance Chief of the Salish tribe, he has taught college chemistry, art, silversmithing, and topics in Native American studies. Recently, he was appointed the department head for the Native American Studies at Salish Kootenai College. He completed his Master's Degree in Education at the University of Idaho in May 2013.

Scholars who come into my community do not understand my culture. Scholars who come into the community do not understand how to come into a community of Natives and talk. They don't understand how to come in and talk. In a non-Native community it is okay to come in and say, "Hi my name is John Smith and I am a researcher from whatever university I am from." In white culture, that is fine. But from a Native culture you walk up and say that, and it means absolutely nothing to them. It is the stereotype of non-Native researchers coming in and taking things. Like the Havasupai there is all these things that have been done in Native communities. Like Jeff Hart (1976). He came in and took all this plant knowledge and wrote a book on it and never gave the people a little bit of credit and sold the book all over the place and the tribes got zero credit for it. So they don't really know how to come in and talk to people and you have to be introduced and you have to talk and you have to pay your time. You may have to wait two or three years before the people will tell you what they want to have researched.

People find out about our community by doing a web search. They look at the www.rezweliveon.com and think they know about stuff or they read CSK&T [the Confederated Salish and Kootenai Tribes] is in the news. There are enough legal cases and things. We are between two big communities, Missoula and Kalispell. Besides it is a beautiful place. Who wouldn't want to do research here? I don't think we are that exciting, really.

Research means doing things over again: "Research: looking. Research: searching things over again...asking a bunch of questions over and over again." It's a linear thought process of the scientific method. You know you make a hypothesis, you do some little experiments. You check your data and in the end you do it all over again with a different question. So it is not curvilinear; it is not circular thought. It is 100% linear. So research is like that. And a lot of people with research, too, I don't think they go back far enough. They always look at the newest things, but some of the older stuff says some of the newer stuff is wrong or that things are wrong so they don't follow the paper trail back and forth.

When researchers want to learn about issues of mental health and psychology here, they probably come in and talk to tribal health and the tribal health psychologist. But I don't think that is very good, because those people are swamped. It takes three or four weeks or a month to get in to see the psychiatrist and all he does is write you a prescription and says, "Here." And you are on Prozac for five years.

With the culture committees, I don't think the elders set the agenda for the researchers or tell them what we want researched. It is a formality to go see the elders here. It is not like it is in Dine [Navajo]. I think they come in and as a formality they go see the tribal council and the tribal council says, "Yes, but you have to go see the elders." So then they come back and say, "Yes, we saw the elders and everything is cool." And they just go ahead and do some of that stuff [their research projects] because we don't have a strong IRB [institutional review board] with the tribe.

The work we have done with Indigenous research methodologies with water quality in Arlee. There was an elder who said, "Oh, you guys just want to come in and look at stuff like the white guys." And as a Native I took offense at that. I had to think really quick, "How can I tell the elder that we really need to look at this for our people. We are looking at this [water problem] for us, not for the EPA [Environmental Protection Agency], the United States, or the University of Montana, or the Department of Agriculture. We are looking at this for the health of our people." So I had to come up with a story and I told the elder that our stories tell us that Coyote will come and get us and take us to the west and take us to the next place. Our stories tell us that. Coyote came and cleared the monsters and made the land safe. Well, now there are these bacteria and these chemicals that are in the water. They are like little tiny monsters and they hurt you from the inside. They can't be seen in the water, so we need to take care of these things so our people will be well when it is time for Coyote to come and get us and take us, and we need to make sure that our people are still here for Coyote to bring. The elder thought for a few minutes. And she was the big stopgap [that would prevent us from doing the research]. She said, "You guys are white guys," and at that moment everybody stopped and there was nothing going forward. But at that point, because I related it with appropriate cultural references, we were told that we could do our project because we were not doing it like the white guys.

We have an IRB at SKC but I don't know if there is a protocol with the tribe. The tribe may have something loosely, but it is not actually followed. To gather data, you have to sign some paper and follow up and provide them with a copy of what you do. That is mostly for physical data, not for physiological, psychological, mental data stuff. The college's IRB is pretty tough and it should be from what I have seen. I don't know if there is any place a researcher can go online or if there is a little pamphlet that says, "Doing Research with the Flathead Tribe." I don't think that exists.

Intellectual property belongs to the tribe in common and so part of the problem with non-tribal researchers is that they don't understand copyrights held in common. How can a group of 7,000 people hold the intellectual property rights for this idea, this concept? How come one person can't own it? And that is the same problem with the Jeff Hart book. He copyrighted that book. That is tribal information. The closest thing that they have on the web is a creative, a copyright on the web where you can use it, but you can't sell it, you can't change it. Credit has to be given to whom it belongs to and that creative commons is the closest copyright thing that I have seen anywhere. It would somewhat fit what we do.

I don't know what researchers do with the information they gather in this community for the most part. I know that people who have interviewed me for one thing or another have given me copies of their research to approve. Academic success, for one reason or another. I guess I am considered an academic success, but because I actually graduated with a degree, but that is not a big thing. There are hundreds of Indians who have done that, but I don't know other than the stuff we have been currently working on with the CBPR [Community Based Participatory Research], that information has been taken out to fulfill somebody's Ph.D. or master's degree. And it may have been given to the tribe, but nobody knows what it is, or what it is for, and it has been written in mumbo jumbo or jargonese for whatever it happens to be for. It is not for plain average everyday people to read or understand.

I don't think they ever come back to clarify the information with the people. I just think we have with the CBPR and when people ask questions, we explain to them until they get really tired, or they have some idea of what is going on. I don't think that we have that many people who have mental health [issues].

I think they are lacking in community. For people with years and years of stuff going on [stress] people withdraw. They don't go out. It's a great community. There is a lot going on. You have to engage. And so the people who have the worst problems are those that don't engage. I think that is something we need to do is to engage more people. Granted we can't fit everyone around one fire anymore, but families, cities, towns because the thing in mental health issues we have right now: depression, suicide, eating disorders, and the profane stuff that goes on, I guess a lot of that stuff could be eliminated if we had an intact community. Because we have people who would be taking care of you, supporting you, looking out for you, getting compassion from everyone else you live with and live around. Do you really know your next-door neighbor? We have had so many people moving in and coming. I bet that half the people here don't know their neighbors on both sides of their house. So if you need a cup of sugar, do you go there or do you wait and go to the store. The entire reservation until the time of the mid 80s was like the 1950s sort of television version of things: Leave It to Beaver. People never locked their houses. There was not a huge amount of violence. You could go to your neighbor's house and borrow sugar even if they weren't home and say, "Ya I took it," because there was a better sense of community. From the latter part of the 80s to the turn of the century that sense of community is gone. For mental health I think that is the biggest thing. People are not connected to their families and they are not connected to the land. Everybody becomes isolated. Some people are connected to their culture and those people are the healthy people, even slight connections, like people who go pick huckleberries, bead, or do something like that, they are connected to the culture at least ephemerally. They have some way to get some feedback from other people. The better the connection [to the culture] the better the people.

Unless you live a traditional life style…the problem is you can't live a traditional lifestyle and pay the rent. You can hunt and fish and dig roots and berries and find all the food you need here…tradition-ally this is the place my dad says they called the "basket." So this is the place where we hunted and fished and picked berries and dug roots and everything. This is the place where we got all of our food and then went back and spent winters in the Bitterroot Valley, which is a lot warmer, a lot friendlier place. We can't do that anymore. We need gas to go back and forth and that is a huge barrier; you can't do it and that is one of the things that affect people's spirits. If you are a tribal member, you can work for the tribe or you might get a job as a convenience store person or a food service. If you are clean and don't have any felonies on your record, you might get that. If you have felonies on your record because you were busy stealing trying to get some money to pay a bill to do any number of things to have some money…Lack of employment is probably…in the domi-nant culture you have to have the almighty dollar to make things work. Even if you did live a traditional lifestyle, you still need some money to buy gas now to go back and forth, because we don't have the horse culture we once had.

I think there was no mental illness back in the day. I think they were all like Narcisse Blood and Ryan Heavy Head, the Blackfeet I know from Siksika, everyone was self-aware, self-actualized. Ev-erybody knew their role in the community and what their place was in the group and what their job was. Not so much, "I work at McDonald's," or "I am a college professor," or "I am a film and media guy" or anything like that. But "I am the guy that goes out and finds fire conchs," and "I know where all the huckleberries are within a hundred miles of here." And that is the thing you take pride in be-cause that is what you are good at. It is the gift that the Creator gives everyone. You are good at something. Everybody is good at something. Some women around here think they are only good at having kids, but maybe that is what they are really good at. Look at me. I am good at learning. I figure things out and I can make stuff. I don't go around bragging to people and say, "Hey look, I can make stuff and you can't." It is an entirely different sort of a thing when you are self-actualized. Look at this lady over here. You take your twenty deer hides and you give her some meat and things, and she will tan those hides, and you take them over to this other person, and she will sew them into a small winter tipi for you. So you have a cover over your head. You are doing other things. You are getting the deer and collecting the things. And then you are taking those bones and trading them with this other person over here and you are trading and bartering with everyone, and you are involved with everyone in the community.

That is the important part in Native culture—is the commu-nity being attached to all the relationships you have to have. That is what would keep you sane. Like Maslow's hierarchy, how many white people are self-actualized, maybe five percent? How many percent of Blackfeet in Siksika were not self-actualized was five per-cent. So why do you have all the deviants? Maslow went to look for all the deviants and found none. No one was acting stranger than anyone else at Siksika. And that was all fine. They all did the things they wanted to do. They were all good at whatever they were doing. "Oh I'm not good at that, and I'm not going to do it." But somebody else would come along and pick that up and be good at it and that was just the way it is. If you are self-actualized you are not going to be the deviant. You are not going to have any mental illness. And even now if you are contrary, that was a specific place in the tribe. If you are the one that's going to wash and dry in the sand, then that, like in Little Big Man, people said, "Huh, that's what they do." And there was no outcry for what they did. Now killing and maiming or hurting other people, those things were not fine in the community. Those things were frowned upon. Those people were sent away, whisked right out of society. You are gone for a year. You come back and you're fine, but without the tribe around you, you are not going to last for a year. Very few people ever did. That's why it was the meanest sentence the worst thing was to be separated from the conclave.

The story should have a different meaning for everybody. Whatever they need at the time. If it is a Native story, it should have a different meaning for whatever you happen to be doing in your life. Sometimes if you're not on any mission or anything, it may be just sharing or for entertainment. It may be just a good story. Other than that, there are lessons encoded in all the stories of one kind or another. Sometimes researchers don't listen to that part of the story. They just think it is really great that Skunk did this thing or that, or Owl did this thing, or Frog did this: "Wow those are really entertaining stories." And they miss the lesson. Well, Skunk really shouldn't have gotten his girlfriend pregnant or gotten Fox's girlfriend pregnant and the kids are going to look different and someone is going to know. It causes trouble. The moral parts of those stories are totally tuned out because the dominant culture is totally tuned into entertainment.

Researchers should come in and say what they are researching for. You can't just come into a Native community and just say, "Hi, I'm this guy and I am from Tufts University or I'm from UCLA," or where ever the hell they happen to be from, the University of Cairo, Egypt. That doesn't mean a thing. You come in and say absolutely nothing and you have someone say, "This is my friend. I know and absolutely trust this person. They have some questions for you. This person is John Smith and I think he is okay." And have a formal introduction, "They are looking at this sort of thing," because from our culture we don't talk about our own things. Somebody else does that for you and explains it to the people. If you come in and say all these things [about yourself] it is bragging. It is saying, "I've got a Ph.D. from a mail order catalog," and that is supposed to be a big deal and it really isn't. It means absolutely nothing. If I go to Crow [Agency] and I have, I have been there and people say, "This is Frank Finley. He teaches at Salish Kootenai College and he's a good guy. He trusts us and he's going to help us, and we want you to listen to him, and, if he needs something, we want you to help him out." When I go to

Fort Belknap, I am treated as an elder because I helped them start their water program and start their environmental science program. I don't really know why they treat me as an elder because I really don't feel like one. But they do. I met Elizabeth, the lady over there. She said, "Oh, I know Frank." And she brought me over there and introduced me. This was pretty funny because she had lived in Namibia for years and had a totally bushman mentality, and they don't mess around when they introduce people, "Hey, this is such and such." And they talk very strongly and the tribes at Fort Belknap, that fit their worldview. And so I would go there and [she would say], "This guy knows science and chemistry and stuff. Listen to him." And they did and they opened their water lab before me. I am at their opening and they brought me food…at their opening.

So that is the way research should be done. You should be brought in, and, by the time you leave, you should be celebrated and be entirely a part of the community. Then you are part of the community, and anything that is going on you have a vested interest in. You can't just come in and say, "Well, we want to look at why all the babies on this reservation have three fingers on their left hand." You don't want to do that. You want to come say, "We have unique children with three fingers on their left hand, and we cherish them, and we don't raise them any different, and they do everything the rest of the children do. We don't see that as a disability, or we don't see it as a superpower or anything. It is just a normal part of everyday life. It means something to us because it is a key for the place we live."

I think an Aboriginal researcher would have an easier time in an Aboriginal community because they would come in and join the community. They would come and try to be part of the group. They wouldn't come in and say, "We do this stuff where we are from. You do this stuff." Indigenous people the world over understand there is one Creator, and he is not a wrathful Creator. Everyone knows the Creator is kind and giving and he made all of us, and the dominant culture just doesn't understand that. Very few of them will ever get to the point of what that means.

To young Indigenous researchers I would say, "Go home. Maintain your culture no matter where you are. Smudge your self and your house when you need it. It ties you to your place. It keeps you tied to your home. Visit your people. Talk to your elders. Ask them for guidance because they have seen a lot more people than you have.

They can tell you how to get along with people who are rude and abrasive, just nasty. They know better ways." Maybe some of them will fly off the handle, but most of the elders I know and people would go off and they would sit and chew their gums or whatever they do when they don't have teeth. And they would wait until they [the rude person] walked off and then they would say, "That was a very rude person and it is no way to act." Then the next person came in and would be gracious and the elder would give them the information they required because they were polite and asked the right things and spent time with the elders instead of swooping and making a big show out of stuff. Whatever research you do, you have to maintain that home. You have to be at home and have that sense of place and know who you are. The research makes no difference if you lose yourself and your place. You always have to know who and where you are.

Leslie Camel

Leslie Camel comes from a family of artists and academics. She left her reservation to attend art school in Boston. She currently works for the tribal newspaper, the *Char-Koosta*.

If scholars come from other reservations [to do research or work at the college] they might understand our culture, but non-Natives I think it is new to them to be around an Indian community and a college on an Indian reservation. Compared to other reservations, we have such a big school and a big campus. So no, unless they are Natives I don't think they understand the culture. I haven't been to a lot of speakers [on campus presentations] but I think Walter Echo Hawk might know about the culture. He did his whole study on the negative things that have happened in the communities. There was a rapper I just seen and, he is a Native rapper from Crow and he was giving positive messaging through hip-hop. He would understand. SKC does a lot of incorporating a lot of different cultures as a sharing of different cultures.

I don't think that researchers from another Indigenous community have similar lifeways and worldviews. I think this reservation has such an infiltration of non-Natives that unless you know or miss the [language highway] signs, you wouldn't know you were on a reservation. We are not as poor as some of the reservations, even in Montana. We are a lot larger. Because of the college we have a lot of different tribes here. So I don't think the experience is the same. They don't see the poverty that is on a lot of other reservations. We are more progressive, but I think what people see in their minds as reservations. I don't think this reservation fits that stereotype.

When I hear the word "research" or "researcher," I usually think of educated people that are educated in some specific field and they always want to get Native feedback and get ideas of how our culture is related to that field. It [the research] is usually something done over a long time. I usually think of non-Natives associated with research and probably a lack of information. They are pretty new to the ideas so they don't really have anything else to base their ideas or their studies on or relate it to [their research] the study of Native ways. It is pretty foreign to them.

When researchers want to learn about issues in mental health or psychology, well luckily we have the college here, SKC, so that they at least can go to people who have been in the community, and it is a resource for them to try and figure out, "Where do we go?" They can go to the college and ask. It is a good place for them to start to find out about the departments, or tribal council to find out some good information. They may also go to cultural events and find out what our cultural beliefs are based on, like powwows or maybe events at the People's Center. I don't think of them as actually going to the mental health department to ask. I think rather it is an observation of the way of life rather than the actual mental health issues. There are a lot of them. It seems like mental health is not really a discussed subject. They talk about domestic violence and alcohol abuse and stuff like that, but I don't think our tribe looks into the why these problems arise or stem from. It is from within the tribe [that these subjects happen]. You see a lot of suicide prevention, relationships of people, parenting classes. I guess those are the effects of mental health, but it's not the cause of it. I think there is really a stigma that goes along with mental health. I know my family has a history of mental health, of depression, and, I don't think we are very different from a lot of people, but I think it is such a stigma, but I think it is more of a stigma for men. I think women are more prone to getting help.

I think that researchers stand back and observe mental health issues rather than question. I think if they were to question, people wouldn't be up front and open about it, because it is just not something that people want to admit, expose. Or they feel like it is something to be ashamed of. I can't say it is just for Native Americans I think it is kind of an American phenomenon. Just the way society is built or based on fear. Our society is based on fear. If you don't go to college, you can't have the car. You won't have a good life. You have to buy a house. You have to have insurance. I'm almost forty and I am just beginning to accept that idea. It is scary. Unless you have good people who are role models to show you that this is important, then you don't think you need it. I don't think Natives are pretty reserved. I am not sure if they [researchers] were asking the right questions, if they would get the right answers [about mental health].

I think this community is very guarded about their resources just because it seems as though the urbanization, they [the elders] don't want it to be as fast. I know the highway was a big deal. Working with the traditional life. Traditional living department…you know like Indigenous plants…they don't want to tell you where they're planted. They want to keep that very private. We always had to ask permission [from the elders], and rarely were we granted it. That is understandable to a point. I think that if they were really sharing it with their own people that would be good, but they don't really share that. It is just guarded, period. That information is not passed along the way it used to be. Society is really changing. Like there isn't much sense of community anymore. I see people not participating in community events very much anymore, or they are not as important as they used to be when I was younger. So I think the elders keep their information guarded. Even as a Native, I am an artist and I need pictures of bitterroot and "Big Medicine" and I had to go to the Salish Culture Committee just to get permission to use their records. So they are really, really guarded about what they share. So I think for researchers it is even less. I think they are really suspicious of their intent, because it can go really wrong. They have been taken advantage of and all that kind of stuff.

The elders would question what is this research being used for. From there they might give them just enough to fulfill that. But I don't think they are gladly open to giving a lot of the information. They are very guarded.

I would think [for researchers who come here], well I used to work for the college and now I work for the tribe, but I have seen situations where people have to go to the tribal council, meet with the council, and tell them what you are doing. I would think that would be the first protocol. That is a recognized entity that they can formally go to and feel like that is a start. After that, I would think the college is another source of who to contact. Other than that, I am not sure. People doing it on their own would get negative feedback. Even if they knew a family and went to the family and said, "Okay, I am going to learn from you," and after that if they came out and said, "Oh I learned this about the community." Well where did you get that information? And they would really be scrutinized for that. I know there was a woman who was online making that she was some kind of a shaman or something and that she learned from Johnny Arlee and the members of the culture committee and she has a website over at the *Char-Koosta* [tribal newspaper]. We get calls all the time with people asking, "Who is she?" She didn't talk to the tribe. So if they make any claims, they [researchers] will really be scrutinized as to where they got that information. So the best place for researchers to start is the tribal council and the culture committee.

Because SKC is a large school I would think that is where people would get interest by being exposed beyond the borders of our reservation. So I think that the college brings in a lot of interest to where our school is today and the fact that we don't just have a few disciplines, but many disciplines and many that are very advanced as far as like IT [information technology] and the science disciplines with NASA [National Aeronautics and Space Administration]. That is awesome. So I think because we are more progressive and we go beyond the borders of the reservation, I think that would get people's attention. Probably the fact that there are so many different tribes that come to the college it would make tribes understand that our students are going over there and what is over there? So I think that would bring people here. I think as far as learning about the community there are a few…there is the People's Center, the culture committee, the [tribal] headquarters right here, the college is right here. So everything is pretty centralized. Luckily they can go to one place and get a bunch of leads.

I think that the researcher owns the information they gather. There is a trust thing that we have to believe that this person [the researcher] and I think that is why information is so heavily guarded because they [the elders or tribal members] don't really know how they are going to be exploited, or how you are going to be perceived. But whatever they are doing with that information, it is their work, their process. It is their [the researcher's] perspective but once you shared it, you kind of shared the information [with the researcher], you share ownership. You have given them a little bit of the information so it is now…from an academic standpoint, it is theirs. A cultural person may think otherwise, but I am not a cultural person. I have gone to school in Boston and Portland and lived in Jamaica and so my perception of those things are mine. It is really not fair for us now [to the researcher] to say, "Okay this is ours now." You can't share it when I have gone to other places and taken what I've learned. Nobody guarded it and nobody said, "You can't share this with anybody." I found that people on the reservation are more closed minded in that way, which I think is a downfall because there is so much we can learn out there, so much to see. I just think, because I am a younger person, that information should be shared. So many could benefit from sharing it more. Even our own could benefit more, but we just keep it so guarded it does get lost, and that is a shame. Just like the language. I don't think people see it as a big need to keep it anymore.

I wish there were more efforts to do it. Like my grandmother just passed away a year ago today, actually, and she was one of the last full Salish speakers and I didn't learn it from her. And so there is one whole generation now that has lost the language and that is really sad. But in my life I can recognize that and feel like I didn't learn it, but what am I going to do if I learn it? You have to keep using it, and the tribe doesn't even use it. It is as if it doesn't even exist. I think they should have all of the signs around here, like the street signs with the names in the language, even the stop signs. Just so people can see it and incorporate it in their daily life because it is not incorporated now. So if you want to learn, it is kind of like you are doing it more symbolically, "I know my language," rather than it being used. I think there are a lot of ways that the language can be integrated into daily life, like the street signs. I think people would be more open to learning it and more ready to learning it rather than going to a class for a couple of months and that's it. Then you have to go to these certain events to use the language. Just them and that's it, otherwise in daily life, no.

How is the research shared with the tribe? Hmmmm, I haven't been exposed of any research done on the tribe. When I was in college and I was in illustration because I wanted to do children's books. My final project was to illustrate the Salish creation story and living in Boston and coming back in the summers it was hard for even me to figure out the creation story and where is it? I did find a copy of it and used that, but years later, in 1996, now I recently did work for Nkwsum [tribal language immersion school] and did their creation story. And one person combined all the different sources of the story, and I went from that which is totally different from the story that I had found years ago. So even as a Native and coming back and trying to get that information, it was not the right information. It went through lots of hands, and now they are trying to figure out how to write the credits for the book, because it has been passed down through so many generations. It is told by these people, but it is a conglomerate of all of these stories so that is kind of interesting. So that is a children's book that will be shared with youth. I was really honored to be part of that. It will be written in English and in Salish. So that is one way of sharing it [the language]. I know that books have been written or sold at the People's Center, maybe Doug Allard's, here at the college. I know if they are doing documentaries they are at KSKC, a public TV station [owned by the tribes], that other people can view it. I think that is all I have seen as far as studies or documentaries. If people write books, it would be nice if they presented it to the community as a lecture so people can come and get their perspective and meet the person, instead of it being some arbitrary name. That would be the respectful way of doing it. And I think that is the way it should be done [shared with the community].

I don't think there is an ethics board or a guide, but I think there is scrutiny. Once they see what you are doing, they will scrutinize it, but I don't think there is anyone in the beginning that says that you can't do this and you can't do that. Hopefully…well that is why it would be smart to go to the college first, because they would be better at ethics than even going to the tribe, because I think sometimes they can be a little proud and just think that people understand what we expect as far as respect and expect that the other people will understand these norms and what is expected of them. Whereas the college, as an education institution, will have a little better idea of how you do go about doing things in a scholarly way. I don't really see the college and the tribe working together [as far as research]. They are two separate entities. Because I work for the newspaper, the tribe knows what is going on here [at the college], but when I worked at the college I never knew what was going on at the tribe. Over here [at the college] seems a lot more open and progressive. So I don't see that there is a lot of working together on things. So a researcher would have to work with both the college and the tribe on things. They would get two different perspectives from both. They wouldn't get one similar ideal of what is going on. The culture committees would have different perspectives. So there are a lot of different perspectives and I would not want to be a researcher; there are a lot of hoops.

[Researchers would look at mental health issues in my community from the point of view of poverty.] I don't think our reservation is as impoverished as other ones. I think there has to be a look at the historical issues that plague the reservation like displacement, genocide; it affects you and just to know where your people come from, and your history and that molds your outlook on life. I am part Native American and I'm part Black and when I was a teenager, I had the worst time. Blacks and Indians have been victimized and at that age you are just coming into this…what do I stand for. I was a pretty mad little girl at that time. But I see, as far as African Americans especially, the men have this victim attitude and somebody owes them something, and they can never get a fair shake at anything. So it really does mold your perception of the world and how you look at things, so I think researchers would have to look at that as far as mental health rather than the poverty. Poverty is an effect or outcome and they would miss the factors of why there is poverty [and mental health problems]. Everybody is a product of the environment and you can either succumb to it or overcome it. It all depends on the strength and perception of the person. That would be where to start. Look at the history that is a big part of it and the whole idea of the reservation is pretty unified across the board as far as reservations in the United States.

I think researchers try to be as objective as they can with the information they gather in our community, but I think there is a lot of stereotypes that exist. I think it is totally hard to go in with a clean slate and just observe and make an unbiased opinion. I would like to see a new and fresh perspective and even Natives if they read would say, "Hay ya, I was really enlightened by this, and I can look at myself and realize something." Instead of, "This is what they observed. It is not really me, but I can see how they see that in some parts of the community." It's kind of like people see the negative and they can focus on those. Because I have been in different parts of the world, like Jamaica, and that was a third world country. I loved it there and I didn't have any preconceived ideas of what it was. I really liked to see how people there were happy. They have less, but they are happy. It took me three months to decompress over there. I always felt like I had to be doing something. And living over there, I saw how they perceive Americans, and I thought, "Ya, I guess we are like that." I think everybody should get off the reservation and go somewhere and get a new perspective. Unless researchers from other countries would have a better perspective of Native Americans than Europeans and white Americans, just because the society here is unique and is very self righteous. I don't like to say they like to conquer everything, but they think they know everything. So I think it is hard to know that and not be suspicious of what they are doing with this information.

I think the smart researchers come back to clarify the information. I don't think that they all do, because I think they feel their research is based on facts. And they wouldn't really feel the need to clarify. They think they have sufficient knowledge of it to fully understand it [their research data]. I know myself as a Native American I would never sit there and go to another culture and think that I know more than them and share that culture with others, "and this is how it is there." Everybody has their own lens of their own experiences. No two are going to be the same. It all depends on how enlightened the researcher is and how much exposure they have had to the world outside the United States to appreciate Indigenous people of any country. Just because a person is smart book-wise doesn't mean they are smart common-sense wise. Some of the most educated people I know are the biggest jerks. They have no social skills at all. It takes a fine balance. I'd like to work with someone who has traveled the world and has done studies on other people and I might be more trustworthy, rather than somebody coming from I don't know where.

For my definition of mental health or mental health: I think mental health, part of it is chemical. My family has a history of depression that we can't control. But I think mental health is also part of a person's maturity level and their understanding of themselves and the world. Experiences that they have had to learn about themselves, also experiences that mold them, whether they are positive or negative. Are they nurtured or are they un-nurtured? That has a lot to do with it, the environment [one lives in]. Unfortunately, living on the reservation there are more exposures and more [cultural] experiences that really help mold people to be full people, rather than to just stay here and maybe not experience other [cultural] stuff. And that has to do with family, relationships, your involvement with the community. So people reaching out to these avenues will have a better mental health rather than somebody that does the same thing over and over again. For a definition I would think it would be a culmination of your experiences and your environment and even for your health as far as what is projected in your community. Like we don't even have Native foods here. So who is really going to live on berries and deer meat and there is so much processed food that really takes a toll on our health. When I lived in Jamaica, and I keep going back to that, even though they seem like times twenty or thirty years ago and even when I walked to the store and get the food and there is somebody next door selling vegetables and you just buy for today and you make your meals and there wasn't a lot of processed food. People were healthy over there. Obesity is not as big. There's not big transportation. People ride bikes or they walk. So they are more healthy over there plus there is a lot of vitamin D because of the sun. Relationships really have a lot to do with it.

I think the things that affect people's minds or spirits definitely are vices. Just last week I came to this realization that I was drinking alcohol and smoking cigarettes, and it was affecting my relationship with my family, and I said to myself that I am not going to use these things anymore. It was not because something bad happened. It was just that I realized it wasn't helping me, so I just quit them. I feel so much better now. I feel like my relationship with my kids is better. I can feel it, and I can see it. I feel more like I want to help my mom and be there for her. My husband was elated that I quit using these vices. He said that his love went from here to here for me. So definitely those are escapes, and people use these vices to fulfill something that they are not getting. They feel like they are getting something out of it [the vices]. So those definitely have negative effects. But I don't consider myself an abuser, but just using them was having a negative effect. And I thought that I need to be a better role model for my kids. I am lucky that I didn't get to the point where I had to go to rehab or intervention and it would be really easy to go down that road and giving up everything. It is scary. So definitely those are things. I am not a religious person. I am a spiritual person. I pray and I believe that there is something bigger out there. Not that I don't believe in a Creator, but something bigger.

Back in the day, I believe the people would not want them [people with mental illness] in the community even though I don't know any instances or stories of that. So to give an example, I think that people would have thought that people who were gay [in those days] were different, and I am not homophobic. Back in the day, those people were made medicine people, and they had more than one spirit in them. So now they are looked on as a mental thing. But that is one instance that back in the day people who were considered different were given more special roles in the community, because they were thought of having more characteristics as gods or spirits or something. Back then I am not sure that there was even a problem with mental health, because the problems that I see people plagued with today are things like genocide, the taking away of our culture and our land, and that has created the mental health problems. So those things didn't exist then, so I don't think there were mental health issues that we have today. I think back in the past the people may have been more reserved than others, but I think like the introduction of chemicals led to ADHD [attention deficit hyperactivity disorder] today. People lived so pure back then, there wasn't all these outside factors, these toxins that created all these diseases and mental issues, so I think that there wasn't the ostracizing of people like that. I don't think that was an issue. I don't want to know what it is going to be like in the future. I look at the younger generations, and they don't even know how to talk anymore. They don't know how to have a conversation. How are they going to be in the future? What is their life going to be like?

The whole idea of community is being lost. They only care about themselves. They don't care about the well-being of somebody else. They can feel sad for somebody on the TV, whatever that story is, and then they go back to life, and they do what they do. Stories have a different meaning to every person hearing the story, depending on their experience and their exposure to the ideas in that culture. You can say something to kids and they just take it as a story, and they don't have that experience to see that more deeply. That is just to show that it depends on your experience and if that person is a person of color or not a person of color has a lot to do with it as well. And how advanced their culture is and their education, their role in society, whether they have kids. Every single person has a different meaning. That is why I don't like to discuss politics or religion, because no two persons will ever agree on the same idea on everything.

I would like to see if researchers were going to come that they would contact the radio station or the newspaper and say, "I am going to do this study. And I would like anyone interested to come." That would be a starting point. Some people would say, "Why don't they ask me. I know, that person doesn't know." It would be nice if they had an open invitation for people to give input. To me that would be the most non-biased way. So if someone comes to me, I would say, "Well go over there." And another person would say, "No go over there." And there goes the different exposures. I would like them to be really open to the community and not just go to the leaders. Somebody else knows something besides Johnny Arlee, different people. If they can go to as many sources as they can and culminate in the protocol.

Top: Ila Bussidor and family. **Middle:** Jessie Anderson, nephew of Ila Bussidor. **Bottom:** Churchill, Manitoba, mainstreet. Photo by Heidi den Haan.

Rachel Bjorklund and Caroline Bjorklund
photo by Sylvia Saunders.

Chapter 10
Steps Along the Journey: Voices from the Arctic: Churchill, Manitoba

Research in Northern Canada, including the Yukon Territory, Northwest Territories, Nunavut, and northern parts of the provinces, is considerably more advanced in terms of ethical principles relating to Indigenous Peoples (Ermine, et al. 2004, p. 36).

Far to the north of the boreal forests, farther north than the taiga or land of little sticks, lies the vast expanse of tundra. One of the coldest regions of the world, the tundra is a dry desert where snow covers the ground for most of the year. When the snows melt in late spring, the tundra comes alive with a profusion of wildflowers, migrating birds, mosquitoes, and herds of roaming caribou. The land has a spiritual quality and I am drawn to its stunning splendor. The love of this land perhaps emanates from my ancestors who were voyageurs in the fur trade, Métis women, Indian people, and donn'es, who were indentured servants. They traveled to New France with the Jesuits and sacrificed their lives working for the Jesuits as laborers, masons, carpenters, and hunters.

Located on the Canadian Shield, Churchill, Manitoba, Canada, is just such a place. Vast expanses of tundra ring the frigid waters of Hudson Bay. In June, polar bears float ashore on huge ice floes and beluga whales begin calving in the warm waters of the Churchill River. Scientific researchers come to the town of Churchill on a yearly or monthly basis to investigate the effects of climate change, the physiology of bears, bird migrations, and for numerous other projects:

> The first people to set foot on what is now Churchill
> and the surrounding area did so thousands of years

ago. It is believed that the Churchill area was a
seasonal hunting ground for hundreds of years.
Artifacts such as tent rings and kayak stands have
been found in the area that remains from Pre-
Dorset, Dorset or Inuit peoples (Travel Manitoba,
2014).

The Thule arrived around 1000 A.D. from farther west, and later
evolved into the present-day Inuit culture. The Dene people arrived around 500 A.D. from the west. Since before the time of
European contact, the Chipewyan and Cree Natives have populated the region around Churchill (Coutts, 1997, pp. 6-7).

Sayisi Dene from the Village of Tadoule Lake, Manitoba

I believe that the members of the Sayisi Dene community are
currently the most marginalized of all the people who participated
in interviews for this research work. Their stories reflect issues of
a horrific relocation that happened in the middle twentieth century. For over 1500 years, the Sayisi Dene—"The Dene from the
East"—led an independent life style. They followed the caribou
herds and had little contact with white society. In 1956, an arbitrary government decision to relocate them catapulted the Sayisi
Dene into the twentieth century. It replaced their traditional nomadic life of hunting and fishing with a slum settlement on the
outskirts of Churchill, Manitoba. Inadequately housed, without
jobs, unfamiliar with the language or the culture, their independence and self-determination deteriorated into a tragic cycle of
discrimination, poverty, alcoholism, and violent death. The scars
of the relocation will take years to heal, and the community continues to grapple with the problems of a people whose ties to the land,
and to one another, have been tragically severed. Their story is one
of stark brutality and the near-destruction of the Sayisi Dene. They
continue today struggling to reclaim their lives, but are plagued
with social issues of substance and spousal abuse (personal communication, Ila Bussidor, former Chief of the Sayisi Dene in 2006).

Ila Bussidor and Jessie Anderson

It was quite by accident that I met Ila Bussidor and her nephew
Jessie Anderson. I am grateful to Svanna, Rachel, and Susan from
Tadoule Lake who advised me that it was essential that I speak with
Ila who is the former chief of the Sayisi Dene. She was in Churchill

to attend her sister's funeral. However, she graciously agreed to meet with me in the Churchill town library. She is a beautiful, intelligent woman who has endured in spite of the hardships she was dealt.

My people were moved by the federal government from Little Duck Lake to Churchill in 1956. This relocation destroyed our independence and ruined our way of life. More than one hundred of my people, one-third of our population, died because of this unplanned, misdirected government action. This didn't happen a hundred years ago, or a thousand miles away, it happened to my people, my family, and it affects us still today.

Researchers who come into Tadoule Lake [where the tribe finally moved] don't quite understand the culture of Tadoule Lake [Sayisi Dene]. I don't think they have a full understanding of that. And of course our culture is not the same any more as it was for my parents and grandparents. And for this young man sitting here [Jessie, Ila's nephew] for him it is even more different than for me.

If the scholar was an Aboriginal they would have a similar worldview and understand better. When I hear the word "research," we have been over researched. There has been so much research on the relocation and nothing has ever been done. We have a relocation claim with the government of Canada but I don't think it is going anywhere soon. But more and more, the people who have survived the Churchill days and the disruption that has happened to them, those people who have suffered, are almost all gone, and where is the compensation for them. Researchers have come to our community to do documentaries and that, and even David Suzuki came to our community, but nothing ever happened with that. I would like to see some research that is accurate and that the voice of the people is there.

When researchers come into the community I don't know how they want to learn about mental health issues; I don't know I have been away from the community for the last five years. But I spent most of my life there and raised my kids there. I don't know if there has ever been research about mental health, but you see a lot of problems in the community and the way the research has been done. For example, the Doug Skoog report on the relocation, and you know you go and interview someone about their past you open up something, and then go away, and is there anyone there to do the aftercare for that person. They need a psychologist and counseling. Health Canada sends a mental heath worker to the community, but how do they expect one person to see 300 people in the few days that they spend there. They need a live-in one. It is forever changing. You go in there today and the next time it is someone different, so how do you expect to gain that trust of the person, so I don't think it is very good.

The elders don't tell the researcher what they want researched. I think the researcher comes in with an idea like with the questions they want. But if they [the elders] say this is the way I want to be interviewed and this is the way I want to provide information to you. I don't think it is like that.

[Indigenous research methodologies holds that the community tells the researcher what the community needs and what the community wants, and then after the research is completed, the researcher comes back to the community to follow up with an action plan in collaboration with the community.]

I don't think anything like that has been set up. I think that if something like that could be set up and individuals could know there was someone they could go to, that could be set up. There is no policy on how researchers come into the community.

They learn about the community through documentaries and that, or they are going to the university and they learn about us, and they want to do more research. But Tadoule Lake has been over researched, but nothing has been given back to the community. There is the book here [*Night Spirits* by Bussidor & Bilgen-Reinart, 1997] but it is just the voice of the people going out there. My name is on it [as the author], but I am just the vehicle for the people. The people [in the community] should own the stories that come from the community, but it never comes back. The researcher never comes back. There has never been one [researcher] that I can see evidence of giving back to the community [where] that research has been taken. Researchers never come back to share their findings with the community.

There is no ethics board that tells the researcher how to do the research in the community, but, I would like to say, because of the way the people have been in the last fifty years, it is like everything is not working in our community. Just about everybody in the community is addicted to something, whether it is booze, alcohol, drugs, or pills. When the research was first done maybe when we were still in Dene Village. If the research should have indicated that there should be something after [like counseling and treatment]. There is just too much pain, and so most of the older people, who made their way back to the traditional ways, have all passed away without any healing, and I don't know I am 56 years old. I won't get another 56 years, but the young people like this young man here [Jessie], and I have a new granddaughter, already she is affected by the damages. How do you start the healing? Something has to happen and it never has. We tried to introduce AA [Alcoholics Anonymous] maybe over 25 years ago, and everyone thought it was a joke. We tried to keep it going and then only one or two people would come. Research should be available to the school, to the people and have it available to the community.

Dene Village is where we used to live. There is a monument there.

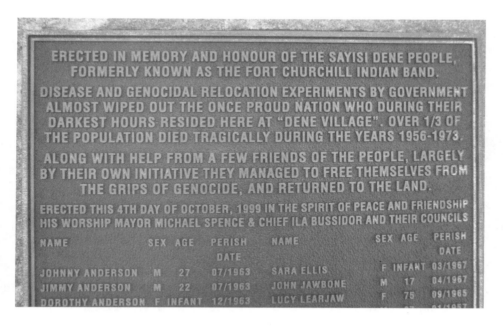

Monument to the Sayisi Dene who died in Dene Village in
Churchill. Photo by Heidi den Haan.

[Ila opens the book, *Night Spirits*. On one of the last pages is a list of Sayisi Dene who died during their stay at Dene Village in Churchill.] I am not sure if you are aware of this. See these names? Right here. These are three names. This is Michael Yassi, Raymond Yassi, Doreen Yassi. That was in January 1971, and in 1972, the following year. These are my parents right here and these are her kids, my sister who just passed away. They all died in a house fire.

We were the bottom of the social ladder in Churchill. When researchers gather information from the community, they put their work together, but sometimes they send us a copy of the work. Our people have no control, and they give their voices out and it rightfully belongs to them. But if they don't say anything, the researchers don't do anything. I don't think that they ever come back to clarify the information with the community. They never come back to the community.

To me mental health is emotional pain that you carry with you, that you live with, and, if it is not taken care of, it leads to more anguish in your life, and you don't understand why you are like this. And to deal with it, people go through bad behavior. The things that affect the spirit and mental health of my people come from relocation, and it is spousal abuse, drug and alcohol abuse. It is sad to say, but Tadoule Lake is in need of so much help. If the community is ever to heal itself something has to be done.

Back in the day, there were no mental health problems. We don't know how they healed themselves. My granny Betsy Anderson, she lived to be over one hundred and was crystal clear all through her life. I asked her many things about how they lived their lives. I asked her about menopause, and I said I read all this stuff about what the white doctors have researched. And I asked her, "What was it like for you in your days?" She did not go into detail because that is not the way they are. She said, "You accepted things as they were. You went about your life and the things you had to do, like work, raise your family. If you were going through menopause no one made a big thing about it." That was the way of life for a woman. I think mental health issues started to affect the people as when the Europeans came. And the influence of them caused a lot of change for us, or the people back then, so I think it caused problems for them.

If a person tells a story to the researcher, I don't think the researcher will interpret it the same way. Let's say you are a white person and you are coming to interview me about something. I think there are very few who can feel or grasp your words. Sure the words can make you cry, but they don't grasp the heart of the story. I think you have to. They try so hard, but they [the researchers] can never understand the heart of our people.

I have been exposed to a lot of researchers. If I could change anything, they would have to live with one of the families. Say that there [were] about three of them that came in—and have them live in their homes so they can get the real feel of the people they are trying to get information from. How do they eat? What kind of structure do they have in the community? In Tadoule Lake is at a loss and if someone doesn't come to help, it is going to continue for another fifty years.

I want Jessie [her nephew] to grow up to be a strong man, get a good education, and never feel he is less than anyone else because he is Native. I want him to be proud and carry himself with dignity because he is a Dene. And I want that for all the young people. But if we are going to start to heal, we need the money to do it. We need to pay someone to come in and do it to help us.

One time I suggested once to have a mobile treatment center. I heard that other communities were using it. They bring their resources with them to heal the people. We need our people to be trained to also help the people.

I would say to young Aboriginal researchers to have an open heart and to respect how they approach the information, and respect the story that belongs to the people. And that has to be number one, and to give it back.

Once the information is in written form, come to the community and present the information to them. When my book came out, there was a big fight and they threw chairs at me. They didn't want the information out. I never was able to take the pride and success of that book, never.

I would love for you to go to Tadoule Lake with your students and see the pain that is there, the pain that causes the dysfunction. It is something that has to be done. Introduce your people to the community and that is the best thing that could happen. I would be honored to come to where you teach and bring the book there and present it to your students.

Suzan, Rachel, Svanna

An informal sharing circle, took place in the Churchill library with Suzan Cheekie Atkins, Rachel Bjorklund, and Svanna Beardly, all of whom kindly agreed to help me by sharing their views on research and researchers even though they were experiencing a lot of emotional pain from the death of an elder. I am grateful for their words.

Suzan: My name is Suzan Cheekie Atkins and I am a teacher. I now live in Split Lake, Manitoba, and I have for the past six years. I have been on the rez for many, many years. I left Tadoule Lake in the year 2005 and I moved on for the purposes of having a family and all that. I went to Brandon University. Scholars who come to my community do not know about the culture of my community. They might do the reading and the research; there are lot of documents and publications done on our community, but they still don't know the community. If a researcher wanted to do real good research, they would have to come in person to the community and get to know the people and meet with the elders, know the history and everything before they can say, "I really understand." A lot of the time the culture and the language is disintegrating now for people who have moved away to the cities. Because of addictions and all the trauma, and the past trauma, that comes with addictions, and you know how that is. People try to escape from it, and it is going from generation to generation. And the culture is disintegrating slowly.

If a researcher is Aboriginal and comes from another rez, they are more likely to have a similar lifeway or way of looking at the world. But if they come from an urban setting, and they come from a different culture, it would be difficult.

When I hear the word "researcher" or "research" what comes to mind is, "What are they trying to pry into?" "What is their purpose?" I don't often see them as white people. They are curious and they come to the north because of the great hunting and fishing. I know it is the curiosity, because I have been in Tadoule for years.

[Our] people learn about our mental health and psychology through the nursing station. That has always been a barrier because of confidentiality. If it was a local person, they would look at it as worrying about gossiping and breaking that confidentiality. Because of what the Sayisi Dene have gone through already, there is a lot of resentment towards white man. For an Aboriginal person to come in and get help with that, there is going to be that barrier there. If there was an Aboriginal man or woman there, that wall wouldn't be so much of a barrier, because they have the Aboriginal background or perspective. There is a difference there. I have worked with white man and I have worked with Aboriginal and I am comfortable with both, but there might be someone who has been on the rez their whole life and never experienced another culture or explored the cities and other cultures, and that they wouldn't be comfortable with a white man. They would be comfortable with an Aboriginal or descendent.

The only researcher I know where elders [set the agenda] and talked to researchers is when they did all those [polar bear research] expeditions. And that is the only time the elders participated in decision making for researchers to come in and whatever. That is when they came up with their last say. So they have done that in the past. So depending on what kind of research you are doing, the protocol for researchers is to go through the elders and the chief and the council.

Rachel: There are some tapes here [in the Churchill library] made into CDs regarding the elders. Louise Lowrie made for the school. There are about ten of them.

Suzan: A lot of our elders are gone now. The old, old ones...our elders...we are losing another family member here. For the past ten or fifteen years we are losing our elders death after death after death. Cancer has taken a lot of our elders, our family members. In the last two decades lots and lots of people have passed from our band. My grandmother had cancer. We lost her in the early 80s, my Mom too. Some by accidents.

You know what they [Ottawa] should be doing is getting doctors in the community. We want to see researchers get an Aboriginal doctor in our community, you know? And stay in the community; don't fly in and take off after a couple of days. They should be staying there and checking up on the people. Check if they have cancer. Check if they have prostate cancer, because men don't check. Check for these things. Have these things for them. But no, they ship them out to Thompson [Manitoba]. Make the doctor travel. Make them [the doctor and health workers] travel. But here the doctor could make a lot of fricken money. I just want to swear!

Rachel: Like with my late Auntie that just passed away, she knew springtime she was sick. She knew. That's when they diagnosed her. She was supposed to go and have chemo. All kinds of cancer and it just spreads like that. It spreads so fast. She recently had a bowel obstruction. They did an X-ray before they opened her up for that surgery, they took X-rays, and they didn't see much, but they could see that [cancer] is spread all over, and they did another X-ray after the surgery, and they could see that it spread all over.

Suzan: After that surgery, she had some strokes and that was it. Her body couldn't take any more. It was just another matter of time. Go back to your colleagues, tell them that there are young people, and we need education and health and community on a big scale. Like you are from a different tribe and like the Crees and the Dene and the Inuit, and they have all gone through the relocation. They have gone through all that destruction, and that destruction now it's a downfall. It is continuous. You can't just go to the nursing station and say, "I need help today. I am fuckin' going crazy." You have to wait for fricken help.

Svanna: Six to eight weeks sometimes.

Suzan: So Svanna is from a different band. She is from Split [Lake] where I live now. And it is almost the same issues. But it is the same bullshit. And then you get the band politics that get into it in there, and they are just in there for themselves and they are not doing anything to help the people and the family and us young people. We are fed up with all the bullshit. When the hell are you going to get off your ass and [start] doing these things for us?

Researchers need to come in and research the positive aspects of our community and see how strong we are as a community rather than focusing on the negative. The women are very strong and the women will be the ones to motivate. So that is a whole other ballgame. It is so fucked up. They don't even have school in Tadoule, and here I was going to go home for a year and teach and motivate the people, because I am good at that, and it is something I did when I was in Tadoule.

[Discussion of the issues that the women want to be researched:]
Svanna: People in Split [Lake] recently had a band meeting and

they are getting fed up because, you know, we are surrounded by riprap from the Nelson River and now all these companies and the hydros and everything, and now to this day all these companies are coming into the community and taking advantage of whatever.

What we are planning to do? My generation and my Mom's generation, is putting their foot up. They are getting sick of all that, and they are posting of what to do, and they are putting it into action. They are getting sick of the government and all like that.

Suzan: This what should be done now and not ten years from now. The Nelson River and the river in Tadoule is contaminated and people should be looking into that. From Stony Lake to our community, there is even mercury.

Svanna: Like now to this day in the community where I come from, there are people who are keeping an eye watching the animals; they go out every summer. They are keeping track of the birds, the fish, the beavers, the birds. They tag the fish nowadays. They never did that before.

Suzan: And Jonathan Kitch [a local fisherman and Svanna's father] found that fucking warped [deformed] sturgeon.

Svanna: That was my dad. You know that Kelsey Dam area? The Kelsey Dam area, the sturgeon got caught up in the dam. They are watching the river all the way from the Kelsey Dam to the Gull Lake. That is where that whole river is, and that is how Split Lake became. There are even grave sites where they used to live along the whole Nelson River. They just fucked it up.

Rachel: The elders say that our whole community of Tadoule Lake was built on a grave site. It shows. That is why our people are the way they are. A lot of our people are bitter. They are very angry.

Suzan: Well, you can understand from that book, *Night Spirits*, that is how it started [the problems in our community]: the whole Canadian government relocated us. Maybe if the Canadian government didn't relocate them, but just introduced them into modern society slowly, maybe all this shit wouldn't be happening now.

That's Manitoba Hydro, that's a multi-trillion company that's contaminating the river, and they are giving some of that energy to the United States. You can't bullshit us. We are the younger generation.

It is so hard to be strong for our community. They have old-fashioned ideas. We are the younger generation, and she [Svanna] went to the band meeting and said, "I am concerned about this, this, this, and this," and the leaders would tell her to fuckin' shut up. How is this supposed to encourage her to move ahead and put action into the community? Some of our elders are cool. It is so hard to be strong for our community.

Svanna: Like us we are slowly getting flooded by the riprap of the Nelson River. That is slowly flooding it.

Suzan: And the band will say, "No money, no money."

[A discussion follows about education with Internet classes:]
Suzan: I have been saying that about Internet classes. We even have UCN [University College of the North] there, and they don't even use it. It took me two years to push the band to get a B.S. and B.A. I want to go back to Tadoule to get motivated to do it.

They always say, "No funds, no money."

Svanna: Our school sponsorship is all paid for. We have it, but our kids may not have it. They are trying to cut that off, and they are trying to cut off our Treaty too, Treaty 10.

Suzan: They are trying to take our treaty away, and they still have control. Indian Affairs has control of the money. We need that money for education and health.

Rachel: I am 37 years old. I had my son when I was 30. I don't get to look after my son. My ex's family is looking after my son. I have stayed in the community, and I am on my way to go back. I was raised here in Churchill; I was born and raised here. When I was 18, I went back to my community. I lost my dad here in Churchill…to cancer. It took its toll. I started drinking and went through that cycle of abuse.

It took me a long time to realize that a Native woman in our community who is abused has nowhere to go. The people in our community just turn their back. There is ignorance. There is no help. When my son was a baby, I left. I was raised in a good home. I wanted to bring him here to Churchill, where I was raised. Through all that I graduated and finished my education and did administrative assistant and did accounting. My goal is to be a certified accountant. But I would like to be a councilor in my community [Tadoule Lake] to help my people. But it is hard to get a home because of housing in the north. It is a very big problem to get housing.

When I go home I always stay with a family member, and that is one of the reasons I don't stay. Like right now, I am going through a personal crisis, but if it wasn't for my sister here—she is more of my sister than anything—and she has helped me out a lot. And these are the kind of things that need to be looked at for women who go through abuse, and to help the little ones who go through their abuse and see it. I can only imagine what my son goes through when I do this. When I take off and leave and come home again.

There is nothing for the kids to do. We need a women's shelter. Our community is 400-500 people. Our band list for Tadoule is 700-800 people. They live outside the community; they have good jobs.

Svanna: There is no way of going home, because there is no housing. When they signed a contract with Split Lake, they promised 200 houses. We haven't seen those houses yet. They never seen them. There is a lot of corruption. And we fight for our kids' education.

Suzan: It took me two years to get those [college] courses into Split [Lake]. Two years to push it, push it, and get off your asses and do it.

Rachel: People learn about our community from the book *Night Spirits*. My Auntie Ila will go and speak to groups. My mom does presentations in this community of Churchill, of how we lived a long time ago. How her life has changed and what she went through and how she lives today. She shows the artwork.

Svanna: Like in my community, people who come there who have never been there, they have to come by boats to travel. And they don't see much housing. There are some old houses, but the reason why you don't see [many] houses is that Split Lake only started in the early 1980s. They all lived around the Nelson River and that is the reason you have to travel by boat. Gull Lake is two hours away by boat, and you have to pass two portages.

Rachel: Our community [of Churchill] is just a fly-in.

Svanna: That is how it was in my community, until they got that road in. Close to 1990 that road finally opened to Thompson and Gillam [neighboring towns]. We were isolated until then.

Rachel: They promised a road into Tadoule, and the people were all for it, and they were promised training and jobs for our people.

Svanna: You know that is how it is. They promise jobs, but others will come in like the Frenchies [from Quebec]. They come in and take those jobs. And they promise our people those jobs. They don't give them to them. They just lie to them.

Suzan: They [companies that work on the rez] have to sign contracts that they will hire our people, but they never follow up on their word. So you see the continuous cycle of destruction. It keeps continuing, and continuing, and continuing.

Svanna: Like in my community, they have a chief in council and they really, really want to start a junior chief in [tribal council] now. There always was one in the school, but now there is a youth center that was given almost $1.2 million. Ya, they use Troy Lake to take kids out there and that, but they barely use the youth center. So they want to get a youth junior chief in council, so they have the youth tell them what they want. So the people know what the youth are expecting when they get older. So that is what they are trying to start. They don't want to depend on the chief in council where I come from. Nobody is listening, and no one wants to volunteer their time. Everyone wants to get paid.

I know a couple of my cousins that want that. They are always complaining about Split Lake and all that. I remember Split Lake when I was growing up. It was nice. But now you don't even see the beach, and when the water hits, the beach is gone. Split Lake is shrinking because of the erosion.

Rachel: Like in my community, when springtime comes, there is always [flooding] on the other side. They were supposed to make it higher, and all the companies pulled out. Something happened with their contribution agreement, so when the winter road came this year, they took everything. The people who were supposed to make our housing, they left and took everything. They promised equipment to maintain these buildings, and it was never kept up.

We have about ten houses in our community that don't even have a furnace or anything. And even the ones that have housing, their houses are starting to get like that because none of these houses were maintained over the years.

Suzan: Indian Affairs [in Ottawa] are cheap. They only send money every six to ten years. They're supposed to send it quarterly. If you and your colleagues would go to all communities and see it, and make these studies and reports to Ottawa to let them see what is happening. They do dick all for the past twenty years. It's disintegrating.

Svanna: Pretty soon all these tribes are going to get together and have a revolution and say, "The hell with it." People from my community are already thinking of going to Ottawa and making a big thing out of it. They are really that close to going.

Rachel: Like our relocation claim, the claim that the people have been doing for years, it is sitting on the desk in Ottawa, at the minister's desk [at Indian Affairs]. We had a group of people that went there in springtime. We had elders. They went to Ottawa. They walked right into the minister's office just to move that paper. We had a lady named Mary, she just recently went to Ottawa to talk for our people to get these papers moving. We need more educated people who are willing to come home in the summer months and do this. I was on the school board to try to make things move. Every time we get something to move, someone [in our community] puts a halt to it, "No, you can't do it."

Suzan: I could have been there already. But you have the board and then because of resentment and the animosity for one person, nothing gets moved. And I could have done a lot already; you know what I mean? I don't know how many times I wrote CBC [Canadian Broadcasting Company]. We got the guys [to do the work].

Rachel: There was a questionnaire on NAPT [National Aboriginal People's Telecommunications] and it was about our drinking water, and I answered that questionnaire. Within our community we do have a water treatment plant and a sewage treatment plant, and these guys are being trained to do that work, but the thing is when it comes to needing things, it takes a long time for them to get here.

Svanna: The reason why it takes a long time to get here is because they are trying to take the treaty rights of what we get or the money. They are trying to cut us off on everything.

Rachel: Like with our medical a lot of things are not covered anymore. Like cough syrup is not covered anymore. Slowly taking away our medical. "You took away our land, you took away this and that."

Svanna: I will tell you something. In Split Lake, there is this binder and it is this thick [four inches] and they had a meeting in there and there was this guy yelling in Cree. He was so mad and so fed up with everything. He brings this bag with him, and he brings this thing with him, and he slams it right in front of the chief in council. And he says, "This is the bylaw that we made when this community started. This is what we follow. This is what we follow and they are trying to change the bylaws on us." He just slammed that book down and said, "This is our bylaw and this is what we go by. We are not losing this. And you are not taking this from us. Everything in there of what we have been given, school, and everything that was promised." And he slammed that book down there. Everybody just started clapping and saying, "Let's go to Ottawa." "We are getting fed up with this." "Let's get funds to go to Ottawa." "I am getting sick and tired of this."

We are not the only community going through this. There are a lot. They don't think about the people, just the money. And some people steal money. That is all they think about is the money.

Rachel: We were told that we have to get this moving [the resettlement claim]. There is a deadline.

Svanna: I cried when I spoke to the chief in council. All I heard was money, money, money. Travel, travel, travel…Instead of wasting money to meet, they should have the all the white people come here. They have all the funds.

Rachel: We just recently had a Manitoba Indian Affairs hydro [meeting] and they just recently came to our community. Just before I left [for Churchill] I told them everything, "We need this for our school." Take a walk in our school. It has been fifteen years since anything has been maintained.

Svanna: Our school [in Split Lake] was burned down. Some kids got ahold of the wiring. Things were different when I went to school. If a kid didn't go to school, they would come and get him and ask why they were not in school. Nowadays if a kid misses school, even for four months, they won't come and ask. They won't even phone. White people are teaching in the school.

Rachel: Most of our teachers come from Newfoundland. And we put a stop to that. We had an incident where a teacher put a video camera in a washroom in his home and we had a student who went there. There was a big stink about it. They went to court. It was in the papers. We put a stop on people who come from there. Our school board, they focus on [getting] people who are Aboriginal to come into our community. They love it when they come into our community, but it is the politics that pulls them away. They try not to get involved, some of them. Even to this day being here lately, people coming into the community [of Churchill] for my Auntie's services.
We used to be called Chipewyan. We are not Chipewyan. There is a difference between the Sayisi Dene and the Chipewyan. Trying to see that while being here. It hurts. My uncle even said we are Sayisi Dene not Chipewyan.

Svanna: When I see that logo on TV that says we are all one, why don't they treat us as one.

Rachel: So after our band meeting [with Indian Affairs], I asked them, "So do you think we are unstable? When we get together and speak we are strong. And what is going to happen when you leave here? Will those papers stay on your desk? You need to make an action plan for those things: our education, our health, the minerals they are mining."

Our community now is very destructive. Not with suicides, but with prescription drugs. We do have band members that come in and sell booze. Like for a mickey in our community is $100.00. How much is a mickey? $15.00? The people who buy that are people who never leave the community, and they live on welfare. The cycle [of alcohol and substance abuse] is still there even though we live on a reserve. We have to stop that cycle, because there are a lot of band members that are going on dialysis. I used to work as a transportation clerk, and I have seen what people go through in dialysis and how those machines work. And it broke my heart to see how many people are going through that.

Even the survivors of the residential schools, they are going for counseling. I recently started going. A lot of what I went through and that, it takes a toll. I release a lot of that when I go there once a month for two days. When you see when a lot of our people are done, they go on a drunk.

There was a lost band member who was released from jail at 2 a.m. But no one has seen him since. He went missing May 9th and he never asked for his welfare check. We just lost another band member. He took methadone. It took his life. The cycle is still there.

We need programs to stop this. We need the services brought to our community and not just once a month. Instead of taking us out, bring the people in!! They get a lot of money for doing the things they do. They would save a lot of money if they brought those programs to our community. When I lost my brother, the psych nurse who comes to our community was there for me. It was to the point where our councilor grabbed me and tried to get me to take medication. I fought it. I told her that is not the way I want to deal with my brother's death and the loss of my brother. I didn't take it. It took its toll on us. It kept me up all night. My brother was lost in a canoe accident and there was alcohol involved. We looked for him for fifteen days. To this day, it will be three years on the 23rd of August [2011]. And that is my dad's birthday. We lost him on my dad's birthday. I didn't even celebrate my birthday that year, because we were still searching for him.

Svanna: That is why alcohol is banned from Split Lake.

Rachel: I remember, he is gone now, late Johnny Yassi. When we found his nephew we were sitting in a church, and he grabbed me. He said, "It is okay. We are going to find your brother too. I can feel it in my heart." He was going through cancer stuff and chemo and we lost him not long after. His words stick to what he said, eh? When we found my brother the next day, that night my Auntie Mary took us to the lake and we put tobacco in the water. And I told my brother, "I'm getting weak I can't do this anymore. Come home so we can put you to rest. It will be easier on grampa." And I cried. And I put that tobacco in the water. The next morning when I went down to the shore, my grandfather and my dad were sitting there. And there is an Island called Ronnie John's Point, my grampa was pointing there and two boats turned and they found him. And we were sitting there quietly and I pointed, "Look they found him." And that is when they brought him to the shore.

[Discussion of Indigenous research methodologies follows and how this way of doing research methodology helps Indigenous communities. I promise to send the data to Ottawa and copies of the book and paper to everyone who was interviewed:]

Svanna: We are the next in line. People their age. I am 24. They are trying to take over. But the elders don't want to let go of their spot. They are supposed to be there to help us. And we are the younger ones trying to help our community. They are not there for us.

I cried at the last meeting in front of everybody and they are arguing about money, "Why money all the time? What about the riprap? Look at these rocks. We are getting nothing. What about the 200 houses you promised us? I'm 24 and look at me and all you guys are arguing about money. We are supposed to be looking after each other. What about my kids? My kids are small. What about our education? It is not always going to be there. What am I going to do for them?"

Every time I go for my grade 12, I can't finish it. I have my grade 9, 10, and 11 but every time I go for grade 12, I keep having kids. And I was supposed to graduate in June, but my boyfriend ripped up my notes and threw my books out. Have your researchers come to our community and see what we go through. There is no place to put you if you come. There is no hotel.

We still have members who are still suffering. I can only imagine what my auntie Donna is going through with all of this with everyone drinking.

Suzan: We need education in our community. The bias is still there for having someone getting an education and going back to help the community. Elijah is the very first Native to step up for all Natives in all Canada and see what they went through when they were doing that referendum. INAC [Indian and Northern Affairs Canada] has so much power, and they have us against the wall.

Rachel: We would not be in this situation if they left us where we were hunting and trapping and fishing. It was them that came to us. We didn't go to them.

Suzan: With my profession, I could go there to Tadoule and teach the old ways of tanning hides. I did it in Split already. They need to do that at UCN [University College of the North]. They do it in Thompson. It came from within the community.

Rachel: Now in our school in our community the Dene language is being taught. They tried to take it away, but we said, "No, we fought for it and we need the proper people to teach it." We had a lady, she died of cancer, but she did the Dene curriculum for our community and it still stands. They still use the materials that she made. How you write the syllabics, how you say this or that in Dene. I can't even read syllabics. It is so beautiful.

I just want to say for myself to you that I am so happy that someone who is of our ancestry who is doing this work, and when I see the results, I will be so proud. These are the things that are needed: our education system, housing, and we want control of the minerals that are on our land. People are trying to take that. The geologists are doing these digs.

Suzan: They are researchers but they are not doing it for us for our community. They are not fucking doing it for us. They are doing it for the white man, so they can get money. That is where all the bullshit is. And that is where the cycle keeps going, and going, and going. They are willing to give us royalties, but excuse me, royalties. That is our land and they are getting a lot of money from that stuff.

Rachel: My nephew is doing that work. He got his license to do that. But when he gets his money he returns to the cycle of drinking.

Suzan: We need money and motivated people to put those programs together for celebrations of sobriety. We need people to do that social work; childhood services have to stop taking children away from the community. We need Aboriginal people to come in and do that work. People will be more comfortable with people of Native ancestry. People our age in our twenties will help. I would be willing to help to introduce you and have people tell you what is needed in our community and then take them.

Rachel: These are things that I want to see happen. I have a lump in my throat because this is what I wanted to see for a long time. There is land up in Nunavut that have Dene names. That land was named by Dene. North Knife Lake has cabins that my dad made. [Traditional gifts were given to the three women in the group.]

Rachel: When I go home, I am going to put this one [dream catcher drum] you gave me on my brother's grave.

Churchill, 2011: Caroline's Story

Following the summer of 2011, I had the opportunity in November to return to Churchill with the Great Bear Foundation of Missoula, Montana, during polar bear viewing season. Caroline Bjorklund is Rachael's mother, and a well known and respected elder. She is an elite crafter of mukluks and moccasins. I am grateful to Jeff Bussidor and Allen Code for helping me connect with Caroline.

It takes four days of travel to reach Churchill from western Montana across the Rocky Mountains, golden prairies covered in snow to the Pas, Manitoba, where our group boards the Via Rail at 2 a.m. The train journey snakes through rolling prairies, through boreal forests, taiga, tundra, and small villages populated by First Nations Cree. It is beautiful country. After two days and two nights, the train finally arrives on the southern edge of the Arctic ecosystem, Churchill, Manitoba.

Caroline and I meet on a cold and snowy morning at Gypsy's, "The Place to be in Churchill." Caroline has a beautiful smile, sparkling eyes, and makes a commanding presence into Gypsy's bakery and restaurant, which is crowded with tourists. It is polar bear viewing season. She arrives on her four-wheeler with her wheeled walker loaded in the back. Because I want her to feel comfortable and to know I care and respect her as an elder, I cut to the front of the ordering line with twenty glaring tourists behind me and ordered her the daily special, a plate piled high with rich lasagna.

Lori: Caroline, thank you for coming out to meet me today. I would like to ask you about how you want to see researchers come into your community. Your advice would help our students to be better Indigenous researchers. I teach at a tribal college on the Flathead Indian Reservation in Montana. I am from the Northeast woodlands. I am from [the Deer Clan] the Abenaki, Mi'kmaq, and Acadian on my mother's side and [the Cord Clan] Wyandot-Huron on my father's. [I tell Caroline my background, which is what all Indigenous people do when they meet an elder or someone from a different tribe.]

I want our students to be better researchers and to understand that research is not a western-European thing. They need to understand how to go into different communities to gather information, to be respectful, to make sure the community owns the data, that the data moves the community forward and heals the community. Last summer I spoke with some women who were at Ila Bussidor's sister's funeral and when I asked them about mental health issues, they told me the story of the relocation of the Sayisi Dene. So I have questions here, if that is okay. Mostly it is about the researcher coming into the community. I want the students to develop their own conceptual framework. A lot of them are working in their own communities with elders, with relocation issues, with alcohol issues, with substance abuse issues, with child abuse issues, and to create a pathway for the students so they will understand what Indigenous communities want researchers to do, especially if they come from a different community.

Caroline's Voice

That is all part of it; the relocation and what it is like when it happened and what it is like for me today. The people have to let go of what happened to us, and there was a lot of mistakes by the government and everything and whoever was involved with all this and everything. A person is better off today than whatever they were, for me anyway. Like me, I changed my life around, and try to live a better life. I was in that mix and a victim of everything that happened, but I couldn't hang on to that. So it must have been about ten to 14 years ago. I know when I go to visit Tadoule Lake, there is a lot of anger, a lot of hate and everything. I haven't gone home. It would be beautiful for me to go to Tadoule and live there. I don't have to pay for rent or for this or that. What is that they want? It just makes me so angry at my own people and the culture is here. Not very many of us left who can practice our culture. I do presentations of what I know, and I have it in three ways: what it was like, what happened, and what it is like for me today. I want to stand up and say, "I want to pass my culture," and have someone take over later on. I want people to recognize not what happened to us, but the things that our ancestors had, the beautiful things that our ancestors had. They lived out on the land years and years ago. They lived out on that land and never complained. So the government made a mistake. What is it that we can't turn around and forget, and it makes me so angry. My own people at times and that is how I feel. It is so hard to make my own people understand, my own relatives, that we can live a better life, if we forget about yesterday.

I probably think, but I can't answer for the other people, but for me in this community it is really hard at times if a white person comes in and starts asking questions. But it doesn't really matter to me. I am in the middle of a lot of people [in Churchill]. But some people are in very touchy situations.

When I hear the word "researchers," I think, "What the hell do they want now." Like I told Jeff [Bussidor], for me to feel that way, "Where were all these people when we needed them?" Nobody looked at us.

We don't have the elders here telling researchers what to do here. Just in the last few years, the elders are just starting to be recognized. When there is a special occasion coming on, the elders are invited and it is really hard. But here [in Churchill] it is a mixed community. There are the frontier Europeans, the Cree, the Métis, the Dene, and the Inuit. We don't have very many elders left in Tadoule. I never lived out there in Tadoule, but I visited out there. And some people are very touchy about it, about research. Like I said to Jeff,

"What do those researchers want now?" I can't speak for them. People learn about our community through the *Night Spirits* book. I don't use it [in my presentations]. I talk about it, but I don't use it. Mary [Code] did a video on the issues. But we have to look at the good things. We have to look at what our ancestors presented and how it was like for them and how it affected a lot of their life.

Not very many researchers will come out [to Tadoule], not very many. To my knowledge all the time I have been here, maybe about four times a researcher asked me to do something. People are very touchy about the Dene culture [in Tadoule]. Only the last few years the community itself started to upset the Native people. It's not only the Dene people but the Native people themselves. At one time we were separated in different ways, but now it is a whole. It is really hard and of course this is a transit place. People stay for a couple of years and then they are gone. We were labeled. We were labeled as "no good Indians and drunks," and who put that on us?

A definition of mental health: I had to overcome the trauma [of relocation] because of my children. I was a suicide victim. Because I had a very strong husband that understood where I was coming from, who helped me overcome it. And then I went to treatment center and I went there two times and when I understood it and once I got that I was involved in AA [Alcoholics Anonymous]. There was a lot of support when I sobered up, so I was very lucky. I had a lot of support not only from AA but from the community itself. I know for example a couple of years ago a young guy went out to a treatment center and came back, and I said, "Did the counselor come to see you?," and he said "No." And I got upset and I called the woman and she said she was waiting for him to come to her. I told her that for them [Native peoples] to feel comfortable, regardless where it is, you have to go see them and get them into the system no matter what it is. Then she said, "Well I don't really have to." And I said, "Okay but what are you getting paid for if you cannot go into the community." Well she never talked to me for over a year and a half.

People like that think we can't do it on our own. And I've proven that I can do it on my own. Number one, you have to have a really strong persistent chief, and you need the three counselors to back you up on. And be consistent, and that is not happening. I see it. A lot of people don't realize that. And it is still, "Poor old me and the government is going to support me and I will sit on my bum and get welfare." That is not the way it is. And just like you were saying about those town girls. They carried that hate for years. When I sobered up I went back to school. At age 36 I went back to school and got my GED [General Education Diploma] and started to work in the community. Then I used to go visit Tadoule Lake, just to talk to the elders to get some information to see what it was like for them moving out onto the land. A lot of them miss being out on the land. It is so sad and only on special occasions would people take the elders out on the land. People don't realize that my ancestors lived out on the land without anything with just what is on the land.

For young researchers who want to research in Indigenous communities, I would say, "What are you going to do with the information? How are you going to tell the story of what happened to us?" A person has to be very strong [to go into the community] and be able to understand a person.

If a person in the community tells a story to the researcher, it depends on the researcher, if they understand the heart of the story. If they go into the community and say, "I want this," or "I want that," [they won't get anything]. They need to care about us, and the community. One of the things that is really important to me is that a young researcher has to go with the flow of the community. If they don't go with the flow, then they [community members] will say, "What the hell are they doing here, if you are not going to help me? What do they want?" As a researcher, you are supposed to hand everything over to them, you know? To me if I went to Montana, if you were in my situation, and I would say, "I want to know what happened to you." Your first reaction would be to say, "What are you going to do with that information?" You are supposed to hand everything over to them.

I know a lot of people don't understand what research is. Happened in Australia. I know these are the things I find out a lot. I meet a lot of people doing presentations. And I meet people that have worked with the Navajo people, and I had the opportunity to go to New Mexico and I met the elders, and we went to a nursing home and I was nobody from Canada, and I felt like I was welcome, and it made me so happy. My dream was to meet the Navajo people, and two people I met in one hour bought me a ticket to go down there. The Navajo language is similar to the Dene. I met with the veterans [Code Talkers] who were selling their books and explained that I was

Dene from Manitoba, Canada, and I told him, "I would like you to say a few words in Navajo to see if I could understand."

So it was so hilarious. Say "snake," and I said, "naduze" and I said, "tł'iish." Then I said, "How do you say 'sugar?'" And he said, "Sugat to you too." It was so similar. It was unbelievable. I think if I sat long enough I would understand. You know not moving out of here I don't get involved with the Dene people as much as I should, because my family is here. But I am planning on a visit out there to visit at the end of the month. But I still hesitate if I should or not, because there is so much drugs up there and it is so sad. And that's why you have to have three or four people who contest that and say, "It is not going to happen." They have to be very strong, and to me if they are strong enough, and if the people see that they are strong, the people will start getting involved…You can't go into the city and go on a good two-week drunk and come back and expect the people to feel sorry for you. You go there because you want to gather information on how you can help these people. But you can't go there and do drugs and everything, so what is the sense? I think it would help if someone from the community went to your college for a substance abuse counseling program. There are young people up there who could do that work. But the community won't support them. They feel the young people are too young. They don't give those kids a chance. The younger generation is about going to school, and they know what they are talking about. I was about seven when the relocation happened. I can recall in 1957 when the people were relocated, the elders would say, "Wish they would take us back to the land." When alcohol started coming into the families and the children were affected, and I can remember them saying, "I wish they would take us back to the land." There are people up there who still remember the old ceremonies and the old ways. I was a victim too. I had to go to the [Churchill] dump [to scavenge for garbage with the polar bears] with my mom, because we had nothing to eat.

One of the first things the government should have done when they brought them [First Nations from Dog Lake] here is to promise them lumber and all. They should have someone who knew how to build houses for them. This is what I think. Maybe something would have been different.

I can't see myself living the life I did before. Allen's [Code] wife is my cousin, eh. She is in Whitehorse and I am in Churchill. I said,

"Mary, you go in as the chief and I will be the first consulate. We could straighten everything out." Number one, do the search before anyone goes back into the community…for drugs, alcohol, and everything even on the winter roads [ice roads]. This is what we would like to see done. And be very consistent. We need to say, "I want to help you to overcome that."

One constable in Thompson at the airport has to do all the search. And they do the scanning now. If I went into there [Tadoule Lake] as a researcher, I would like to say, "I would like to hear some of your stories and why you are depressed, because I care about you." Say, "I can see the people are still struggling. What can we do?" That would be what I would do. I pray every day for my daughter [Rachel]. She has a real good education. She has to overcome that drug.

For young researchers who go into [Indigenous and First Nations] communities, they go in there and say who you are and then ask, "What do you want? This is what I would like the people to present to me and the information." If you go in there and say, "This is what I want." They will send you out. We don't need that now.

Chapter 11
Connecting the Stories: Themes and the Development of a Conceptual Framework

Our Common Journey

There were 25 amazing Indigenous people who shared their views on research and researchers. They live in communities in Queensland, Australia; Manitoba, Canada; and Montana, United States. Their stories brought to light common themes across these Indigenous communities. Similar themes are echoed in the writings of other Indigenous researchers: Smith, 1999; Menzies, 2001; Medicine, 2001; Weber-Pillwax, 2004; Wilson, 2008; Kovach, 2009.

Over the past few years, Indigenous scholars have shared their perspectives on research to mainstream universities. Indigenous interests, knowledge, and experiences must be at the center of methodologies in the construction of knowledge about Indigenous people. Smith (1999) wrote that the process of decolonization is about centering our concepts and worldviews, then coming to know and understand theory and research from our own paradigm. We believe that the knowledge produced in Indigenous research must build capacity in Indigenous communities. Knowledge is power; our knowledge as Indigenous researchers challenges the imperialism and hegemony of traditional academic thinking. It is research that makes sense to Indigenous people and students:

> Aboriginal research is an opportunity for us to create innovation and change for our people. If we develop an approach to research, which is unique and reflects our values and beliefs, we will be reflecting the spirit of our ancestors, the spirit of our people who are alive today, and the spirit of our

Aboriginal children who are yet to be born (Kenny,
2000, p. 148).
The application of Indigenous research methodologies to research
in tribal colleges with Indigenous students is making meaning for
them, their communities, and lately for western science:

> Who decides on the values on which most re-
> search is based? How can the values of Aboriginal
> peoples and communities be acknowledged? Are
> we always aware of our own values? How can out-
> siders understand the values embedded in oral
> traditions—values that are rarely explicitly stated?
> (Letendre, & Caine, 2004, p. 4).

What is a conceptual framework and why do we need one? Just
like a hunter or explorer needs a map, a conceptual framework is
the path the researcher follows to complete the project. Think of
gathering data as hunting. One wouldn't go out into the wilderness
without some way to find the path. The conceptual framework is
grounded in an Indigenous paradigm, a methodological approach
and a perception of reality that informs our reality. As Kovach's
work indicates, "Conceptual frameworks make visible the way we
see the world" (2009, p. 41). Just like the hundreds of Indigenous
cultures, each researcher will develop their own individual framework based on worldview, culture, place, and heart of the research
process. The conceptual framework reflects the researcher's perceptions of reality, what counts as knowledge and values and how this
impacts the way we gather data, the questions we ask, the interpretation of the data and dissemination (Chilisa, 2012).

One of the teachings from some First Nations in North America
(Mi'kmaq, Cree, Ojibewe, Algonquin, Passamaquoddy, Malicete,
Lakota, Blackfeet, Salish) is the symbolism in the Medicine Wheel.
Within these teachings is an understanding of health, balance, and
well-being. A healthy state is based on balance between four inter-
connected realms: the physical, mental, emotional, and spiritual
(Crowshoe, 2005).

When I began my research career as a medical ecologist, I
sought to collect data in four different areas: ecological data, epidemiological data, cultural data, and clinical data. I worked with
Arctic Native women who were survivors of breast cancer. I turned
to the four directions and the colors of the Medicine Wheel for
my framework. The center of the framework was the specific tribal

culture of the women who helped me, women from the Inuit culture.

Medicine Wheel Model

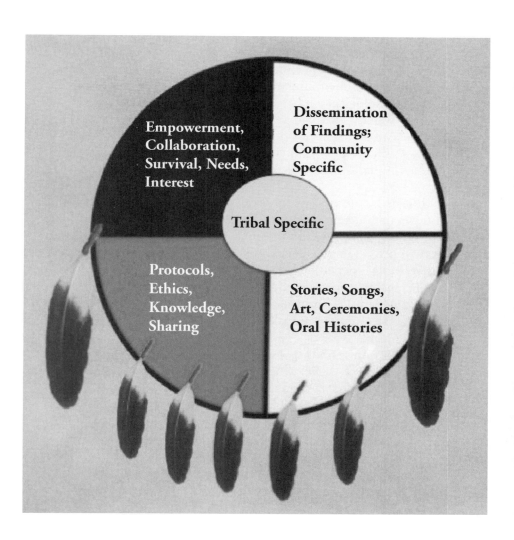

I assessed the data from the four areas of the Medicine Wheel by examining the following data sets:

Cultural Data
* Medicine plants destroyed.
* Animal habitat contaminated or compromised.
* Ceremonial areas and spiritual places for vision quests, Sun Dances.
* Sweat lodges free from trash, pollution.

Clinical Data:
* Signs and symptoms of cancer and disease.

Environmental Data:
* External environment.
* Home environment.

Epidemiological data
*Where is this happening?
*Are there clusters of cancer?
*What types of cancer?
* What other kinds of diseases are prevalent?

But as I continue to indicate, every tribe is unique and not all tribes or Indigenous groups hold to the teachings of the Medicine Wheel. So for each Indigenous group, for each researcher, and for each project, a new conceptual framework must be developed. Native/Indigenous knowledge or epistemology is tribal and place specific and that is one of the first elements of Indigenous research methodologies. The information, the relationship with the knower, and how the questions are asked are all part of this element. Wilson wrote:

> An Indigenous paradigm comes from the fundamental belief that knowledge is relational. Knowledge is shared with all creation. It is not just interpersonal relationships, not just with the research subjects I may be working with, but it is a relationship with all of creation. It is with the cosmos; it is with the animals, with the plants, with the earth that we share this knowledge...you are answering to all your relations when you are doing research (S. Wilson, 2001, pp. 176-177).

In Indigenous communities, knowledge that is acquired from the research is owned by the community. In working with Australian

Aboriginal communities, I developed the boomerang model. A boomerang is the oldest hunting tool on the planet. Once it seeks out its prey, it returns to the community. Just like the knowledge that the researcher gathers, it is returned to the community. The following conceptual framework was used with this community:

Australian Indigenous Research Model

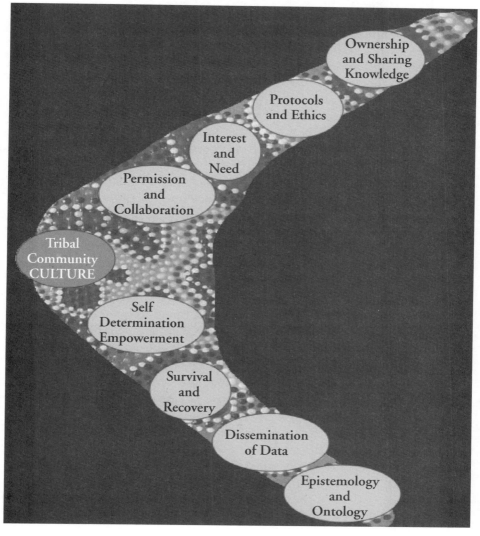

Themes or "Thinking Alike"

Several of the participants in this project are professionals who are working in the fields of mental health, education, and nursing. They have undertaken their own research projects and understand what Indigenous communities want from researchers. The members of the Indigenous communities validated what was surmised about Indigenous research from Wilson, 2008; Kovach, 2009; Smith, 1999; Chilsea, 2012; although the questions asked in the interviews were not focused on the themes per se. The voices from the participants in Australia and Canada showed that they have been marginalized by the dominant culture, and this project gave them a voice and empowered their communities to take control of research and researchers flowing in and out of their communities.

The members of the Sayisi Dene community appeared to be the most marginalized of all the peoples who were interviewed. Their stories reflect issues of a recent horrific relocation that happened in the middle of the twentieth century. For over 1500 years, the Sayisi Dene, "The Dene from the East," led an independent life style. They followed the caribou herds and had little contact with white society. In 1956, an arbitrary government decision to relocate them catapulted the Sayisi Dene into the twentieth century. It replaced their traditional nomadic life of hunting and fishing with a slum settlement on the outskirts of Churchill, Manitoba. Inadequately housed, without jobs, unfamiliar with the language or the culture, their independence and self-determination deteriorated into a tragic cycle of discrimination, poverty, alcoholism, and violent death. The scars and soul wounds of the relocation will take years to heal. Today, the community continues to grapple with the problems of a people whose ties to the land, and to one another, have been tragically severed. Their story is one of stark brutality and the near-destruction of the Sayisi Dene themselves. They continue struggling to reclaim their lives, but are plagued with social issues of substance and spousal abuse (Ila Bussidor, personal conversation, 2011).

The stories from the participants reflected ten common themes. I used these themes to create the conceptual framework for student researchers at Salish Kootenai College, and for other researchers who enter communities in Australia and Canada. Recall that frameworks, or the path the researcher follows to complete the research journey, are winding, and perspectives on that path may also change with the community. It is essential for researchers to follow a conceptual framework, because as Kovach has indicated and I have stressed in previous pages, "Conceptual frameworks make visible the way we see the world" (Kovach, 2009, p. 41). Each researcher will follow her own framework. It provides beliefs about knowledge production, how that impacts the research project, and how the researcher views the data. It gives insight into the worldview of the researcher. But, keep in mind that the path on the research journey is winding and fluid, and perspectives on that path will change as part of the process.

The themes are key for Indigenous researchers doing research in Indigenous communities. The themes are the foundation for the Spider Web conceptual framework, which is appropriate for many Indigenous communities. We all have spiders and everything on the earth is connected in the web of life.

Theme #1: Perception that historical trauma is the major cause of mental health issues in Aboriginal communities.

"The things that affect the spirit and mental health of my people come from relocation and it is spousal abuse, drug and alcohol abuse. It is sad to say, but Tadoule Lake is in need of so much help. If the community is ever to heal itself, something has to be done. I think mental health issues started to affect the people when the Europeans came. And the influence of them caused a lot of change for us, or the people back then, so I think it caused problems for them" (Ila Bussidor: Manitoba, Canada/Sayisi Dene).

"My people were moved by the federal government from Little Duck Lake to Churchill in 1956. This relocation destroyed our independence and ruined our way of life. More than one hundred of my people, one-third of our population, died because of this unplanned, misdirected government action. This didn't happen a hundred years ago, or a thousand miles away, it happened to my people, my family, and it affects us still today" (Ila Bussidor: Manitoba, Canada/Sayisi Dene).

"The loss of culture, the loss of identity and family structure, I think probably was the cause of mental issues" (Whisper Camel: Montana, United States/Pend d'Oreilles).

One of the major themes from all of the communities emanates from the perception that most negative coping behaviors, suicides, substance and spousal abuse, and other mental health problems among Indigenous communities stem from historical trauma. This trauma is described as language loss, culture loss, and being devalued as an Indigenous person through the residential (Canada), mission (Australia), and boarding school (United States) experiences. In that respect, researchers who enter Indigenous communities to research mental health issues need to be aware of this.

Theme #2: The researcher needs to respect and understand the culture of the community.

"Researchers must have a cultural guide so they can learn the community; all research is community specific. When the elder determines that the researcher is competent to understand the community, the researcher is issued a black card after being paired with an elder and the elder determines that the researcher is culturally competent. Scholars who come into our community may know nothing about our culture. They may know generally, but nothing specific. They may have some competency" (Kevin McNulty: Queensland, Australia/Australian Aboriginal/Murri).

"Culture is an interesting word. I'm sure that most people research a little bit on what Aboriginal culture is, but most of them don't really grasp what is going on here in Australia. When we talk about culture, we can talk about the way things were [before contact] and another thing about how things are today, and the reason why we are in the situation we are in today. They can break that barrier by introducing themselves and telling about their family and where they come from. Scholars don't really understand what I see as our culture; they do not know about the diversity of Aboriginal Australia. Some people may know what it is like in different parts of Australia or the Northern Territory, but they certainly don't grasp the complexity of what has happened here in Queensland as a result of dispossession, and everything that's happened to our people here. It is a complex thing. Researchers come into communities and they don't know anything about our culture. They need to live in our community for a few months to find out what our culture is all about" (Laurie Armstrong: Queensland, Australia/ Australian Aboriginal/Murri).

"I met a few people that come through and try to get a grasp on our culture and cultural identity and how we discipline. So they [researchers] come in and observe and, try to integrate, and try get a grasp on what is our culture" (Graeme White: Queensland, Australia/Australian/Aboriginal/Murri).

"I don't think people who come into my community understand the South Sea Island culture. Our relatives were brought here from the Republic of Vanuatu, formerly called the New Hebrides, to work on the sugarcane fields in the 1880s. They were kidnapped much like the Black African slaves were kidnapped to work the cotton fields in the American South" (Mark Warcon: Australia/ Cheyenne/South Sea Islander/Aboriginal).

"When scholars come into our community, I think they have done their homework [to learn about our culture] or had a bit of a think about the community. They come in with pretty general broad understanding of what Australian South Seas Islanders are" (Evan Sirris: Queensland, Australia/South Sea Islander).

"To be honest, I do not think that scholars or researchers who come into the reservation understand the culture here. Not all of them, but the majority of them. I feel like we are in a lab being looked at. And this is my own personal opinion. And it makes me feel like I am not normal, that I am something to be studied… and neither are my children, or my grandchildren or my tupias. You know we are not here to be studied. We are a unique people. I get really, really defensive sometimes" (Evelyn Matt Hernandez: Montana, United States/Flathead Salish).

"I don't think scholars who come into this community to do research understand the people here. They have to be exposed and learn as they go along. If they are from here or if they have read some books or talk to the people they may, but when they first initially come, I don't think they understand the people. Depending on where they are from, they may understand culture, but a lot of them come with an open mind so I think a lot of them are willing to learn" (Kiana: Montana, United States/Flathead Salish).

"Sometimes I think that scholars who come to the reservation don't understand our culture. I am thinking of things that I have seen. I am a wildlife biologist and one time as I was driving up around St. Mary's Lake and I saw people from the University [of Montana] doing some sampling in some of the streams. And I know that we have permits that the tribe puts out for these people that we go through our own protocol if they are doing any kind of sampling or any kind of research. I went back [to the tribe] and asked them and no one ever heard of these guys or given any permits or anything. So I think there are people who come here unbeknownst to us and do work, which I don't think is right because it is our land, and we are supposed to be co-owners and the majority of things where we say you can go ahead and take data from us" (Whisper Camel: Montana, United States/Pend d'Oreilles).

"Scholars who come into my community do not understand my culture. Scholars who come into the community do not understand how to come into a community of Natives and talk" (Frank Finley: Montana, United States/Flathead Salish).

"So no, unless they are Natives I don't think they understand the culture" (Leslie Camel: Montana, United States/Pend d'Oreilles).

"Researchers who come into Tadoule Lake don't quite understand the culture of [Sayisi Dene] in Tadoule Lake. I don't think they have a full understanding of that. And of course our culture is not the same any more as it was for my parents and grandparents" (Ila Bussidor: Manitoba, Canada/Sayisi Dene).

"Scholars who come to my community do not know about the culture of my community. They might do the reading and the research; there are lot of documents and publications done on our community, but they still don't know the community. If a researcher wanted to do real good research, they would have to come in person to the community and get to know the people and meet with the elders, know the history and everything before they can say, 'I really understand'" (Suzan Cheekie Beardly: Manitoba, Canada/Sayisi Dene).

When researchers understand, and are familiar with the culture and the history of the place, their presence will be more acceptable, and the community will trust the researcher and the data. Participants indicated that researchers should attend functions when they are invited, eat the food, live and participate in community life. Don't just go to observe!

Theme #3: The researcher must contribute to community empowerment and self-determination.

"They are researchers but they are not doing it for us for our community. They are not fucking doing it for us. They are doing it for the *white man* so they can get money. That is where all the bullshit is. And that is where the cycle keeps going and going and going. They are willing to give us royalties but excuse me, royalties. That is our land and they are getting a lot of money from that stuff" (Suzan Cheekie Beardly: Manitoba, Canada/Sayisi Dene).

"Researchers got rich off of us. It is way different now. I am kinda old and I kinda know some things because of past researchers that came in. I want to have knowledge, but people came in at the turn of the [twentieth] century and took knowledge and information and robbed graves to get information, get people drunk to get information, and take things. Up until the mid 1900s, until our people started to know, we could control our own lives and not have BIA or government assume that they have our best interest, as our people became smarter in dealing with those academia people" (Roy Bigcrane: Montana, United States/Flathead Salish/Pend d'Oreille).

"For young researchers who want to research in Indigenous communities I would say, 'What are you going to do with the information? How are you going to tell story of what happened to us?' A person has to be very strong [to go into the community] and be able to understand a person" (Caroline Bjorklund: Manitoba, Canada/Sayisi Dene).

By being part of the community, researchers will gain an understanding of the epistemology and ontology of that community and how the historical knowledge of the community goes back into

time immemorial. The research and researcher should demon-
strate an understanding of these concepts as they pertain to mental
health.

**Theme #4: The research data should contribute to the commu-
nity survival and recovery.**

"I believe that research that is done in Aboriginal communities must be done from the cultural values of that community. The
research must be to move the community forward, to heal issues
of historical trauma, to promote self-determination, and to make
visible the issues in those communities, so we can come together
as a community and make a plan to remedy the issues. I thought
that telling my story would be my way of being part of reconciliation for my ancestors who've gone, for the family that's still here
and for my future family" (Dr. Pam Croft-Warcon: Queensland,
Australia/Aboriginal/Murri).

"I think we need a much more political push for mental health
issues. South Sea Islanders need to be put on the agenda for mental
health issues. I have never seen anything for mental health, skin
infections, heart disease, diabetes, social diseases. I have never seen
anything specific for Australian South Sea Islanders. That's where
it has to get identified, health positions specifically for Australian
South Sea Islanders. We need research for education. We have been
on the back burner for years" (Mark Warcon: Queensland, Austra-
lia/Northern Cheyenne/South Sea Islander/Aboriginal).

"All that, and historical trauma. Boy we are kind of a messed
up people. We're fighting our way back to stability. We're fighting
our way back, but it is still pretty tough, because some people don't
even know they are traumatized. They think, 'Well, I'll beat up the
old lady, and kick the dog and smack around the kids and drink in
front of them and have parties here.' How many of them do really
understand that this isn't right? It isn't right. My kids should be
first" (Roy Bigcrane: United States, Montana/Flathead Salish/Pend
d'Orielle).

The key to decolonization and empowerment of the community is
by asking research questions focused on resilience rather than on

negativity. In this regard, the data that focused on resilience will move the community through survival and recovery from historical trauma. I believe that when the community understands their strengths, more effort will be made to counter maladaptive behaviors regarding their own families and tribes.

Theme #5: The research must focus on community interest and need.

"They need to speak to the elders and have them tell the researchers what they need to do when they are doing this research and how to be respectful and to honor our traditions instead of coming in and listening and not writing the real truth about our people, because they [the researchers] don't know the real truth. The only ones who know the real truth are the elders and the tribal people" (Evelyn Matt Hernandez: Montana, United States/Flathead Salish).

"If they go into the community and say, 'I want this' or 'I want that.' They need to care about us, and the community. One of the things that is really important to me is that a young researcher has to go with the flow of the community. If they don't go with the flow, then they [community members] will say, 'What the hell are they doing here, if you are not going to help me? What do they want?' As a researcher, you are supposed to hand everything over to them, you know? To me if I went to Montana, if you were in my situation, and I would say, 'I want to know what happened to you.' Your first reaction would be to say, 'What are you going to do with that information?' You are supposed to hand everything over to them" (Caroline Bjorklund: Manitoba, Canada/Sayisi Dene).

The research must meet the needs and interest of the community, rather than be focused on the needs of the researcher.

Theme #6: The community must be in collaboration and give permission for the research to be done.

"People need to have council approval, which should include a board that would keep an eye on the ethics and any issues that might come up, whether it is wildlife or mental health" (Whisper Camel: Montana, United States/Pend d'Oreilles).

"I don't think the elders will set the agenda for the researchers, but they will help guide us in what not to do. If the researchers asked the wrong question that would quell the research because once the door is closed, the community themselves may not open the door. They may not allow the research. If they have an elder that is involved with research and guides the type of questions of what can and should be asked and how it is asked and where they can find the research. When a researcher comes in to gather information, and this is where the elders come in, it is important to have the elders agree on it [the research proposal]. The researcher has to make sure that the information they are receiving is accurate. Without having the guidance from the culture committee or whatever, the tribe won't know the information is accurate" (Virgil Braverock: Alberta, Canada/Blood First Nations).

"I don't know if the researchers are involving the elders like they should be. The elders don't tell the researchers what they want researched. I would like to say that the tribe has some say about what is being done with the results of the research, and it has to go through council before they are allowed to print" (Kiana: Montana, United States/Flathead/Salish).

"Here the researchers have to go through council and generally the council will direct you to the culture committee to make sure it is okay with them. And you give a presentation to the council and the culture committees. They like to be informed and they can ask questions about what you are looking for, and they can tell you what [information] you can use and what you can't use" (Whisper Camel: Montana, United States/Pend d'Oreilles).

"I don't think the elders set the agenda for the researchers or tell them what we want researched. It is a formality to go see the elders here. It is not like it is in Dine [Navajo]. I think they come in and as a formality they go see the tribal council and the tribal council says, 'Yes, but you have to go see the elders.' So then they come back and say, 'Yes, we saw the elders and everything is cool.

' And they just go ahead and do some of that stuff [their research projects] because we don't have a strong IRB with the tribe" (Frank Finley: Montana, United States/Flathead Salish).

"People have to go to the tribal council, meet with the council, and tell them what you are doing. I would think that would be the first protocol" (Leslie Camel: Montana, United States/Pend d'Oreilles).

"The elders don't tell the researcher what they want researched. I think the researcher comes in with an idea, like with the questions they want. But if they [the elders] say this is the way I want to be interviewed and this is the way I want to provide information to you. I don't think it is like that" (Ila Bussidor: Manitoba, Canada/ Sayisi Dene).

"There is no one protocol. It can be disjointed when different tribes are all in one place. In those communities you have things like alcohol. Again, it is around respect and learning about someone's culture. If a researcher wants a successful outcome for all parties, they would go to find out about the protocols and have a successful outcome. It is important for researchers entering the community…that they touch base with the right community members or the right community organizations and social groups, especially in terms of mental health" (Graeme White: Queensland, Australia/ Australian Aboriginal/Murri).

In that respect, researchers have to collaborate with the community and gain permission from the administrations of each community to determine their needs. Researchers are obliged to get approval from the Institutional Review Board (IRB). If there is no IRB, they must obtain approval from the council or governing body of that community.

Theme #7: The researcher should be required to do the work with an understanding of the community's epistemology and ontology.

"It is all about respect. Researchers need to participate and live in the community and not just watch. People will accept them better if they participate. They are bringing something to the community. They are not stand offish. They may have a picture in their head about Aboriginal people" (Graeme White: Queensland, Australia/Australian Aboriginal/Murri).

"...and the researchers need to respect us as tribal people and what we believe in" (Evelyn Matt Hernandez: Montana, United States/Flathead Salish).

"...and to be respectful of our culture and our community" (Whisper Camel: Montana, United States/Pend d'Oreilles).

"You will get very negative feedback if you don't know how that community works. So understanding the culture is key. And coming from a cultural background they will accept you" (Kiana: Montana, United States/Flathead Salish).

"We also need to take into account our spiritual beliefs and our culture. Because these are contributing to our mental health or can be contributing to our mental health, but others may not see it that way" (Graeme White: Queensland, Australia/Australian Aboriginal/Murri).

"People are very touchy about the Dene culture [in Tadoule]. Only the last few years the community itself started to upset the Native people. It's not only the Dene people, but the Native people themselves" (Caroline Bjorklund: Manitoba, Canada/Sayis Dene).

Theme #8: The community must own the data.

"Our stories belong in the community. They do not belong to the university or the government. They are ours, our data, and they belong to the Aboriginal community where the research is being carried out" (Dr. Pam Croft-Warcon: Queensland, Australia Australian Aboriginal/Murri).

"The people [in the community] should own the stories that come from the community, but it never comes back. The researcher never comes back. There has never been one that I can see evidence of giving back to the community that research has been taken" (Ila Bussidor: Manitoba, Canada/Sayisi Dene).

The community has to own the data. Researchers are borrowing the stories and the data from the community members and should return and acknowledge the members of the community who shared their stories and interviews.

Theme #9: The researcher must disseminate the data in ways that the community can understand.

"The researchers write up reports and send it to where it needs to go, but I never see any good come from it. Dissemination takes place through working groups, written papers, and community groups. Men versus women have different roles in each community, and perhaps a male researcher cannot speak with a female member of the community" (Kevin McNulty: Queensland, Australia/Australian Aboriginal/Murri).

"Researchers at first may be quite clinical in their approach and how they approach us. And that never works because of our culture, and our way of learning, and our way of absorbing information. It doesn't collate with the non-Indigenous community and that may make it quite difficult for researchers. They have to give respect to the culture" (Graeme White: Queensland, Australia/Australian Aboriginal/Murri).

"The researchers write up their reports and make recommendations and how to best address the problem...Small steps, not large steps to address the problem" (Evan Sirris: Queensland, Australia/South Sea Islander).

"We were the bottom of the social ladder in Churchill. When researchers gather information from the community, they put their work together, but sometimes they send us a copy of the work. Our people have no control, and they give their voices out, and it rightfully belongs to them. But if they don't say anything, the researchers don't do anything. I don't think that they ever come back to clarify the information with the community. They never come back to the community" (Rachel Bjorklund: Manitoba, Canada/ Sayisi Dene).

"Once the research project is finished, and this is only my opinion, sometimes when the researchers come, the one thing they have to do is go before the tribal council and the council will tell them that they also have to go before the cultural committees, because they need to know what the research is. They need to know what questions the research is going to ask. There are some things that we will never share with the researchers and they will never know. There have been a few researchers who have come back to share, but I am always really suspicious of researchers because Indian people are so great and some of the researchers come in here and take that stuff, information, in order to make money and that is totally wrong" (Evelyn Hernandez Matt: Montana, United States/ Flathead Salish).

Theme #10: The integrity of the story and the storyteller or the informant are keys to knowledge.

"The stories that community people give to the researcher are always open for interpretation. If it is a non-Indigenous person, they will interpret it from their worldview as opposed to an Aboriginal world view" (Kevin McNulty: Queensland, Australia/ Australian Aboriginal/Murri).

"When a researcher hears a story from someone, I do not think that the researcher hears the story in the same way it was told. It doesn't have the same meaning. When the elders tell you something, their words are sacred when they come out of their mouth" (Evelyn Matt Hernandez: Montana, United States/Flathead Salish).

"When the story is told to the researcher, I think there is a loss of communication. Elders have a different way to telling stories and how the story should be told. So that is why it is so important to give a copy of the interview to the person so they can add or clarify. A lot of people are not willing to let the elder tell the whole story with the point of the story at the end. They want the point made now. I love how the elders tell the story. Society has changed us a lot, and we are not as patient as we once were" (Kiana: Montana, United States/Flathead Salish).

"The story should have a different meaning for everybody. Whatever they need at the time. If it is a Native story, it should have a different meaning for whatever you happen to be doing in your life. Sometimes, if you're not on any mission or anything, it may be just sharing or for entertainment. It may be just a good story. Other than that, there are lessons encoded in all the stories of one kind or another. Sometimes researchers don't listen to that part of the story. They just think it is really great that Skunk did this thing or that or Owl did this thing or Frog did this. 'Wow those are really entertaining stories,' and they miss the lesson. Well, Skunk really shouldn't have gotten his girlfriend pregnant or gotten Fox's girlfriend pregnant and the kids are going to look different and someone is going to know. It causes trouble. The moral parts of those stories are totally tuned out because the dominant culture is totally tuned into entertainment" (Frank Finley: Montana, United States/Flathead Salish).

"Stories have a different meaning to every person hearing the story depending on their experience and their exposure to the ideas in that culture. You can say something to kids and they just take it as a story, and they don't have that experience to see that more deeply. That is just to show that it depends on your experience and if that person is a person of color or not a person of color has a lot to do with it as well, and how advanced their culture is and their education, their role in society, whether they have kids. Every single person has a different meaning" (Leslie Camel: Montana, United States/Pend d'Oreilles).

"If a person tells a story to the researcher, I don't think the researcher will interpret it the same way. Let's say you are a white person and you are coming to interview me about something, I think there are very few who can feel or grasp your words. Sure the words can make you cry, but they don't grasp the heart of the story. I think you have to. They try so hard but they [the researchers] can never understand the heart of our people" (Ila Bussidor: Manitoba, Canada/Sayisi Dene).

"I think that stories can be different from the one telling the story to the researcher hearing the story. They might strike from something that they experienced in their own life or something that they heard from someone else previously, that they heard and they did some research on it. I think the gist of it might be there, but there are personal biases whenever anyone hears a story. If I hear a story and you hear a story and we go retell that story, it will be different because we are going to focus on different aspects of it. I think that is just oral knowledge that things are fluid and change" (Whisper Camel: Montana, United States/Pend d'Oreilles).

"If a person in the community tells a story to the researcher, it depends on the researcher, if they understand the heart of the story" (Caroline Bjorklund: Manitoba, Canada/Sayisi Dene)

The researcher is obliged to disseminate the data in ways the community can understand, perhaps by a Power Point presentation or a video where the whole community is invited and can ask questions.

Parting Words: Lori

Each ethnic group will have their own cultural concepts for treatment. Healing for Indigenous people in the area of mental health ought to include the power of communities, spiritual ceremonies, connections to the land, and restoration of traditions such as hunting, fishing, and trapping, and the spiritual aspects related to these traditions. Clinical psychologist, educator, and researcher, Dr. Joseph Gone/Cree, calls this "Integrated treatment" (J. Gone, presentation at Montana State University, Bozeman, Montana, 2013).

Members of the communities where the research was carried out discussed their rights in controlling research and researchers. The members of the Australian South Sea Island Community indicated a need to develop stronger protocols for their own community, since they do not fall under the umbrella of Indigenous Australians. In the Sayisi Dene community, several women indicated that they need protocols developed to protect their people. Although protocols for this community come from the Association of Canadian Universities for Northern Studies (2003), members of the community did not realize their rights. More communication regarding researchers should be done with Ottawa and the Aboriginal Affairs Department. The one goal, which has yet to be realized, is the improvement of mental health services to Indigenous communities. More Indigenous students need to be trained and educated in the areas of counseling, substance abuse, and social work. More researchers must learn how to research from an Indigenous epistemology. As well, much more research needs to be carried out in other communities. This project interviewed only 25 individuals in four communities. There is a great need to do more.

More Indigenous students need to be trained and educated in the areas of counseling, substance abuse counselors, and social work. Students at SKC are moving forward in these careers. We founded the American Indigenous Research Association, which is based at SKC. In October of 2013, the Association held its first conference with participants coming from India, New Zealand, Australia, Hawaii, and throughout the United States. It is an exciting time for Indigenous research to be at the forefront of academia.

The Development of the Conceptual Framework

Based on the stories, information and needs of the communities, my model for a conceptual framework has evolved into the spider web model. In the past I wrestled with models based on the Medicine Wheel and the boomerang, however these models are not applicable to each community in each country. I pondered over this dilemma over the years and thought about what we all share in common and what ties us together. As a medical ecologist, I know that spiders in different forms and species exist in all continents except Antarctica, therefore the spider web model fits with the work I am doing internationally.

Spider Web Conceptual Framework

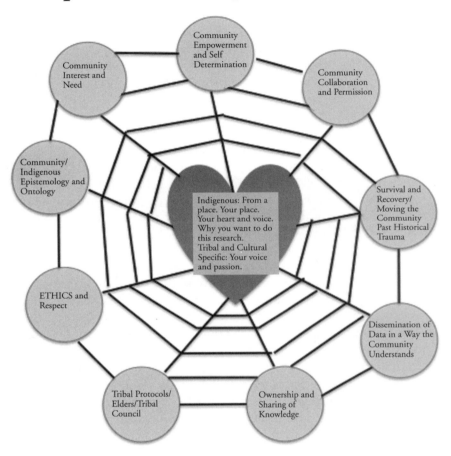

Afterword
by Dr. Thundering Hill

Dr. Thundering Hill is my very good friend and colleague. We have known one another for over twenty years. Her career spans being a professor, researcher, and consultant. She was trained in Western science. Her personal story echoes the similar issues of land loss, culture loss, and soul wounding that all Indigenous groups have endured. Because of her Western training in science, I invited her to write the afterword from her cultural point of view about research, this book, and other issues that were on her mind.

My story is a little like that of the people of No Place in the South Seas, who live on the coast of Australia, that you spoke with. But I am from North American land. My people were removed from their land, parted forcibly from it like lovers separated by war or prison camp, nearly 200 years ago. This changed everything for my family, even to this sixth generation that I am in. It has made things unspeakably difficult for me, as an individual person. But it has also been a gift, because it has given me a point of view that I think could be important to all of us trying to live in this world, which is so lethal to the world in which we truly belong. I have never shared my story before, but reading your words makes me think that I should do that now. Perhaps it has meaning that can help contribute now, a little bit, to the important work you are doing.

My people are Choctaw. I grew up being told our family stories. I grew up being taught, "This is how we do this." "See how this thing does that, how this bird does such-and-such, how this plant reacts to this-and-that thing, how we live in relationship and respect with everything around us because it is all sharing its wisdom with us if we are still enough to listen and to look, to pay attention and to reflect, and to ask politely and with respect for more chances to learn when we do not understand."

But I also grew up without any community other than just my father teaching me these things. When my great-grandmother died, she was the family Matriarch, my family scattered like bugs running every which way when you pick up the stone beneath which they are living. No one else I knew but my father was Choctaw. When I asked my mother certain things, she would say, "This is a thing I do not know about. You have to ask your father about this. He understands these kinds of things. He thinks like that. He has that kind of experience. He has those kinds of dreams. He will understand what you are talking about. I don't understand it at all. It makes no sense to me. It sounds crazy to me. Talk to your father." That's how I learned that there were two cultures in my house. And then when I went to college and met people without a father like my father, that is the first time I realized there was only one culture in many other houses. And that is when I began to feel very much alone, out in a world where there was no one to go to when I had a question. My father was far away. And there was no one else.

I worry what will happen to the people who are so strong now in their cultures, who live on their ancestral lands, when they are dispossessed and scattered to the four winds like we were. I know they are strong and that they have a firm legal grip on the land where they live. But I know we thought we had this all figured out, too, 200 years ago. The impact of my family's losses culminated in 1958 when everyone finally gave up and ran every which way on the wind. But it started when we were dispossessed of our tribal homelands in 1831. When the people in the dominant culture to ours decide they want the oil and gas and lumber and water on those people's lands, they will take them. They will dispossess the people living there like they did us. Legal will not matter. Fighting will not matter. History shows us this. It makes me worry a great deal about the future for all these people. Because the dominant culture is using up all the things they have, and they are starting to look with greedy eyes at what these other people have preserved. This is not a new story. But I see every People who still have their land, and I hear them say, "This cannot happen to us." I fear they underestimate the power of greed that drives the dominant culture that surrounds them like the sea around small islands. And this great sea of greed has everything to do with our mental health.

I grew up being told about my great-grandmother's own grandmother, her very mother's mother, dying on the Trail of Tears. I knew my great-grandmother, who I called Gramma. I remember her very, very well. She was telling me a story of her own mother's mother. Two hundred years is not such a long time as it sounds like it is. Because of the things that happened, Gramma decided our family would be white. She decided we would speak only English forever, never more Choctaw. She decided to protect us from harm in this way. Yet she was still Choctaw. For instance, she always knew she was not in her homeland. She felt the dispossession. There were ancient Mound-builder mounds just across the border in Arkansas, only a few miles from her house. But she always said, "Those are not our mounds." She never once went to visit them. Because of the way she saw things, which this combination of bits of information helps to express, she made me know that our family was cast out or disenfranchised from our true home. We could never go back. There were people who somehow got to stay there. They kept the old ways. They kept the language. But there was always a feeling of "How is it they got to do this? We don't know. We can't say. But the government forced us out. It made us die. It pushed us around when it did not do such things to those people. So we are not sure how we feel about them being there, on our Land. We are not sure how we feel about them getting to keep all the things that were taken away from us." This is a very uneasy feeling. It is one that I fear more and more Indian people will feel. And meanwhile, the people who get to remain where they were, who get to somehow keep the pieces of culture they keep, can be tempted to feel better and more proud, maybe even a little smug. And I think that is just as dangerous as feeling cast out and dispossessed. Both are two sides of a single coin. And I fear both of them are detrimental to our mental health as both individuals and communities.

But what I have gained from being dispossessed, being raised without the whole tribal community that I should have been among, is perhaps precious. I understand the importance and power of the Land itself. People can say that the Land is the source of story and language, but unless that is all they have to be their teacher, I think it is hard for them to really know what this means at a gut level. Here is one example: rattlesnakes have interacted in unusual ways with me, several different times in my life. Things have happened that made even people with me, white people with me, wonder what was going on. So I began to think about what was going on. I could feel it was not a personal relationship. It was something else. I began to wonder if there was a tribal relationship between us. Then, much later, I learned about a pattern that is put on many Choctaw clothes and baskets and beadwork. It is the diamond pattern on a rattlesnake's back. It's there because the rattlesnake has a special relationship with the Choctaw people. (This shows one reason why the written records being made now are so important, by the way.) The point is that this relationship between rattlesnakes and Choctaw people exists. It is there. It is there even when the Choctaw person around a particular rattlesnake, and maybe even that particular rattlesnake, have never been told about it. But it still exists. And it influences their behavior, both of them. That is because the relationship comes from the land itself. The culture recognizes and acknowledges and codifies (in a basket pattern, for instance) that relationship. But the culture did not invent this relationship. And, in that regard, the relationship does not belong to the culture. Instead, the culture, and the people of that culture, belong to the relationship. This is a very important distinction.

For many years I struggled to help open up academia and Western science to a greater diversity of ideas and viewpoints. My concern was that academia and science were increasing the physical racial and ethnic diversity of their participants, but demanding such thorough acculturation to survive the system that it nullified any possible gains in cultural diversity. Worse, this acculturation seriously, even lethally, damaged the identities and therefore the health and well-being of the people involved. When it got to the point that I could no longer support diversity-enhancement programs that I knew would put young people into career tracks in which they could not succeed, and that would in fact be life-destroying, I finally realized there was no integrity behind Western institutions' stated willingness to diversify ideas, approaches, and methodologies. So I retired in anger and disgust from academia and science, both. I now do public education as I can, and write some as I can, trying to find ways to help people encounter the Reality we Indigenous people know in a way that might plant seeds of hope for the very dark future we all face. For my greatest concern at this time is that when the dominant culture fails, it will take the rest of the Earth's peoples, plant as well as animal, with it.

Dr. Thundering Hill, Colorado, 2012

Endnotes

1. Indigenous research is any research that touches the lives, communities, environment, or culture of Indigenous people. I use the word Indigenous in this work to refer to Aboriginal, Native, or marginalized people living in their particular community.

2. In this work, I use the terms ethno-psychology and Indigenous psychology interchangeably.

3. The Wobanaki Confederation is composed of Mi'kmaq, Maliseet, Passamaquoddy, Penobscot, and Abenaki.

4. Micmac spelling is found in Maine and the spelling Mi'kmaq is found in Canada. There are 28 bands of Mi'kmaq people in Canada and one band of Micmac in Aroostook, Maine. Recently the language has changed Mi'kmaq to Mi'gmaw when referring to the tribe. I will use Mi'kmaq in this work.

5. Elders are the persons most educated in the oral tradition; they carry credentials that are recognized within their community; they enjoy respect as sources of wisdom and culture and they transmit these values to those who seek advice (Castellano, 2004).

6. Attitash: Abenaki word meaning blueberries.

7. Continued: (4) It advocates use of multiple methods. (5) It advocates the integration of "insiders," "outsiders" and multiple perspectives to obtain comprehensive and integrated understanding. (6) It acknowledges that people have a complex and sophisticated understanding of themselves and it is necessary to translate their practical and episodic understanding into analytical knowledge. (7) It is part of a scientific tradition that advocates multiple perspectives, but not multiple psychologies or absolute relativism. (8) Although descriptive analysis is the starting point of research, its final goal is to discover psychological universals that can be theoretically and empirically verified. (9) It is a part of the cultural sciences tradition in which human agency, meaning and context are incorporated into the research design. (10) It advocates a linkage of humanities (which focus on human experience and

creativity) with social sciences (which focus empirical analysis and verification).

8. Kakadu National Park in Northern Territories, Australia.

9. Woorabinda: A community started by missionaries on the central coast of Brisbane. There are people of many Aboriginal cultures who were brought to the mission by the government.

10. Gumbi gumbi is Pittosporum phylliraeoides, a bush medicine used in Central Queensland. It is rare because it is slow growing and cattle eat it.

11. Permission was given to tell this story. Usually Coyote stories are told in winter

References

Abatto, S. (2011). *Community profiles for health care providers.* Brisbane, QLD, Australia: Queensland Health.

Aboriginal Healing Foundation. (2002). *The healing has begun: An operational update.* Ottawa, ON, Canada: Aboriginal Healing Foundation.

Aboriginal Health and Medical Research Council of New South Wales. (2013). *Annual Report 2012-13.* Surry Hills, NSW, Australia: Aboriginal Health and Research Council of New South Wales.

Absolon, K., & Willett, C. (2005). Putting ourselves forward: Location in aboriginal research. In L. Brown, & S. Strega (Eds.), *Research as resistance* (pp. 97-126). Toronto, ON, Canada: Canadian Scholars' Press.

Adams, D. W. (1995). *Education for extinction: American Indians and the boarding school experience, 1875-1928.* Lawrence, KS: University Press of Kansas.

American Indian Higher Education Consortium. (2012). *AIHEC AIMS Fact Book, 2009-2010.* Alexandria, VA: American Indian Higher Education Consortium.

Association of Canadian Universities for Northern Studies. (2003). *Ethical principles for the conduct of research in the north.* Ottawa, ON, Canada: Association of Canadian Universities for Northern Studies.

Australian Human Rights Commission. (2010). *The community guide to the UN declaration on the rights of indigenous peoples.* Canberra, Australian Capital Territory, Australia: Australian Human Rights Commission.

Australian Institute of Health and Welfare. (2012). *Aboriginal and Torres Strait Islander health services report, 2010-11.* Canberra, Australian Capital Territory, Australia: Australian Institute of Health and Welfare.

Bailey, J. (2005). *You're not listening to me! Aboriginal mental health is different–don't you understand?* Paper presented at the 2005 National Rural Health Conference, Alice Springs, NT, Australia.

Baranowsky, A. B., Young, M., Johnson-Douglas, S., Williams-Keeler, L., & McCarrey, M. (1998). PTSD transmission: A review of secondary traumatization in Holocaust survivor families. *Canadian Psychology/Psychologie canadienne, 39*(4), pp. 247-256.

Barnes, H. W. (2000). Collaboration in community action: A successful partnership between indigenous communities and researchers. *Health Promotion International,* 15(1), pp. 17-25.

Baskin, C. (2005). *Circles of inclusion: Aboriginal worldviews in social work education.* (Ph.D. dissertation). University of Toronto, Toronto, ON, Canada. (Proquest 30537377).

Battiste, M. (Ed.). (2000). *Reclaiming indigenous voice and vision.* Vancouver, BC, Canada: UBC Press.

Battiste, M., & Henderson, J. Y. (Eds.). (2000). *Protecting indigenous knowledge and heritage: A global challenge.* Saskatoon, SK, Canada: Purich Publishing Ltd.

Beals, J., Manson, S. M., Croy, C., Klein, S. A., Whitesell, N. R., Mitchell, C. M., & AI-SUPERPFP Team. (2013). Lifetime prevalence of posttraumatic stress disorder in two American Indian reservation populations. *Journal of Traumatic Stress,* 26(4), pp. 512-520.

Bigart, R., & Woodcock, C. (Eds.). (1996). *In the name of the Salish and Kootenai nation: The 1855 Hell Gate Treaty and the origin of the Flathead Indian Reservation.* Pablo, MT: Salish Kootenai College Press.

Bigcrane, R., & Smith, T. (Directors). (1991). *The Place of Falling Waters* (DVD). Pablo, MT: Salish Kootenai College Media Department.

Biser, J. A. (1998). *Really wild remedies: Medicinal plant use by animals.* Retrieved from http://nationalzoo.si.edu/publications/zoogoer/1998/1/reallywildremedies.cfm.

Blood, N., & Heavy Head, R. (2007). *Blackfoot influence on Abraham Maslow.* Presentation at University of Montana. Missoula, Montana. Retrieved from www.blackfootdigitallibrary.org.

Brant-Castellano, M. (2000). Updating aboriginal traditions of knowledge. In G. J. S. Dei, B. L. Hall, & D. G. Rosenberg (Eds.), *Indigenous knowledges in global contexts* (pp. 21–36). Toronto, ON, Canada: University of Toronto Press.

Brasfield, C. (2001). Residential school syndrome. *BC Medical Journal,* 43(2), pp. 78–81.

Brayboy, B. M. J. (2005). Toward a tribal critical race theory in education. *The Urban Review,* 37(5), pp. 425-445.

Bretherton, D., & Mellor, D. (2006). Reconciliation between aboriginal and other Australians: The "stolen generations," *Journal of Social Issues,* (62)1, pp. 81–98.

Bruchac, J. (2005). *Foot of the mountain and other stories.* Duluth, MN: Holy Cow! Press.

Bussidor, I., & Bilgen-Reinart, U. (1997). *Night spirits: The story of the relocation of the Sayisi Dene.* Winnipeg, MB, Canada: University of Manitoba Press.

Cajete, G. (2000). *Native science: Natural laws of interdependence.* Santa Fe, NM: Clear Light Publishers.

Canada, Public Health Agency of Canada. (2006). *The human face of mental health and mental illness in Canada.* Ottawa, ON, Canada: Minister of Public Works and Government Services Canada.

Canada, Royal Commission on Aboriginal Peoples. (1996). *Report of the Royal Commission on Aboriginal Peoples: Vol. I, Looking forward, looking back.* Ottawa, ON: The Commission.

Canadascope: Canadian Tourism Product e–Bulletin, May 24, 2011. Retrieved from http://www.canadascopebulletin.com/May2411.html.

Canadian Council on Learning. (2008). *Lessons in learning: Aboriginal and rural under-representation in Canada's medical schools.* Retrieved from http://www.ccl-cca/ccl/Reports/LessonsInLearning/html.

Cardinal, T. (2010). *For all my relations: An autobiographical narrative inquiry into the lived experiences of one aboriginal graduate student.* (master's thesis), University of Alberta, Edmonton, AB, Canada.

Cariboo Tribal Council. (1991). Faith misplaced: Lasting effects of abuse in a First Nations community. *Canadian Journal of Native Education,* 18(2), pp. 161-197.

Castellano, M. B. (2004). Ethics of aboriginal research. *Journal of Aboriginal Health,* 1(1), pp. 98-114.

Catanzaro, F. B. (2002). *With the 41st Division in the Southwest Pacific: A foot soldier's story.* Bloomington, IN: Indiana University Press.

Chiasson, P. (2006). *The island of seven cities. Where the Chinese settled when they discovered America.* New York: St. Martin's Press.

Chilisa, B. (2012). *Indigenous research methodologies.* Los Angeles, CA: Sage.

Close, D. (2009). *What the Abenaki say about dogs.* Warren, VT: The Tamarac Press.

Cole, P. (2002). Aboriginalizing methodology: Considering the canoe. *Qualitative Studies in Education,* 15(4), pp. 447-459.

Corrado, R. R., & Cohen, I. M. (2003). *Mental health profiles for a sample of British Columbia's survivors of the Canadian residential school system.* Ottawa, ON, Canada. Aboriginal Healing Foundation.

Coutts, R. (1997). *On the edge of a frozen sea: Prince of Wales' Fort, York Factory and the fur trade of western Hudson's Bay.* [Winnipeg, MB, Canada?]: Parks Canada, Department of Canadian Heritage.

Crowshoe, C. (2005). *Sacred ways of life: Traditional knowledge.* Ottawa, ON, Canada. First Nations Centre, National Aboriginal Health Organization.

Cruikshank, J. (1990). *Life lived like a story: Life stories of three Yukon native elders.* Lincoln, NB: University of Nebraska Press.

Dana-Sacco, G. (2010). The indigenous researcher as individual and collective. *American Indian Quarterly,* 34(1), pp. 61-82.

Day, A., Nakata, M. N., & Howells, K. (2008). *Anger and indigenous men: Understanding and responding to violent behaviour.* Leichhardt, NSW, Australia: Federation Press.

Deloria, V., Jr. (1995). *Red earth, white lies: Native Americans and the myth of scientific fact.* New York: Scribner.

Deloria, V., Jr. (2006). *The world we used to live in: Remembering the powers of the medicine men.* Golden, CO: Fulcrum Publishing.

Duran, E. (2006). *Healing the soul wound: Counseling with American Indians and other native peoples.* New York: Teachers College Press.

Duran, E., & Duran, B. (1995). *Native American postcolonial psychology.* Albany, NY: State University of New York Press.

Durie, M. (2001). *Cultural competence and medical practice in New Zealand.* Paper presented at Australian and New Zealand Boards and Council Conference. Wellington, NZ.

EDSITEment! National Endowment for the Humanities. (n.d.). *Australian Aboriginal art and storytelling.* Retrieved from http://edsitement. neh.gov/lesson-plan/australian-aboriginal-art-and-storytelling

Elder, B. (1998). *Blood on the wattle: Massacres and maltreatment of aboriginal Australians since 1788.* (Expanded ed.) Sydney, NSW, Australia: New Holland Publishers.

Elliott-Farrelly, T. (2004). Australian aboriginal suicide: The need for an aboriginal suicidology? *Australian e-Journal for the Advancement of Mental Health,* 3(4), pp. 138-145. doi: 10.5172/jamh. 33.138.

Ermine, W., Sinclair, R., & Jeffery, B. (2004). *The ethics of research involving indigenous peoples: Report of the Indigenous Peoples' Health Research Centre to the Interagency Advisory Panel on Research Ethics.* Saskatoon, SK, Canada: Indigenous Peoples' Health Research Centre.

Fanon, F. (1965). *Studies in a dying colonialism, or a dying colonialism.* New York: Monthly Review Press.

Fetterman, D. M. (2010). *Ethnography: Step-by-step.* (3rd ed.). Los Angeles, CA: Sage.

Fixico, D. L. (2003). *The American Indian mind in a linear world: American Indian studies and traditional knowledge.* New York: Routledge.

Fred, R. (1988). Foreword. In C. Haig-Brown, *Resistance and renewal: Surviving the Indian residential school* (pp. 11-20). Vancouver, BC, Canada: Tillacum Library.

Fredericks, B. (2006). *Pamela Croft and "bothways" philosophy.* Qwaruba Seva Foundation. Queensland University of Technology Digital Repository. Retrieved from http://eprints.qut.edu.au.

Fuller, A. (2012). In the shadow of Wounded Knee, *National Geographic,* 222(2), pp. 30-67.

George, D. (2012). Chief Dan George (1899-1981). In G. Welker (Ed.), Indigenous people. [Internet site] Retrieved from http://www.indigenouspeople.net/dangeorg.htm.

Gone, J. P. (2013, April). *Traditional healing and counseling interventions: Bridging the cultural divide in behavioral health services for Indian country.* Presentation at INBRE Network of Biomedical Research Excellence, Research and Training Symposium, Bozeman, Montana.

Gone, J. P., & Alcantara, C. (2007). Identifying effective mental health interventions for American Indians and Alaska Natives: A review of the literature. *Cultural Diversity and Ethnic Minority Psychology,* 13(4), pp. 356-363.

Gonzalez y Gonzalez, E. M., & Lincoln, Y. S. (2006). Decolonizing qualitiative research: Nontraditional forms in the academy. In N. K. Denzin, & M. D. Giardina (Eds.), *Qualitative inquiry and the conservative challenge.* (pp. 193-214). Walnut Creek, CA: Left Coast Press.

Grande, S. (2004). *Red pedagogy: Native American social and political thought.* Lanham, MD: Rowmen & Littlefield Publishers, Inc.

Grayshield, L., & Mihecoby, A. (2010). Indigenous ways of knowing as a philosophical base for the promotion of peace and justice in counseling education and psychology. *Journal for Social Action in Counseling and Psychology,* 2(2), pp. 1-16

Guilfoyle, A. (2008). Embedding indigenous content into qualitative research in psychology in reflective case studies: A case for social change. In *Proceedings of the EDU-COM 2008 International Conference. Sustainability in Higher Education: Directions for Change* (pp. 201-211). Edith Cowan University, Perth, Western Australia, Australia. 19-21, November 2008.

Hager, S. (1895). Micmac customs and traditions. *American Anthropologist,* A8(1), pp. 31-42.

Haig-Brown, C. (1988). *Resistance and renewal: Surviving the Indian residential school.* Vancouver, BC, Canada: Tillacum Library.

Hanam, A. (2006). *Island of 7 cities exposed.* Retrieved from http://www.1421exposed.com/html/exposed.htm.

Harding, S. (1991). *Whose science? Whose knowledge? Thinking from women's lives.* Ithaca, NY: Cornell University Press.

Hart, Jeff. (1976). *Montana native plants and early peoples.* Helena, MT: Montana Historical Society and Montana Bicentennial Administration.

Henderson, J. Y. (2009). Ayukpachi: Empowering aboriginal thought. In M. Battiste (Ed.), *Reclaiming indigenous voice and vision* (pp. 248-278). Vancouver, BC, Canada: UBC Press.

hooks, b. (1981). *Ain't I a woman: Black women and feminism.* Boston, MA: South End Press.

hooks, b. (1984). *Feminist theory from margin to center.* Boston, MA: South End Press.

Huggins, J. (1998). *Sister Girl.* St. Lucia, QLD, Australia: University of Queensland Press.

Johnston-Goodstar, K. (2012). Decolonizing evaluation: The necessity of evaluation advisory groups in indigenous evaluation. *New Directions for Evaluation,* 136, pp. 109–117. doi:10.1002/ev.20038.

Kawagley, A. O. (1995). *A Yupiaq worldview: A pathway to ecology and spirit.* Prospect Heights, IL: Waveland Press.

Kenny, C. (2000). A sense of place: Aboriginal research as ritual practice. In R. Neil (Ed.), *Voice of the drum: Indigenous education and culture* (pp. 139-150). Brandon, MB, Canada: Kingfisher Publications.

Keoke, E. D., & Porterfield, K. M. (2002). *Encyclopedia of American Indian contributions to the world: 15,000 Years of inventions and innovations.* New York: Facts on File, Inc.

Kidd, R. (1997). *The way we civilize: Aboriginal affairs—the untold story.* St. Lucia, QLD, Australia: University of Queensland Press.

Kim, U., & Berry, J. W. (1993). *Indigenous psychologies: Research and experience in cultural context.* Newbury Park, CA: Sage Publications.

Kim, U., Yang, K. S., & Hwang, K. K. (2006). *Indigenous and cultural psychology: Understanding people in context.* New York: Springer.

Kimmerer, R. W. (2013). *Braiding sweetgrass: Indigenous wisdom, scientific knowledge and the teachings of plants.* Minneapolis, MN: Milkweed Editions.

Kirmayer, L., Simpson, C., & Cargo, M. (2003). Healing traditions: Culture, community and mental health promotion with Canadian aboriginal peoples. *Australasian Psychiatry,* 11(supplement), pp. s15-s23.

Kirmayer, L. J., & Valaskakis, G. G. (Eds.). (2009). *Healing traditions: The mental health of aboriginal peoples in Canada.* Vancouver, BC, Canada: UBC Press.

Kovach, M. (2009). *Indigenous methodologies: Characteristics, conversations and contexts.* Toronto, ON, Canada: University of Toronto Press.

Kowanko, I., de Crespigny, C., Murray, H., Groenkjaer, M., & Emden, C. (2004). Better medication management for aboriginal people with mental health disorders: A survey of providers. *Australian Journal of Rural Health,* 12(6), pp. 253–257.

Krippner S., & Welch, P. (1992). *Spiritual dimensions of healing: From native shamanism to contemporary health care.* New York, NY: Irvington Publishers.

Kuokkanen, R. (2010). The responsibility of the academy: A call for doing homework. *Journal of Curriculum Theorizing,* 26(3), pp. 61-74.

Laenui, P. (2009). Processes of decolonization. In M. Battiste (Ed.), *Reclaiming Indigenous Voice and Vision* (pp. 150-160). Vancouver, BC, Canada: UBC Press.

Lambert-Colomeda, L. A. (1996). *Through the northern looking glass: Breast cancer stories told by northern native women.* New York: NLN Press.

Lavallée, L. F. (2009). Practical application of an indigenous research framework and two qualitative indigenous research methods: Sharing circles and Anishnaabe symbol-based reflection. *International Journal of Qualitative Methods,* 8(1), pp. 21-38.

Lavallée, L. F., & Poole, J. M. (2010). Beyond recovery: Colonization, health and healing for indigenous people in Canada. *International Journal of Mental Health and Addiction,* 8(2), pp. 271-281.

Le Clercq, C. (1910). *New relation of Gaspesie with the customs and religion of the Gaspesian Indians.* Toronto, ON, Canada: The Champlain Society.

Lescarbot, M. (1907). *The history of New France* (3 vol). Toronto, ON, Canada: The Champlain Society.

Letendre, A., & Caine, V. (2004). Shifting from reading to questioning: Some thoughts around ethics, research, and aboriginal peoples. *Pimatisiwin: A Journal of Aboriginal and Indigenous Community Health,* 2(2), pp.1- 31.

Little Bear, L. (2000). Foreword. In G. Cajete, *Native Science: Natural laws of interdependence* (pp. ix-xii). Santa Fe, NM: Clear Light Publishers.

Loppie, C. (2007). Learning from the grandmothers: Incorporating indigenous principles into qualitative research. *Qualitative Health Research,* 17(2), pp. 276-284.

Louis, R. P. (2007). Can you hear us now? Voices from the margin: Using indigenous methodologies in geographic research. *Geographical Research,* 45(2), pp. 130-139.

Luiggi, C. (2012). The stuff of nightmares. *The Scientist.* Midland, ON, Canada, 26(8), pp 15-17.

McCarthy, T. (2000). The Stolen Generation. *Time,* 156(14), p. 50

McDonald, S. (1999). The impact of contact on culture: The Newfoundland Mi'kmaq perspective. In I. Bulgin, (Ed.), *Cabot and his world symposium, June 1997* (pp. 121-125), St. John's, NF, Canada: Newfoundland Historical Society.

Macintyre, S. (1999). *A concise history of Australia.* Cambridge, UK: Cambridge University Press.

McKay, H. F. (Ed.). (2001). *Gadi mirrabooka: Australian aboriginal tales from the dreaming.* Englewood, CO: Libraries Unlimited.

Magoulick, M. (n.d.). *Native American world view emerges.* Retrieved from http://www.faculty.de.gcsu.edu

Mann, C. C. (2011). *1491: New Revelations of the Americas before Columbus.* (2nd ed.). New York: Random House, Inc.

Martin, K. (2003). Ways of knowing, being and doing: A theoretical framework and methods for indigenous and indigenist re-search. *Journal of Australian Studies, 27*(76), pp. 203-214, 256-257.

Matsumoto, D., & van de Vijver, F. J. R. (Eds.). (2011). *Cross-cultural research methods in psychology.* Cambridge, England: Cambridge University Press.

Medicine, B. (2001). *Learning to be an anthropologist and remaining "native."* Urbana, IL: University of Illinois Press.

Mehl-Madrona, L. (2003). *Coyote healing: Miracles in native medicine.* Rochester, VT: Bear & Company.

Mehl-Madrona, L. (2009). What traditional indigenous elders say about cross-cultural mental health training. *Explore: The Journal of Science and Healing, 5*(1), pp. 20-29.

Mehl-Madrona, L. (2010). *Healing the mind through the power of story: The promise of narrative psychiatry.* Rochester, VT: Bear & Company.

Mehl-Madrona, L. (2011). *Intergenerational and historical trauma: Day 4 of the Australian journey.* Retrieved from http://www.futurehealth. org/populum/page.php?f=Intergenerational-and-Hist-by-Lewis-Mehl-Madrona-110313-34.html.

Menzies, C. R. (2001). Reflections on research with, for, and among indigenous peoples. *Canadian Journal of Native Education, 25*(1), pp. 19-36.

Mihesuah, D. A. (Ed.). (1998). *Natives and academics: Researching and writing about American Indians.* Lincoln, NB: University of Nebraska Press.

Miller, J. R. (1996). *Shingwauk's Vision: A history of native residential schools.* Toronto, ON, Canada: University of Toronto Press.

Moeke-Pickering, T., et al. (2006). Keeping our fire alive: Towards decolonising research in the academic setting. *WINHEC Journal.* World Indigenous Nations Higher Education Consortium, Honolulu, HI. Retrieved from www.win-hec.org.

Moon-Stumpff, L. (2010). *Hantavirus and the Navajo nation: A double-jeopardy disease.* Retrieved from native cases.evergreen.edu/collection/cases/hantavirus-navajo.html.

Mundell, K. (2008). *North by northeast: Wabanaki, Akwesasne Mohawk, and Tuscarora traditional arts.* Gardiner, ME: Tilbury House, Publishers.

Nabigon, H., Hagey, R., Webster, S., & MacKay, R. (1999). The learning circle as a research method: The trickster and windigo in research. *Native Social Work Journal,* 2(1), pp. 113–137.

National Congress of American Indians. (2009). *Research that benefits native people: A guide for tribal leaders: Module I: Foundations of research: An indigenous perspective.* Washington, DC: National Congress of American Indians Policy Research Center.

Nebelkopf, E., & Phillips, M. (2004). *Healing and mental health for Native Americans: Speaking in red.* Walnut Creek, CA: AltaMira Press.

Oberklaid, F. (2013). *Promoting early childhood development: Planning and implementing a social strategy.* Retrieved from www.earlyyears.org.au_data/assets/pdf_file/0005/203000/Frank_Oberklaid_Presentation.pdf.

O'Nell, T. D. (1996). *Disciplined hearts: History, identity, and depression in an American Indian community.* Berkeley, CA: University of California Press.

Organista, P. B., Marin, G., & Chun, K. M. (2010). *The psychology of ethnic groups in the United States.* Los Angeles, CA: Sage.

Pohl, F. J. (1974). *Prince Henry Sinclair: His expedition to the new world in 1398.* New York: Clarkson N. Potter, Inc./Publisher.

Porsanger, J. (2004). An essay about indigenous methodology. *Nordlit,* Tromso University, Tromso, Norway, 15, pp. 105-120.

Prairie Research Associates. (2013). *Canadian University Survey Consortium: 2013 First-year university student survey: Master report.* Winnipeg, MB, Canada; Canadian University Consortium. Retrieved from www.cusc-ccreu.ca/publications.htm.

Ranzijn, R., McConnochie, K., & Nolan, W. (2008). Steps along a journey: The growth of interest in the relations between psychology and indigenous Australians. In R. Ranzijn, K. McConnochie, & W. Nolan (Eds.), *Psychology and indigenous Australians: Effective teaching and practice* (pp. 9-18). Newcastle, UK: Cambridge Scholars Publishing.

Restoule, J. P. (2004). *Male aboriginal identity formation in urban areas: A focus on process and context.* (Ph.D. dissertation). University of Toronto. Toronto, ON, Canada. (Proquest 305070238).

Reyhner, J. (1992). American Indians out of school: A review of school-based causes and solutions. *Journal of American Indian Education,* 31(3), pp. 37-56.

Reynolds, V. (2005). *The chimpanzees of the Budongo forest: Ecology, behaviour, and conservation.* Oxford, England: Oxford University Press.

Robertson, M. (1969). *Red earth: Tales of the Mi'kmaq.* Halifax, NS, Canada: Nimbus Publishing Ltd.

Running Wolf, P., & Rickard, J. A. (2003). Talking circles: A Native American approach to experiential learning. *Journal of Multicultural Counseling and Development,* 31(1), pp. 39-43.

Salish-Pend d'Oreille Culture Committee and Elders Cultural Advisory Council, Confederated Salish and Kootenai Tribes. (Eds.). (2005). *The Salish People and the Lewis and Clark expedition.* Lincoln, NB: University of Nebraska Press.

Sams, J. (1994). *Earth medicine: Ancestors' way of harmony for many moons.* San Francisco, CA: HarperSanFrancisco.

Shortal, J. (1987). *Forged by fire: Robert L. Eichelberger and the Pacific war.* Columbia, SC: University of South Carolina Press.

Shweder, R. A. (1991). Menstrual pollution, soul loss, and the comparative study of emotions. In R. A. Shweder (Ed.), *Thinking through cultures: Expeditions in cultural psychology* (pp. 241-265). Cambridge, MA: Harvard University Press.

Silko, L. M. (1977). *Ceremony.* New York: The Viking Press.

Simard, S. (1997). Net transfer of carbon between ectomycorrhizal tree species in the field. *Nature,* 388(6642), pp. 579-582.

Smith, L. T. (1999). *Decolonizing methodologies: Research and indigenous peoples.* London: Zed Books Ltd.

Starks, P. T. B., & Slabach, B. L. (2012). The scoop on eating dirt. *Scientific American,* 306(6), pp. 30-32.

Stevenson, J. (1999). The circle of healing. *Native Social Work Journal,* 2(1), pp. 8-21.

Suzack, C., Huhndorf, S. M., Perrault, J., & Barman, J. (Eds.). (2010). *Indigenous women and feminism: Politics, activism, culture.* Vancouver, BC, Canada: UBC Press.

Tafoya, T. (1997). At the center of the dance. In L. Crozier-Hogle, & D. B. Wilson (Eds.), *Surviving in two worlds* (pp. 132-141). Austin: University of Texas Press.

Thomas, R. A. (2005). Honouring the oral traditions of my ancestors through storytelling. In L. Brown, & S. Strega (Eds.), *Research as resistance* (pp. 237-254). Toronto, ON, Canada: Canadian Scholars' Press.

Travel Manitoba (2014). *Everything Churchill* [Internet site]. Retrieved from http://everythingchurchill.com/about-churchill/history.

Trepanier, F. (2008). *Aboriginal arts research initiative: Report on consultations.* Ottawa, ON, Canada: Strategic Initiative Division, Canada Council for the Arts.

Trimble, C. E., Sommer, B. W., & Quinlan, M. K. (2008). *The American Indian oral history manual: Making many voices heard.* Walnut Creek, CA: Left Coast Press.

Trimble, J. E., & Medicine, B. (1993). Diversification of American Indians: Forming an indigenous perspective. In U. Kim, & J. W. Berry (Eds.), *Indigenous psychologies: Research and experience in cultural context* (pp. 133-151). Newbury Park, CA: Sage Publications.

Tseng, W. S. (2001). *Handbook of cultural psychiatry.* San Diego, CA: Academic Press.

Tuck, E., & Yang, K.W. (2012). Decolonization is not a metaphor. *Decolonization:Indigeneity, Education & Society,* 1(1), pp. 1-40.

UC Davis Center for Reducing Health Disparities. (2009). *Building partnerships: Conversations with Native Americans about mental health needs and community strengths.* Davis, CA: UC Davis Health System.

United Nations Food and Agriculture Organization. (2005). *Building on gender, agrobiodiversity and local knowledge: A training manual.* New York: U.N. Food and Agricultural Organization.

United States Department of Health and Human Services, Indian Health Service. (2013). *Fact sheets: Behavioral health.* Retrieved from http://www.ihs.gov/newsroom/factsheets/disparities/.

University of Alaska Fairbanks, Center for Alaska Native Health Research. (n.d.). [Internet site] Retrieved from www.uaf.edu/canhr.

U.S. Statutes at Large (1887) [United States Congress: General Allotment Act or Dawes Act] 24, pp. 388-91.

van den Berg, R. (1998). Intellectual property rights for Aboriginal people in Australia. *Mots Pluriels,* 8. Retrieved from http://www.arts.uwa.edu.au/MotsPluriels/MP898rudb.html.

Videbeck, S. (2014). *Psychiatric-mental health nursing.* (6th ed.). Philadelphia, PA: Wolters Kluwer Health/Lippencott Williams & Wilkins.

Walters, K. L., et al. (2009). "Indigenist" collaborative research efforts in Native American communities. In A. R. Stiffman (Ed.), *The field research survival guide* (pp. 146-173). New York, NY: Oxford University Press.

Warne, D. (2008). Warne: A new hope for Indian health. *Indian Country Today Media Network.com.* Retrieved from http://indiancountrytodaymedianetwork.com

Weber-Pillwax, C. (2004). Indigenous researchers and indigenous research methods: Cultural influences or cultural determinants of research methods. *Pimatisiwin: A Journal of Aboriginal and Indigenous Community Health,* 2(1), pp. 77-90.

White, L., Warren, J., & Hickey, T. (2008). Developing a structured and appropriate program to support parents who have had their aboriginal children removed by the state and the process that they need to engage in to have their children returned. In R. Ranzin, K. McConnochie, & W. Nolan (Eds.), *Psychology and indigenous Australians:*

Effective teaching and practice (pp. 157-163). Newcastle upon Tyne, Great Britain: Cambridge Scholars Press.

Whitehead, R. H. (1991). *The old man told us: Excerpts from Micmac history 1500-1950.* Halifax, NS, Canada: Nimbus Publishing Ltd.

Wilson, C. (2001). [Review of the book] Decolonizing methodologies: Research and Indigenous peoples by Linda Tuhiwai Smith. *Social Policy Journal of New Zealand* 17, pp. 214-217.

Wilson, S. (2001). What is an indigenous research methodology? *Canadian Journal of Native Education,* 25(2), pp. 175-179.

Wilson, S. (2008). *Research is ceremony: Indigenous research methods.* Halifax, NS, Canada: Fernwood Publishing.

Wohlforth, C. P. (2004). *The whale and the supercomputer: On the northern front of climate change.* New York: North Point Press.

Yellow Horse Brave Heart, M. (2003). The historical trauma response among natives and its relationship with substance abuse: A Lakota illustration. *Journal of Psychoactive Drugs,* (35)1, pp. 7–13.

Index

Dr. Lori Lambert is an enrolled member of the Nulhegan Abenaki Tribe of Vermont and a descendant of the Mi'kmaq and Huron Wendot people. For the last twenty years she has been a faculty member of the Salish Kootenai College on the Flathead Indian Reservation, Montana. Dr. Lambert is the founder of the American Indigenous Research Association and is the chair of the annual conference.